Born February 10, 1849
Died February 4, 1926

NEW TESTAMENT CHRISTIANITY

VOL. II

Edited by

Z. T. SWEENEY

NEW TESTAMENT CHRISTIANITY BOOK FUND, INC.
COLUMBUS, INDIANA

Printed in the United States of America

To Joseph I. Sweeney, son of Mr. and Mrs. Z. T. Sweeney, who was taken out of this world just as he was preparing to enter the ministry of the gospel, this book is lovingly dedicated.

TABLE OF CONTENTS

Contents

4

FOREWORD

THIS is the second volume of a series of three to be issued on *New Testament Christianity*. Like the first book, it is for gratuitous distribution among preachers of the Christian Church. The purpose as previously explained is twofold:

1. To let our preachers—especially our young preachers—get a clear insight into the aims of the Restoration movement. 2. To arm them for the defense of the movement.

The two books can be freely drawn upon without fear of plagiarism. The articles making up the contents have, most of them, been out of print for many years. They are in no sense private property, but the legacy of us all.

It was while completing the present volume that my husband died suddenly at his home in Columbus, Ind. During the latter days of his life he organized and incorporated the New Testament Christianity Book Fund as a means of carrying on the work he had undertaken, and a third volume will be issued and distributed as planned by Mr. Sweeney.

The first volume was given a most cordial reception, and the interest so enthusiastically expressed by recipients was a great inspiration, not only to Mr. Sweeney, but to his associates in the Book Fund.

MRS. Z. T. SWEENEY.

Columbus, Ind.

CHURCH OF THE FIRST CENTURY

By H. W. EVEREST, LL.D.

THE agencies through which God would bring to man the spiritual renovation are all embodied in the kingdom of heaven, the kingdom or church of Christ, "the Church of the living God, the pillar and ground of the truth."

I ask your attention to the kingdom of heaven as a great fact, as an actual existence among men, as something most wonderful in its *conception* and still more wonderful in its *realization.*

Moses, before he laid down the scepter, pointed to the coming Messiah, to a prophet like unto himself, mediator, law-giver and ruler. *Israel's greatest poet* spoke of one who should sit on David's throne and at the right hand of God. *Daniel,* standing among the ruins of ancient empires and with the horoscope of coming ages before him, said: "In the days of these kings shall the God of Heaven set up a kingdom which shall never be destroyed; and the kingdom shall not be left to other people, but it shall break in pieces and consume all these kingdoms and it shall stand forever."

7

John the Baptist proclaimed that the kingdom of heaven was at hand. *The young carpenter of Nazareth* had a divine conception of this kingdom, and no thought of man can ever equal the sublimity of that conception; a kingdom not of this world, yet including all nations—a dominion over the hearts and consciences of men; a kingdom of truth and love; a kingdom universal and eternal; a kingdom which He would found in His own ignominy and death, and the scepter of whose authority He would never lay down.

While to all outward seeming He was but a wretched Jewish peasant, without a soldier at His beck and without a single denarius to pay for His burial, when as yet not a word of His teachings had been written, and while the blood was trickling down His face from the many wounds of the mock crown of thorns, to the scornful question of the Roman governor, "Art thou a king?" He said: "I am a king, and hereafter you shall see the Son of Man seated at the right hand of power and coming in the clouds of Heaven."

In answer to Peter's confession that He was the Christ, the Son of God, He said: "On this rock I will build my church, and the gates of hell shall not prevail against it." And yet He died on a Roman cross, He was buried in a borrowed grave, a great stone was rolled to the door of His sepulchre, His mother's heart was pierced through with many sorrows, and His few disciples were scattered abroad.

8

Miraculous though it be, the conception of the Nazarene was more than realized. On that memorable day of Pentecost, the disciples at Jerusalem were all with one accord in one place. There was a sound as of a rushing mighty wind. The Holy Spirit came in baptismal power and testified with tongues of flame that God had made that same Jesus both Lord and Christ.

This was *the inauguration* of the kingdom of heaven. The prophetic utterances and symbols were fulfilled, the long ages of preparations were justified, the human cry for grace and mercy was heard, and three thousand conversions signalized this auspicious beginning.

Is Jesus a *king?* He reigns more gloriously than did Cæsar or Napoleon. Has He a *kingdom?* Millions of subjects bow the knee before Him and submit to His sway. Is His kingdom *universal?* He rules from shore to shore and from zone to zone. Is His dominion an everlasting dominion? It will be as lasting as the beatitudes of the Sermon on the Mount, and cannot perish until truth and love shall die. The miracle of His kingdom is only less than the miracle of Christ Himself.

My theme, thus introduced, "The First Century of the Church of Christ," I shall discuss not as a matter of church history, but as related to the religious movement with which myself and nearly a million of my brethren stand identified.

The first Christian century is the beginning

9

corner where we must place our theodolite if we would measure correctly the boundary lines of heaven's kingdom. It is the *pow sto* where we must place our fulcrum if we would effectively use the lever of the Gospel. It is the center whence streams forth the light of revelations over all the past and all the future, and around which all Bible truth revolves in more than astronomic harmony. That the first Christian century was all this and more is evident from several points of view.

First. This century was the period of inauguration and confirmation. When did the kingdom of heaven begin on earth? Not when Daniel said: "In the days of these kings will the God of Heaven set up a kingdom;" not when John the Baptist proclaimed: "The kingdom of heaven is at hand," for the least in the kingdom of heaven was greater than he; not when Jesus said: "On this rock I will build My church;" not when the dying malefactor prayed: "Lord, remember me when thou comest in Thy kingdom." Jesus was not exalted to the right hand of power until He had suffered the humiliations of the scourge and the cross, and not until He had conquered death and hell did He enter heaven leading captivity captive.

The kingdom of heaven was not possible until it was announced on earth that "God had made that same Jesus both Lord and Christ." Prophets and Apostles bear witness that Jerusalem was the place and the last Jewish Pentecost the time. Isaiah pre-

10

dicted that "the law should go forth from Zion and the word of the Lord from Jerusalem."

Peter declared that Joel's prophecy concerning the last days began to be fulfilled on that Pentecost, and that that was the beginning of the new dispensation. Thence forward in the sacred history the kingdom of heaven is referred to as an accomplished fact; sinners "are translated from the kingdom of darkness into the kingdom of God's dear Son," and saints rejoice in the kingdom and patience of Jesus Christ.

This position in regard to the beginning of the church of Christ is impregnable. All that preceded, whether it be the law of Moses, the utterance of the prophets, or the work of Jesus, was but preparatory, while all that followed, under the guidance of the Apostles, was but a development and confirmation of its power.

Moreover, this century was the heroic age of the church—heroic like that of a nation when it declares its independence and sovereignty and makes that declaration good in successful warfare. The Christ had been humiliated and exalted—crowned with *thorns* and crowned with *glory*. His kingdom had been proclaimed by the Holy Spirit sent down from heaven. It was to be sustained by the power of truth and the attractions of divine love. Its conquests were to be won, not by the sword, but by the preaching of the Gospel.

Will this new and unique kingdom of the

11

Nazarene stand? Will it increase? Will it triumph? The first hundred years gave proof that it would stand, that it would break in pieces all other kingdoms and endure forever.

A second point of view presents the first Christian century as the culmination and expansion of all that had gone before in the history of redemption. As the geological ages with their rising series of living forms were without meaning till man appeared, so Jewish laws and institutions have little meaning except they stand revealed in the light of the Gospel.

What was the meaning of sacrifice? It seems obscure and heathenish till we see "the Lamb of God that taketh away the sin of the world." What the meaning of the Mosaic tabernacle and its priestly services? None until we see its mysteries illumined by the correspondence between type and anti-type. Even some of the parables of Christ are not intelligible except in the light of subsequent facts: The sower who went forth to sow and who gathered a harvest according to the condition of the soil; the mustard seed and the full-grown tree; the king who went into a far country to receive a kingdom and to return.

The results of this century fully justify the facts of redemption, the divine love, the humiliation of Jesus, the ministry of angels, the mission of the Holy Spirit, the garden and the cross, the darkness and the earthquake, the resurrection and the ascension,

12

the mission of the Apostles and the Saviour's prediction of their triumph over all opposition. If the Bible student shall master the history of this century, the past will be clear and the future glorious.

A third consideration of much importance is the fact that during this century the church was under the miraculous guidance of the Holy Spirit, Jesus promised His Apostles and their immediate followers the baptism of the Holy Spirit. He told them that He would send them another comforter, even the spirit of truth, whom the world could not receive.

He commended them to wait at Jerusalem until they were endued with power from on high. He left the elements of His kingdom in chaotic conditions; Jewish ritual and prophecy were the only historic facts not yet built into the scheme of redemption; the sublime truths which He had taught rested only in the memories of a few devoted disciples and were liable to perish utterly.

His sun had been obscured at noonday and had gone down in blood; His followers were disorganized and dispersed. It was at this juncture, when all things seemed to be at the worst and needing more than ever before His presence that Jesus was taken from the earth.

But the Spirit was to come and bring order out of this chaos. It was to lead the Apostles into all truth, to convince the world of sin, of righteousness, and of judgment, to follow the Apostles with signs and wonders, with demonstrations and with power.

13

The church of the first century was under the immediate supervision of the Holy Spirit. In fulfillment of the Saviour's promise it came upon the waiting disciples with baptismal power. Peter and the other apostles spoke the Gospel as the Spirit gave them utterance.

It was the source of *wisdom*, determining the matter and form of the Gospel proclamation, opening the door to the Gentiles, settling the question of difference between Jews and Gentiles, edifying the church through spiritual gifts, interpreting the Scriptures, directing the movements of evangelists, and disclosing the future.

It was the source of *power;* power to heal the sick, cast out demons and raise the dead; power to confirm the Word with miraculous manifestations; power to organize the church, determine its officers, its sacraments and its methods of worship and work.

Let it also be emphasized that the miraculous presence and power of the Holy Spirit were peculiar to the Apostolic age, to the first century of the church. The only authentic record of such supernatural phenomena is in the New Testament. In the earlier and later Christian fathers, fact and fable are so intermingled that human wisdom cannot separate them. It is beyond controversy that no miraculous endowments are now in possession of the church.

Such supposed manifestations now, whether public or private, whether in a Quaker meeting or a camp-meeting, whether prophesied by Christian Scientist or faith healer, and whether of Protestant or Roman Catholic endorsement, are a delusion and a dishonor, are of man or the devil, are modifications of epilepsy or hypnotism, and originate in weak heads or in wicked hearts.

As nature began in a miracle, but now stands in the clear light of science, so did Christianity begin in these superhuman phenomena, but it now moves on under the guidance of beneficent law.

If anyone claims the baptism of the Holy Spirit, let him speak with tongues, if he arrogates to himself the authority of Jesus, let him prove his apostleship by presenting his miraculous credentials; if he claims to be the vicegerent of Christ and lords it over God's heritage, let him show that Heaven confirms his word by signs and wonders following.

These pretenders, these fanatics and cranks, male and female, with their lying relics and mock miracles are descendants of Jannes and Jambres, who withstood Moses, and are a disgrace to the church of the nineteenth century.

A fourth proposition is a logical inference from what I have said. The Christianity and the church of this first century, as revealed and perfected by the Holy Spirit, are presented as a finality.

Now for more than eighteen hundred years the heavens have kept silence, a silence not again to be broken until the trump of God shall sound and the dead shall rise.

15

What God has done cannot be improved upon. It has no deficiencies and no redundancies, and hence the apocalyptic curse falls on him who shall add to this finished work, or who shall dare to take from it. There can be no need of change in any respect since God and man, sin and righteousness, heaven and hell are forever the same. No authority has been delegated to any man, pope or council to amend or abolish any portion of this perfect system. It is the anti-Christ, that hierarch of heresy, that has presumed to change times and laws.

These are the "last days," the last dispensations of the grace of God. We are to contend earnestly for the faith which was once for all delivered to the saints. The Pauline anathema is terribly conclusive: "Though we or an angel from Heaven preach any other gospel unto you than that which we have preached unto you, let him be accursed." "As I said before, so say I now again: if any man preach any other gospel unto you than that ye have received, let him be accursed;" and this anathema comes not from the vatican, but from the throne of God.

"All flesh is as grass, and the glory of man as the flower of the grass; the grass withereth and the flower thereof falleth away, but the word of the Lord endureth forever; and this is the word which by the Gospel is preached unto you."

This brings us logically and relentlessly to a fifth point of view, to the all-important conclusion that the first century of the Church of Christ, that the inspired record of this century left us by the Holy Apostles and evangelists who were under the guidance of the Holy Spirit, is the only source of authority in religious matters.

"The Bible and the Bible alone is the religion of Protestants." Everything must be measured and approved or disapproved by the Divine standard of the New Testament. If creed and dogma, if sacrament and ritual do not agree with these Scriptures, it is because there is no light in them.

What question can be greater than this one of religious authority? Who can forgive sins? Who can give commands which reach forward into eternity? Who can bind the conscience? Who can establish law for the day of judgment? Who can decree ordinances and governments for the church? And on whose rod and staff shall we lean as we go through the valley and shadow of death?

The risen Christ said: "All authority in heaven and in earth is given unto me; go ye therefore."

To the Apostles this authority was delegated, but to none others. Episcopacy and papacy alike are unsupported pretensions; the chain of succession lies in broken fragments which cannot be welded, nor is it linked to the throne of Christ.

Councils, whether ecumenical or otherwise, and assemblies, whether general or provincial, are without legislative authority, for a voice has come to us from the excellent glory, "This is my beloved Son; hear ye Him."

Nor has any man or class of men been authorized and inspired to interpret the New Testament for the rest of the world. This is no revelation which requires another revelation to reveal it. God has not put into the hands of any mortal man such an instrument of oppression.

The assumption that he has done so has been productive of evils the most tremendous; it has divided Christendom into hostile sects and united church and state; it has built up great systems of priestcraft and converted the institutions of religion into sources of revenue; it has drawn up creeds and enforced them with the sword; it has kindled the fires of martyrdom and invented the horrors of the Inquisition; it has persecuted churchman and dissenter with equal ferocity, and drenched many a battlefield with fraternal blood.

Notwithstanding pope or priest, creeds or ecclesiastical anathemas, every man has free access to the Word of God. Not only may every man interpret for himself, but he must do so and will do so; for thought is eternally free, and neither men nor devils can put it in chains.

This right and duty of every man and church to come to the New Testament as the only source of authority this side of the throne of God has made it necessary that this shall be a science of interpretation. Coming to the same book and following the same rules of exposition, we shall come to the same conclusions.

As in science, so in theology; the inductive system of investigations will bring contending dogmas and factions into harmony. Hence with us, as a people, this science of interpretation has always occupied a prominent place.

We build on the best text and translations of the Holy Scriptures; we would apply the strictest logical and grammatical law to the words and sentences; we would recognize the progressive character of revelation and the three distinct dispensations of the grace of God, Patriarchal, Jewish and Christian.

We ask who speaks, to whom, and for what purpose? We distinguish between law and custom, between the permanent and the temporary, between the precedent and isolated facts. We feel bound where the Apostles have bound us; but where they have left us unbound to any custom or method of administration we are determined "to stand fast in the liberty wherewith Christ has made us free."

Still further, the first century of the church is a remarkable period because the nineteenth century so regards it, because it is the central point toward which all the great currents of religious thought and reformation are tending.

Every institution of the church has been changed and marred by unholy hands; we must go back to the first sources. All the streams of religious teaching have been polluted by theological speculations

19

and priestly abuses; we must go up and drink at the fountain head. All the offices and organizations of the church have been prostituted to worldly ambition and worldly gain; we must again stand in the presence of the Apostles and see how they administered the kingdom of heaven.

Coming back thus to the first century of the Church of Christ, what shall we find? What were the characteristics of that divinely constituted church, and what the sources of its power? The Apostolic church was remarkable for its absence of several things: There was no pope, no papal palace, no papal bulls, no papal anathemas, no papal decrees, no papal nuncios. Who was Paul and who was Peter but ministers by whom they believed?

It cannot be shown from the New Testament that Peter was ever at Rome. The Peter who would not receive the homage of Cornelius, but said: "Stand upon thy feet; for I also am a man," could not have endured to be called "Christ's Vicegerent," or "Lord God the Pope."

The Roman pontiff was developed in after years out of an overgrown metropolitan bishop. The only New Testament prototype of the pope is Diotrephes, who loved to have the pre-eminence. And this is asserted to be true, not as a matter of controversy, but of unquestioned scholarship.

There was no hierarchy, no gradations of priestly honor, metropolitan archbishop, bishop, priest, monk and layman. Christ was the only high priest, with no vicar on earth or in heaven, and the Apostles had no successors.

All Christians were kings and priests unto God. The work of the church was divided among the servants of Christ, but there was no ecclesiastical ladder of promotion to tempt an unholy ambition to deeds of pride and oppression.

We do not read of the "Right-Reverend John Mark," or of "Cardinal Timothy," nor of "Arch-Bishop Titus." These titles and the things they signify arose far this side of the first century.

There was no ecclesiasticism, no complicated system of church government formed after the model of the Roman Empire; no "Great Iron Wheel" to crush out individualism; no Ferris wheel to elevate the few above the many. There was no tyranny of one church over another and no danger that some arch-heretic might be brought to trial and so disrupt the whole church.

There was no speculative theology. They were so busy preaching Christ and Him crucified that they had no time to write out a system of divinity. They deferred many interesting questions until they should no longer "see through a glass darkly." They gave heed to Paul's instruction: "That they strive not about words to no profit;" that they "shun profane and vain babblings;" "neither give heed to fables and endless genealogies, which minister questions rather than godly edifying which is in faith."

There were no anxious-seat conversions. Then faith came by hearing, and hearing by the Word of God. Then men received assurance of pardon through obedience to the commands of the Gospel. Then none who wanted to become Christians went away unblessed and doubting the word and mercy of God. In all the Book of God you will find nothing that corresponds to some modern revival scenes, unless it be the one enacted by the prophets of Baal on Mt. Carmel.

There was no infant membership. They did not practice baptismal regeneration. Faith and repentance were essential to discipleship. The New Testament furnished not a single example of infant membership.

There was no six months' probation. The same day that they made confession of faith in Jesus they were added to the church. They took the lambs into the fold and did not leave them exposed to him who goes about as a roaring lion, seeking whom he may devour.

There were no pseudo baptisms. Those who were baptized in the Holy Spirit spoke with tongues. They did not think that affusion was a mode of immersion. They did not try to bury a man in a few drops of water. It was always preceded by a change of heart and life. It is conceded by all competent scholars that immersion was the Apostolic practice and that the Saviour Himself set the example. All

22

the substitutes for New Testament baptism came up in subsequent times.

There was no Sabbath. The Jewish Christians continued to observe it as they did circumcision, but it had been taken out of the way. The Lord's day, the first day of the week, was observed by the ancient church, not as a Sabbath, not as a day of rest, but as a day of worship, a day consecrated to the Lord, a day of great religious activity.

There was no "auricular confession," no "transsubstantiation," no "extreme unction," no "purgatory," no "holy water," no "Mariolatry," no worship of the saints, no "papal infallibility." If you would learn about these inventions, you must go to an encyclopedia and not to the New Testament.

There was no human creed. They had a creed but it was divine; announced from heaven; demonstrated by the Holy Spirit; needing no revision; embodying the central formatives built of Christianity, the belief of which gave men the power to become the sons of God.

What were the positive characteristics of that Apostolic church?

It was a Christ church. That Jesus was the Christ, the Son of the Living God, was its creed and foundation, a creed announced by the Father, predicted by the Prophets, preached by the Apostles and confessed by every disciple. They were baptized into Christ; they put on Christ; they walked in Christ; they died in Him. They bore His name,

23

were imbued with His spirit, followed His example and looked forward to His coming a second time without a sin-offering to salvation. They gave Christ the pre-eminence in all things.

It was a Gospel church. They accepted the Gospel facts that Jesus died for our sins, that He was buried and that He rose the third day according to the Scriptures. They obeyed the Gospel commands to believe on the Lord Jesus, to repent, to confess His name, and to be baptized by His authority. They rejoiced in the Gospel promises, the remission of sins, the gift of the Holy Spirit and eternal life. They were saved by the Gospel, and though to the Jews a stumbling-block and to the Greeks foolishness, to those who believed it was the wisdom of God and the power of God.

It was a people's church. It was not for the aristocratic or learned few, but for every man. Hence the conditions of the discipleship were very simple and level to the comprehension of every one who needed to be saved. They were to believe in Christ, turn away from sin and give a test of this faith and repentance in their ready obedience in baptism.

They were not required to become experts in introspection until they could analyze their own state of mind and measure the degree of faith and feeling. They were not required to fathom the mysteries of the Trinity and the nature of Christ, nor to unravel the perplexities of election and free grace. They were not required to examine thirty-nine articles, more or less, and settle the most obtuse theological problems; if such had been the hard conditions, many youthful and ignorant sinners could not have been saved.

It was not controlled by a body of priests; but all matters not legislated upon by the Apostles were decided by the whole body of believers. It was a people's church because nothing was done to exclude the poor and the wretched.

The members were gathered in from the highways and the hedges. They had no splendid cathedral, so elaborate in furnishing and with audiences so richly dressed that the poor man was put to shame. It did not have to build mission churches and come down to people, for it was itself a mission church and was already down among the masses.

It was an obedient church. Its life began in obedience. It continued steadfastly in the Apostles' doctrine, in the partnership, in the breaking of bread, and in prayer. The Lord's death and resurrection were commemorated every week. They were intent on carrying out the great commission. They went forward in the path of obedience though that path might lead to prison and to death.

It was a free church. It did not form an unholy alliance with the state; was not the slave of priestcraft and superstition; did not manacle itself with rigid creeds and customs until growth and knowledge in grace were impossible; was not subject to fate, either through an eternal election, or through the impotence of total depravity; but it was free to receive the Gospel, and just as free to reject it; free to use the best methods and means in carrying out the commands of Jesus; free in this respect to avail itself of all progress in science and art; free to declare the whole counsel of God though martyrdom might be the consequence; free in the highest sense, for the truth had made it free.

It was a praying church. Christ, though Lord of all, set the example. It was while in prayer that the Holy Spirit came; they prayed without ceasing. No theory of God, which makes Him an iceberg in the sides of the north, no theory of law, which makes God as well as man its victim, which binds the Almighty so that He cannot hear and answer prayer, kept them from the throne of grace.

It was a united church. They built on the foundation of Prophets and Apostles, Jesus Christ Himself being the chief corner-stone. They were united by the "one Lord, one faith, the one baptism, by the one body, the one spirit, the one hope and the one Father of all." They were not divided over men, nor neither Paul, nor Peter, nor Apollos was willing to become a leader in any schismatic movement. They were not divided over opinions, for their differences were not exalted into tests of fellowship. They did not press the heads of all believers into the same mould, nor seek to connect their necks into cast iron so that they could not turn to take a new view of any subject.

They did not seek to introduce the horrible monotony of perfect uniformity. Even Jew and Gentile gathered and worshiped in the same congregation, for Christ was their peace, who had broken down the middle wall of partition between them. The prayer of Jesus for the unity of His disciples was gloriously answered, for the times of sectarian division and strife had not yet come.

It was a missionary church. They seemed constantly to hear the Saviour saying: "Go ye into all the world and preach the Gospel to every creature." Their energies were concentrated on mission work. When scattered abroad from Jerusalem, they went everywhere preaching the Word. Deacons like Stephen and Philip gained great boldness in the Gospel. Women were prophetesses and helpers. Evangelists were everywhere, depending on their own labor, supported by single churches or by the combined aid of large districts. Missionary church? Why, the church of the first century did scarcely anything else. They did not spend their time in learning to pronounce the party shibboleth correctly, nor spend the Lord's money in building up contending factions.

It was a suffering church. Its founder was crucified, its Apostles were murdered and thousands of its members were slaughtered to make a Roman holiday, but the blood of the martyrs was the seed of the church.

It was a triumphant church. The combined

27

hostility of Jews and Gentiles, of high-priest and Roman governor, of Pharisees and Greek philosophers, of depraved human nature and satanic agencies, only served to prove that the gates of hell could not prevail against it.

It went forward from conquering unto conquest. Converts multiplied with wonderful rapidity—three thousand, five thousand, a great company of the priests, and millions before the close of the century.

Country after country fell before it—Judea, Samaria, Phœnicia, Cyprus, Asia Minor, Macedonia, Greece, the Roman Empire, Babylon, Arabia and Ethiopia. Before the death of the last Apostle, the whole world had heard the wonderful proclamation; and all this without armies, without steamships and railroads, without printing presses and libraries, without colleges and favoring Christian governments —all this in the midst of heathenism and against the most bloody opposition.

Could we but reproduce the church of the first century in its spirit and power, with our millions of money and our millions of men, and with our peaceable access to all tribes and nations of the earth, how soon all the kingdoms of this world would become the kingdom of our Lord and Saviour Jesus Christ.

As a brotherhood, nearly a million strong, this is our position, this is our endeavor. We present no human creed and no human plan of confederation, but we say: "Let us go back to the days of inspiration and infallible teaching, let us sit at the feet of the Apostles, let us rally around the cross.''

Here we stand; we can do no otherwise, so help us, God. And, if in the good time coming, whose auspicious signs are already apparent in the ecclesiastical sky, the contending churches of christendom shall drop creeds or revise them out of existence, cease to glory in party names, and return to the church of the first century, to the foundation of Apostles and Prophets, they will find us a people tenting on that ground and lifting the banner of the cross higher and still higher.

THE MANIFESTATION OF FAITH

By J. Z. TYLER

What doth it profit, my brethren, though a man say he hath faith, and have not works? Can faith save him? If a brother or sister be naked or destitute of daily food, and one of you should say unto them, Depart in peace; be ye warmed and filled; notwithstanding ye give them not those things which are needful to the body, what doth it profit? Even so faith, if it hath not works, is dead, being alone. Yea, a man may say, Thou hast faith and I have works; show me thy faith without thy works and I will show you my faith by my works.—James ii:14-18.

WE are required not only to believe, but to manifest our faith to the world. God does not permit any one to hide his faith. It is something too precious to be concealed. Though the exhibition of it should bring upon us the hatred of men, and lead us through bitter persecution, even to a violent death, still we are required to confess and deny not. Moreover, a strong, living faith cannot *consent* to be silent. It cannot live shut up in one's heart. It must out. It will show itself. When a genuine faith takes hold upon us we are compelled to speak and to act under its directions. It will not suffer

30

us to be idle. It enthrones itself in the heart, and then, by the words of the lips and the works of the hands it proclaims its presence and its power. We cannot be possessed of a living faith without at the same time being characterized by obedient lives. Faith alone is dead. It cannot benefit any one.

The comparison in the text is obvious and striking. The sense of this Scripture is, that, faith in itself, without the acts fitly corresponding to it, and to which it would prompt, is as cold, and heartless, and unmeaning as it would be to *say* to one who is destitute of the necessaries of life, "depart in peace; be warmed and filled," and not give then the things which are needed. Faith is not, and cannot be shown to be genuine, saving faith, unless it be accompanied with corresponding acts; just as our good wishes for the poor and needy (when we have it in our power to help) cannot be shown to be genuine but by actually ministering to their necessities. He who refuses to give to the needy, when he is able to do it, shows, beyond a doubt, that he has no genuine sympathy for them, although his profession of sympathy may be very great; so he who does not work, shows that he has not genuine faith, though he may lay great claim to it.

But what kind of works is to be given and accepted as proof of faith? Clearly, those works which spring from faith and can be produced by nothing else. There are many good works which may exist, and actually do exist, where there is no

2   31

faith. An infidel may be generous, liberal, kind, affectionate and philanthropic. The natural and noble impulses in men often bring forth good fruit to bless others. Such works, therefore, cannot certainly prove the presence and power of faith within us, since they often are where faith evidently is not. Faith, however, is not in the least opposed to such good works, but by strengthening the good already within, makes us abound more and more in doing good to all men as we have opportunity. We may become so fruitful in self-sacrifices for the good of others as to leave little room to doubt the genuineness or strength of our faith. A man who lives by faith will be more affectionate and forbearing in his family, more sympathetic and charitable toward the poor and needy; more willing and gracious in forgiving, and more ready to expend his energies and his means in every good word and work.

There are works, however, which spring from faith, and which can be produced by nothing else; and these, after all, must furnish the clearest proofs of the presence of faith. These works may be classified under one general head—*works of obedience.* Faith looks up to God and is guided by him. It resolutely and persistently rejects all other guides. To it, God's will is the highest law possible. But it is not sufficient to say, in this general way, that the works which furnish the best proof of faith are works of obedience. This is sufficiently exact, but is not sufficiently minute and specific. Let us de-

scend into a more detailed description of some of
their characteristics, and illustrate our meaning by
incidents in the lives of those who have lived by
faith. I do not undertake, however, to point out all
the marks peculiar to these works, nor do I hold that
all the features of them which I may present are to
be seen in any one single act of faith. Works of
obedience are:

1. *Where there is no apparent reason for doing
the thing commanded, and where we are, therefore,
compelled to do it simply and alone because God has
commanded it.* Were any other reason apparent,
save the fact that God has commanded it, then that
other reason might be the motive which prompts us
to do it, and hence the doing of it could not certainly
prove our faith. For instance, when Abram was
commanded to leave his native land, and go forth,
he knew not where nor why, he obeyed the divine
injunction and thus gave proof of his faith. There
was no apparent reason why he should leave his
home and become an exile. No doubt he loved his
kindred and the land of his birth. He saw no
reasonable prospect of improving his circumstances
by seeking a new place. Why then should he go?
Why did he go? For this reason, and for this alone:
God had commanded him *to do it.* Again, when,
many years after this, God said: "Take now thy
son, thine only son Isaac, whom thou lovest, and get
thee into the land of Moriah; and offer him there for
a burnt offering upon one of the mountains which

33

I will tell thee of''—what reason could have induced him to do this? There were many apparent reasons why he should not, but there was only one reason why he should. God had commanded it. Of this there could be no doubt. The command was emphatic and specific. He obeyed simply and alone because God had commanded. What higher reason could any one have? Faith says this is the very highest possible.

2. *Where there is no apparent connection between the thing commanded and the end to be gained.* A certain end is to be accomplished. We are commanded to do certain things in order to reach this. But there is not the most remote connection, so far as we can see, between the end and the means. They are not related to each other as cause to effect. Take, as an illustration of this, the capture of the city of Jericho. That city was taken by *faith.* We read, that, *"by faith* the walls of Jericho fell down, after they were compassed about seven days.'' But how does it appear that the taking of that city was an act of faith? The Israelites took many other cities, and they took them, too, in obedience to God's command, yet these other cases are not mentioned as acts of faith. What is there peculiar to this, which marks it as an evidence of faith? Evidently, this, that there was no apparent connection between the means to be employed and the end to be gained. God said to Joshua, "Ye shall compass the city, all ye men of war, and go round about

34

the city once. Thus shalt thou do six days. And seven priests shall bear before the ark seven trumpets of rams' horns: and the seventh day ye shall compass the city seven times, and the priests shall blow with the trumpets. And it shall come to pass, that when they make a long blast with the rams' horns, and when ye hear the sound of the trumpet, all the people shall shout with a great shout: and the walls of the city shall fall down flat, and the people shall ascend up every man straight before him.'' This was the divine plan for the siege. But in all the history of wars, and in all the science of warfare, who had ever adopted such a plan? What apparent connection between the means and the end? The adoption of the plan was a trial and a triumph of their faith. Their own judgment and experience would certainly have suggested some plan more apparently rational. But God intended they should walk by faith, and so while he clearly presents the end to be accomplished, and reveals in detail the means to be employed, he hides from sight and from reason the link which unites the one to the other. We may find, in the conclusion of this discourse, that he sometimes applies to *our faith* the same severe test.

3. *Where there is no apparent necessity for doing the thing commanded, and where reason and experience pronounce it foolish.* The faith of Noah furnishes a striking illustration of this. He was a man of remarkable faith. ''By faith, Noah, being warned

of God of things not seen as yet, moved with fear, prepared an ark to the saving of his house; by the which he condemned the world, and became heir of the righteousness which is by faith." What necessity presented itself? What signs of a universal deluge? What reason for expecting one? What, in his own experience, or his research into the experience of those who had lived before him, could suggest even the probability of a coming flood? What prophecy in the movement of the waters above the firmament or what ominous sign in the movement of those beneath? None! For sixteen centuries man had lived upon the earth, and there had been no deluge. The earth had moved steadily on in its appointed course. The seasons had come and gone in their regular order. There had been sunshine and shower, making fruitful fields. The sowing at seed-time had been followed by the gathering of the golden grain at the time for the harvest. The laws of nature are moving on with their usual exactness and are producing their uniform results. But God said to him, "Behold, I, even I, do bring a flood of waters upon the earth, to destroy all flesh, wherein is the breath of life, from under heaven." He commanded him to build an ark. He gave him the dimensions therefor, and told him of what material he should make it. Now, see him prove his faith. He goes to work doing as God had directed him. The ignorant laugh at him. He works on. Away up in the high land he is felling trees. He says he is preparing to build a great vessel. There is no large body of water near, but he says he intends to build it right there. They call him crazy. He works on. He tells them a great flood is coming, by which both lowland and highland will be covered. He exhorts them to repent. They mock him and turn away. Their wise men seek to instruct him. They tell him there never has been a flood. They lecture him upon the uniformity of the operation of the laws of nature. They argue that such a flood is a physical impossibility. But he answers all this by telling them what God has said, and works on. Years come and go. There are yet no signs of the fulfillment of the prophecy. Still he preaches to the people and works on. O, the patience, and the long suffering and the heroism of his faith! Ridicule, and wit, and sarcasm, and logic, and science, and philosophy, and everything, brought against him—nobody is converted, and nobody pays him for his preaching—yet, he preaches on and works on! O, for a faith like that!

4. *Faith endeavors to do everything God commands, and to do it exactly as God commands it to be done.* This is an important feature of genuine faith. When faith affirms that the will of God is the highest law possible, it teaches, at the same time, by necessary implication at least, that there is no other power or authority in heaven or upon earth which can excuse us from obedience to that will as it is expressed in the very least of all his command-

37

ments. If God's will is supreme and universal law, then, that will, so far as revealed to us, must be supreme law to us, in matters both great and small. If he has right to command that anything be done, then, clearly, he has right to tell exactly how it shall be done, and if he condescends to give the details of the manner in which it shall be done, then faith will, with the same diligence and energy, seek to follow out the details and specific directions, that it employs in accomplishing the general end. Let us recur, for a moment, to the faith of Noah. He was commanded not only to build an ark, but God gave him specific directions as to its size, proportions, and the materials of which it should be made. Now, his faith is shown perhaps more in the exactness with which he followed out all the details than in his obedience to the general command to build an ark. Again, when Moses had received instructions to build the tabernacle, God said, "See that thou make all things according to the pattern showed to thee in the mount." It was, therefore, as clearly his duty to make it according to the pattern as it was to make it at all. This point must be clear. So, at least, it appears to me.

Before leaving this point, however, let me indicate one or two applications of it. First, its bearing upon the theory of essentials and non-essentials. This distinction arises, I apprehend, from a failure to draw the line accurately which marks the boundary between the province of faith and the province

The Manifestation of Faith

of reason. Reason may be employed in deciding
whether God has commanded me to do a certain
thing. But it cannot, without being guilty of usurpation, go further and undertake to decide whether
it is essential or not, and thus decide whether it is
binding or not. A strong and intelligent faith protests against such usurpation and ignores all such
classifications of divine law. A second application
of this point is to the popular idea of Christian
charity. There is certainly great need of charity,
and there is a legitimate field for its exercise. But
I submit that those cases, in which God clearly tells
us both what to do and how to do it, cannot properly be included in this field. In such cases there
is no room left for us to be charitable, or unchar-
itable; liberal or illiberal. The only question is
whether we will be faithful or faithless. When once
it has been decided that a command has been given
to us by divine authority, then whether it be great
or small, apparently important or unimportant, in
harmony with the dictates of reason or above reason,
necessary or apparently unnecessary, a genuine and
intelligent faith urges us to obey, and to perform
the duty with scrupulous exactness.

5. In the last place I notice this test of faith:
*Where the thing commanded requires great self-de-
nial, and self-sacrifice.* This may be regarded as a
test of the strength of faith. It is equally a test of
its genuineness. The greater the difficulties which
lie in our way, the brighter shines that faith which

enables us to surmount them. The darkness of the night brings out the stars, and so the trials and difficulties of life cause our faith to shine with unusual lustre. How often may we see this? Time would fail me to mention the illustrations of it which appear on the pages of the history of God's people in all ages—of the martyrs and confessors who were tortured, not accepting deliverance, who had trials of cruel mockings and scourgings, yea, moreover, bonds and imprisonment. They were stoned, they were sawn asunder, were tempted, were slain with the sword. They wandered about in sheepskins and goatskins; being destitute, afflicted, tormented (of whom the world was not worthy). They wandered in deserts, and in mountains, and in dens and caves of the earth.

Faith led Saul of Tarsus to turn from his friends and admirers, and the bright prospect of earthly honor opening before him and to condemn himself to perpetual exile. He was a despised and homeless wanderer on the earth. He was troubled on every side, yet not distressed; he was perplexed, but not in despair; persecuted, but not forsaken; cast down, but not destroyed. The faith which led him through the furnace of fiery trial sustained him. God never forsakes those who are faithful to him. When the three Hebrew children were cast into the white blazing fire of the furnace God did not take them out, but he did that which was much better. He came down and walked with them through the flames. So he will do with us, my brethren, if only we walk by faith.

Faith led Moses to forsake royal honors, the pleasures of the palace, the treasures of Egypt, and the high social standing of the house of the Pharaohs, and to identify himself with the poor enslaved people of God. He endured as seeing him who is invisible. It caused faithful old Abram to offer his son, his beloved Isaac, in obedience to God's command. O, how much stood in his way! With a father's warmest affection he loved that boy. Must he now offer him as a burnt offering? It was morally wrong to kill. Must he slay his own son? Moreover, God had promised that through Isaac his seed should become as the sands upon the sea shore, and as the stars in the heavens—innumerable—must all this fail? Can faith surmount all these difficulties? It did. I do not know how theologians classify his faith—whether it was evangelical, or historical, or faith in the mere word—I don't know, and less do I care—but give me just such a faith.

Having described and illustrated some of the features of those works which furnish the highest proof of the presence and power of faith within, let me hasten to a conclusion, by making a brief application of these principles to present duties. Not only in living the Christian life, but also in coming to Christ for the pardon of our sins and adoption into the family of God, we must walk by faith. The first question to be answered is always this, What

41

does God say? What are the commandments of
Christ? What is the divinely appointed way of
coming to the Saviour? What are the conditions of
admission into the Church of Christ? After a careful study of the teachings of Christ and the practice of his apostles, I present this answer: First,
you are required to believe, with all your heart, on
the Lord Jesus Christ. Second, you are required to
repent of all your sins. Third, you are required to
confess with your mouth the faith of your heart;
and in the fourth place, you are required to be baptized into the name of the Father, and of the Son,
and of the Holy Spirit. These are the divine requirements and this the divine order. All these are
for, or in order to the remission of sins.

For proof and illustration of this I refer you to
Christ's conversation with Nicodemus (John iii:5),
to the great commission given to the apostles (Matt.
xxviii:19; Mark xvi:15,16; Luke xxiv:46,47); to
the conversion of the three thousand on the day of
Pentecost (Acts ii:37,38); to the conversion of
the Samaritans under the preaching of Philip (Acts
viii:12); to the conversion of the Ethiopian (Acts
viii:35-39); to the conversion of Saul (Acts ix:1-18;
xxii:16); to the conversion of Cornelius (Acts x:44-
48); to the conversion of Lydia (Acts xvi:14,15);
to the conversion of the Philippian jailor (Acts xvi:-
25-34); to the conversion of the Corinthians (Acts
xviii:8); to what Paul wrote to his brethren in Rome
about the faith of the heart and the confession with

the mouth (Rom. x:10); and finally, to what he wrote to these same persons about having been made free from sin through obedience (Rom. vi:17-18). I submit these Scriptures without argument. How, now, may we show our faith?

1. *By striving to do all that God requires.* If there are four steps required we will not take three and then stop. The Israelites were required to march around the walls of Jericho once every day for six consecutive days, and then on the seventh to march around them seven times, and then when they heard the sound of the trumpet they were to raise a loud shout. When all this was done they could rest assured that God would fulfill his promise. But would it have have done for them to march around the city only once on the seventh day, and then having raised the shout expect God to fulfill his promise? Could they have claimed it? Would they have shown their faith while thus manifestly disregarding divine directions? Why march around the city for seven days? Why march around it seven times on the seventh day? Yea, why march around it at all? There can be only this answer: *God said do it.* But would he not have delivered the city into their hands if they had encompassed it only once on the seventh day? I do not know. I know that in such an event they would have had no right to claim the fulfilment of the promise. I know still farther that faith would not lead them to try such an experiment.

2. *By striving to do it just as God has ordained*

43

it should be done. Faith seeks neither substitutions
nor modifications of ordinances. It asks for the divine mode, and having found it; it clings to it. Now,
Christ has ordained Christian baptism. Sinners are
commanded to be baptized before they are received
into the kingdom of Christ. The command is not
generic, but specific. *One certain, definite thing* is
commanded. Faith seeks to find what that one, definite act is, and having found it resolutely rejects all
proposed substitutions. What, therefore, is baptism?
It will not do to trifle with this question. What do
we *know* about the primitive practice? We know
that those who went out to hear the preaching of
John the Baptist were "baptized of him in the river
Jordan." (Mark 1:5). We know that after this
John baptized in Enon near to Salim, "because there
was much water there." (John iii:23). We know
that after Jesus was baptized he "went up straightway out of the water." (Matt. iii:16). We know
that when Philip went to baptize the Ethiopian noble-
man, "they went down both into the water, both
Philip and the Eunuch," and after the baptism they
came up out of the water. (Acts viii:38,39.) We
know that Paul, writing of this ordinance says, "we
are buried with him by baptism." (Rom. vi:4.) We
know that in another place he says, "buried with
him in baptism, wherein ye are risen with him."
(Col. ii:12.) These are some of the things which all
may *know* if they will read. Now, put them together
and what do we have? We have going to a river, or

44

place where there is much water, a going down into the water, a burial, a resurrection, and a coming up straightway out of the water. This is the divine way. We must show our faith by accepting the divine way, and persistently rejecting all proposed substitutions.

3 *We may show our faith by obeying when there is no apparent connection between the things commanded and the result to be secured;* between the means to be employed and the end to be gained. Now in the case before us the result to be secured is the forgiveness of past sins. The things commanded are faith, repentance, confession and baptism. Not one of these alone, but all of these together are for remission of sins. But is there any apparent connection between the end and the means? Is there between faith and forgiveness? between repentance and forgiveness? between confession of Christ and forgiveness? Were I to answer these in the affirmative perhaps few, if any, would object to the answer. I now ask, is there any *apparent* connection between Christian baptism and the forgiveness of sins? I answer most emphatically, No! But is there any connection? Have they been joined together by the divine will? Has baptism been commanded for salvation or in order to the remission of sins? The word of God only can answer this. In Mark xvi:16, Christ says, "he that believeth and is *baptized* shall be saved;" and in his conversation with Nicodemus he said, "Except a man be born of water and the

Spirit he cannot enter into the kingdom of God.''
When those on the day of Pentecost cried out, ''Men
and brethren, what shall we do?'' Peter answering
said: ''Repent, *and be baptized,* every one of you,
in the name of Christ, *for the remission of sins.*'' I
might add passage after passage to the same effect.
These are enough. The baptism of a proper subject
is for the remission of sins. This makes baptism a
test of faith. It must be an act of faith. The connection between faith, repentance, confession, *and*
baptism, and the forgiveness of sins, is no more apparent than was the connection between marching
around the city of Jericho and the falling of its walls.

4. *Show your faith by following Christ in his
appointed ways,* great as may be the self-denial and
the sacrifice required. We are not threatened with
persecution now as were those who followed Christ
during the infancy of the Church. I thank God that
we are not. But there is self-denial and sacrifice
even now in being a true disciple.

O for that faith which says:—

> "In *all* my Lord's *appointed ways,*
> My journey I'll pursue,
> Hinder me not, you much loved saints,
> For I must go with you.
> *Through floods and flames, if Jesus lead,*
> *I'll follow where he goes."*

Begin to follow Christ now. Begin the work of
faith tonight. Our glorious Lord and King is

coming. It is written, "Behold, I come quickly, and my reward is with me to give to every man according as his work shall be." "The Lord is not slack concerning his promises, as some men count slackness; but is long-suffering to us-ward, not willing that any should perish, but that all should come to repentance. But the day of the Lord will come as a thief in the night; in the which the heavens shall pass away with a great noise, and the elements shall melt with fervent heat; the earth also and the works that are therein shall be burned up." You may not believe this, but it is true. It is God's truth. Men would not believe Noah. When he warned them, they laughed and mocked him. They said: "Has such a thing ever been. What sign is there in the heavens above, or the earth beneath?" That did not change God's truth. At last the time came. It was the day of doom. The Ark was closed. Then were the windows of heaven opened and the fountains of the great deep were broken up, and the earth became one mighty, boundless, shoreless sea. The same God who foretold the deluge of waters and told Noah to preach, now foretells the deluge of fire and bids me call you to the Ark of Safety. That Ark is Christ. The way to him stands open tonight. Who will come? Who will enter in and be saved?

THE CONVERSION OF THE WORLD TO CHRIST

ALEXANDER PROCTOR in Lard's Quarterly,
January, 1866

WHEN Jehovah promised Abraham that in him and his seed all families of the earth should be blessed, there was planted the germ of that faith which has constituted the chief element in the life of his posterity, both natural and spiritual, from that day to this. Very early in the history of his descendants the impression began to unfold itself that it was the purpose of God that they should in the end become the rulers of the world.

In the time of David this conviction had taken root in the national mind, and was already strong enough to express itself with great distinctness. It constitutes the subject of some of the sweetest songs of the shepherd king. Especially is it the foundation of inspiration of that splendid vision of his illustrious son, in which he beholds upon the throne of Israel a monarch to whom "The kings of Tarshish and of the isles shall bring presents; the king of Sheba and Seba shall offer gifts; yea, all nations shall fall down before him; his name shall be continued as long as the sun; all nations shall call him blessed.'' The spirit of this prophecy was the faith of the nation—a faith which was so deeply rooted in the hearts of all faithful Israelites, that no change could possibly remove it. *About three hundred years after David* had established his throne in Jerusalem, had blended his spirit with Hebrew literature; and, with the deep faith of his own heart, inspired the songs of the people, came the prophet Isaiah. But not until the fortunes and future prospects of Israel were darkly changed. The kingdom was rent, and both parts of it were in ruins. The royal seed of David, the priesthood, and the people had apostatized, until not a trace of the glory of the reigns of David and Solomon had remained. Assyria, Babylon, and Persia were successively spoiling Samaria and Jerusalem. Even Edom, Moab, and Tyre scorned and insulted the degenerate children of Abraham, Isaac, and Jacob. Yet, from the depths of such hopeless ruin, the son of Amoz, with exulting eloquence, proclaims the hope of Israel: ''And it shall come to pass in the last days, that the mountain of the Lord's house shall be established in the top of the mountains, and shall be exalted above the hills; and all nations shall flow unto it. In that day there shall come a root out of Jesse which shall stand for an ensign of the people; to it shall the Gentiles seek; and his rest shall be glorious.'' ''He shall not fail nor be discouraged till he have

49

set judgment in the earth; and the isles shall wait for his law." "Thus saith the Lord God: Behold I will lift up my hand to the Gentiles and set up my standard to the people, and they shall bring thy sons in their arms, and thy daughters shall be carried upon their shoulders, and kings shall be thy nursing fathers and their queens thy nursing mothers. They shall bow down to thee with their face toward the earth and lick up the dust of thy feet." "Arise, shine, for thy light is come and the glory of thy Lord is risen upon thee, and the Gentiles shall come to thy light, and kings to the brightness of thy rising." "For the nation and kingdom that will not serve thee shall perish; yea, those nations shall be utterly wasted." *A hundred and fifty years after* one of the seraphim had touched with a live coal from off the altar the lips of Isaiah, and long after the heavens were opened to Ezekial, among the captives of Israel by the river Chebar, and the eye of Jeremiah had trickled down without ceasing because he saw the city solitary that had been full of people, appeared the prophet Daniel, the counsellor of Nebuchadnezzar, and the ruler of the province of Babylon. The Assyrians had made the mountain of Ephraim a wilderness, and "Judah had gone into captivity because of affliction and because of great servitude." "The Lord had covered the daughter of Zion with a cloud in his anger, and cast down from heaven unto the earth the beauty of Israel." Her enemies had passed by and clapped their hands at her. They had hissed and wagged their heads at the daughter of Jerusalem, saying: "Is this the city that men call the perfection of beauty, the joy of the whole earth?" Her princes, her priests, and her people had "sat down by the rivers of Babylon; yea, they had wept when they remembered Zion. They had hanged their harps upon the willows in the midst thereof," and mourned in songless silence over the buried hopes of their wasted nation. Thus when the Hebrew nation was destroyed, when, according to the calculations of human sagacity, even the hope of its reorganization and of its human triumphs had utterly perished; and when the monarch of the world's empire, who had carried them into captivity and dispersed them through the provinces of Babylon, that their name as a people might be forgotten, was lying in his palace and dreaming of his future greatness, his spirit was troubled by the appearance of a great image, whose brightness was excellent and the form thereof was terrible. And when all the wise men of his kingdom failed to show him his dream or the interpretation thereof, then there was found a man of the captives of Judah who showed the dream, described the great image, and revealed the interpretation. The interpretation of the king's dream was a sublime procession of the great empires that were to fill the then inhabited earth. As these vast monarchies, with their subjects, provinces, and captive nations passed in stately session across the field ot the prophet's vision, what could a captive Hebrew, whose nation as such had been swept away by their power, hope for the future of his people? Yet, while Daniel was still beholding the last and greatest of them all, devouring, breaking in pieces, and bruising all the nations of the earth, the deathless faith given by promise to Abraham, sung by David and proclaimed by Isaiah, came out of his heart in these remarkable words: *"And in the days of these kings* shall the God of heaven set up a kingdom which shall never be destroyed; and the kingdom shall not be left to other people, but it shall break in pieces and consume all these other kingdoms; it shall stand forever."

This great man seems to have been intentionally placed by Providence in the position most favorable for observing the movements of the kingdoms and empires of earth, that from these he might educe his prophecies concerning the future history and destiny of all nations in all coming ages, by a sort of divine sequence. Standing at the right hand of the throne of the greatest power on the earth, he lived to see the rise and fall of some of those mighty kingdoms whose fortunes he had beheld in his wonderful visions. In the first year of the reign of Belshazzar, King of Babylon, there was given him another vision of the four great empires, at the close of which he expressed, still more clearly and strongly, the faith and the hope of Israel: "And the kingdom and dominion, and the greatness of the kingdom under the whole heaven shall be given to the people of the saints of the Most High, whose kingdom is an everlasting kingdom and all dominions shall serve and obey him.''

These predictions and a multitude of others like them, formed the ground on which rested the expectation of the Messiah. It is true that, by construing the prophecies literally, the Jews misconceived the nature of the kingdom promised them, and then of necessity the character of the king who was to fulfill these sublime predictions. But it can not be said that the faith which filled the Hebrew heart, from which, as from a never-failing fountain, has flowed all Hebrew life, which gave form and color to all their literature, and which time and its revolutions have found to be indestructible, was wholly false. The final domination of Israel over all the inhabitants of this globe is as clearly predicted as the coming of Christ, and belief in the fulfillment of the one involves belief in the final fulfillment of the other.

The actual coming of the Christ has not changed *the fact* of such a faith in the hearts of men, but only *the form* of it. From the day that Jesus called to him, from their boats on the waters of Galilee, the sons of James and Zebedee, there has been in the hearts of his disciples a deep and ever-increasing conviction that the human race would in some way or other be brought under his dominion.

Listening daily to his words and witnessing his mighty works while he was with them on earth, the

53

confidence that it was he who was the blessing of Abraham, the Son of David, the King foretold by Daniel, was growing stronger and deeper. The disappointment expressed in those touching words of some of the disciples, "We trusted that it had been he who should have redeemed Israel," shows the strength which their faith had attained; and after his resurrection was known by them, and they had collected again about him, the question, "Lord, wilt thou at this time restore again the kingdom to Israel?" reveals the same faith still looking to the supremacy of Israel over the nations of the earth, but expecting it now through him.

Precisely in harmony with the prophecies to which we have referred was the commission received by the apostles from him who was now come to fulfill them. Sanctioned by all authority in heaven and upon earth. It read: "Go ye, therefore, disciple all the nations." They waited in Jerusalem until they were endued with power from on high, and then in the fulness of the inspiration of the Holy Spirit, with the higher interpretation of the Hebrew prophets, and with the whole life of Christ brought afresh to their remembrance, with every act and word with all its mighty import to them and to the world lying forever open before the eye of the soul, they went forth armed to the conquest of the nations. And when they saw the whole creation travailing and groaning together in pain under the weight of its inward evils and outward griefs, and felt that

54

the grand purpose of their mission was to make known the life, the death, the resurrection and the coronation of him who had come to bring glad news to the poor, to heal the broken-hearted, to open the prisons of them that were bound, and to set at liberty them that were bruised, is it not wonderful that they should have thought such a message, before such a world, would draw all men after their Redeemer and King?

Can the language of the Hebrew prophets, illuminated and extended to its true signification by the Dayspring from on high, and the vast meaning and purpose of the life Christ expressed in the words of the commission of the twelve apostles, fail to establish in the hearts of all who receive the Old and New Testament Scriptures as true, the belief that it is the clearly expressed purpose of Jehovah to give the empire of the world to the saints? Such, we have already seen, has been their faith and their hope in the ages past, and such it must ever be until the trumpet of the seventh angel shall sound, and there will be great voices in heaven saying: "The kingdoms of this world are become the kingdoms of our Lord and of his Christ, and he shall reign for ever and ever." If it be said that the kingdom of Christ is spiritual, and therefore has nothing to do with the kingdoms of this world as such, it will be enough to reply, that to the extent to which the reign of Christ over the spirits of men shall become universal, to that extent will it become outward in its manifestations. This thought is so well expressed by Trench, that I am induced to avail myself of his language. Alluding to the examination of the Savior by Pilate, he says: "The practical Roman saw as much as the natural man could see of this in a moment, that the question at issue between Christ and the world was not a question of one nation and another, but of one kingdom and another; and seeing this, he came at once to the point: 'Art thou a king then?' And that empire which tolerated all other religions would have tolerated the Christian, instead of engaging in a death-struggle with it to strangle it or be strangled by it, but that it instinctively felt that this, however its first seat and home might seem to be in the hearts of men, yet could not remain there, but would demand outward expression for itself, must go forth into the world and conquer a dominion of its own, a dominion which would leave no room in the world for another fabric of force and fraud!"

With the word of prophecy made more sure by voices from the excellent glory, and with a commission bearing with it the authority of Him whose power they had so often witnessed, and whom, after he had led captivity captive, they had seen ascend to the right hand of the Majesty on high, giving them, as he arose, a pledge of his presence and co-operation to the end of the world; let it not surprise us if, with these transcendent facts immediately before them in the freshness and power of their faith, and the strength and splendor of their first hopes, they contemplated the conquest of the world as near.

This lengthened introduction will prepare us for some questions which will constitute the real subject of this article. Have the prophecies, that shone in starry beauty over the darkness of those long past ages, ever found their fulfillment? Or, have the hopes which put forth their blossoms in the dawning light of the rising Sun of Righteousness ever found their realization? Christianity has been in the world now nearly 2,000 years; how far have the results of the labors of all those long centuries corresponded with the promises made at the beginning? Has the world ever been converted to Christ? The thoughtful reader of the history of Christianity is compelled to answer: No. Notwithstanding the nature of the message contained in the glorious gospel of the blessed God, the preaching of the apostles, the sufferings of martyrs, and the toil and sacrifices of the disciples in succeeding ages, but a comparatively small fraction of the human race has ever acknowledged the power and authority of Him who was declared to be both Lord and Christ.

Still another question meets us; one which, most of all, commands our interest, namely: Does the present condition of the religious world point to the fulfillment of our hopes? The religious powers now at work on the globe, do they give us any assurance that they *can convert* any large portion of mankind to Christ? A serious examination of the available data necessary to render a candid answer to this question turns our hearts into sadness. Truth compels the statement, however solemn and painful to Christian philanthropy, that the world, considered as to its whole population according to its best calculation that human wisdom can make, is not even in the process of being converted to Christ. Does this startle you, Christian reader? If so, wait and hear me. If true, it ought to startle and alarm all Christendom. Look with me at a few facts, and then think.

In the April number of the *Millenial Harbinger* for 1863 is published the latest statistical report that has come under the observation of the writer. The facts published in that paper purport to have been taken from a table prepared by Prof. Schem, editor of the *National Almanac*. In that report the total population of the globe is estimated at about one billion, 300,000,000 of which, the total Christian population, counting in all the sects laying claim to the name, is about 357,000,000, leaving the earth's unconverted masses about 943,000,000. Now in all the estimates made in the early part of this century from the best data that could be furnished from all sources, the latter number was set down at 800,000,-000, so that if such estimates can be taken as even approximately true, the unchristianized population of the globe has gained on all the churches in the world, nearly 150,000,000 in a little more than half a century. But if we take what is here called the Christian population of the globe, and subtract from it the unconverted, the result is more painfully discouraging. For if we should say that but a small proportion of the Greek Church, the Roman Catholic, and some of the other national establishments of the Old World, into which children are born and grow up as they did in the Jewish Commonwealth, are converted, facts would sustain the statement; but, if we subtract one half, we have only 178,500,000 out of the entire population of the globe converted, and who will say that there is even that number? Leaving 1,250,000,000 of the earth's inhabitants, of whom it can be said every moment, so far as Christianity is concerned, they are dying unsaved.

What is Christianity doing to convert America today? The census of the United States shows that in the decade between 1900 and 1910 the population of our country increased twenty-one per cent and Christianity increased twenty-one per cent. In the land most favored by the Christian religion we have barely held our own with the increase in population. Going into more detail, I notice that the great Methodist Episcopal Church during the year 1912 increased only about two members to each congregation. This is one of the most vital, aggressive and active religious bodies among us today. The average increase in the membership of the Northern Presbyterian Church is a little over one for each of its churches. The average increase in the Protestant Episcopal Church is a trifle over two for each church and the Disciples of Christ would probably number about the same. According to Dr. H. K. Carroll, the average increase in all the Churches in America for the year 1914 was only two per cent. This much for Christianity in America.

What is its condition in England? A religious census recently taken by one of the large daily papers of Liverpool shows that in the previous decade the Anglican Church made a decline of 9,900 members, the Non-conformist bodies made a decline of 14,200 members; among these the Congregationalists show a decline of 1,850, the English Presbyterians of 1,500, the Welsh Calvinistic Methodists of 400, the United Methodists of 700, the Primitives of 150, the Wesleyans barely held their own; the Roman Catholics held their own with the increase in population.

If we leave England and go to the heathen countries we find a still more startling condition of things. When William Carey, after careful study, made a report one hundred and twenty-five years ago, he gave the population of the non-Christian world at 550 millions; Warneck today gives the population of the non-Christian world at 1,050 millions. If these figures be correct, the heathen world has increased since foreign missions have been prosecuted 500 millions of people. Allowing for mistakes in Carey's estimate, we can safely put the increase of the non-Christian world at 300 millions.

In short, after one hundred and twenty-five years of our missionary propaganda, we find less than three millions of converted heathen and three hundred millions more heathens than when we began; and these facts are no reflection upon our foreign missionary work. We have accomplished in that direction all that could be hoped for under existing conditions. I am a hearty supporter, with tongue and pen and purse, of our foreign missionary work, but I must recognize the fact that for every heathen that has been converted to Christianity, heathenism has brought 100 others *into its darkness.)

These are a few of the facts that have forced the melancholy and startling statement already made, namely, that the world, looked at in relation to its whole population and the religious potencies now operating upon it, is not even in *the process* of being saved. Preachers and other religious partisans who hasten every year to report the numbers they have gained in particular communities, and to publish the rate of increase in their respective little parties, fail to tell how much the great world outside of the churches has grown at the same time. It is certain that the most favorable estimate in behalf of the churches of Christendom will show that the world is gaining on them every year.

What then? Have the promises to Abraham, by which he looked for a city which hath foundations, whose builder and maker is God, proved, after all, vain illusions? Shall the sweet strains of the Hebrew

*Above facts supplied by the Editor.

minstrel, which have charmed the evil spirit of dis-
sands of the human race, charm no more? Are the
cord and gloom from the hearts of so many thou-
enraptured visions of Isaiah, by which his soul was
borne away from the evil days of Ahaz to behold
with exultant joy the coming of the Wonderful, the
Counselor, the Father of the everlasting age, and the
Prince of Peace, to be regarded as the fantasies of
a wild imagination? And those most marvelous
dreams of the prophet Daniel, by which the tears of
the exile were dried, and Jerusalem still remembered
above his chief joy, are they to be considered as
nothing but dreams? Have all those holy men who
walked by the light of these promises, seeing them
afar off, being persuaded of them and enduring as
seeing Him who is invisible, lived and died in a vain
faith? And is it in vain that the Redeemer has come
to Zion travailing in the greatness of His strength,
mighty to save? Has He borne our griefs and carried our sorrows—was He wounded for our transgressions and bruised for our iniquities, and yet not
to see the travail of His soul and be satisfied? Have
the everlasting doors been opened wide to receive
the King of Glory, and yet is the dominion under
the whole heavens not to be given to Him? To all
of these questions we say : *No! They do not form the
conclusions* to the premises stated above. But there
is an answer to the question, what then? which is
so palpable and overwhelming that it is forcing its
way into the minds of the best thinkers of the age.

It is this: The present religious organizations of Christendom have *no power in them* to save any large proportion of mankind. It is not that Christianity is a failure. The gospel is adapted to all the wants of human nature. It is the power of God for salvation, and it can and will save all men who believe. But the religious powers on the globe, after having ample time to make a full trial of what they can do to save the human race, have demonstrated clearly the fearful fact that they are *wholly inadequate* to its accomplishment. To a thoughtful mind this conclusion is solemn beyond expression, and it forces from the heart the painful inquiry: Why is this? Is it a revealed purpose of God that any large part of mankind is to be converted to Christ, or are we to be driven to the dreadful alternative that nearly all of our race are to be excluded from the great redemption? Who is prepared for this conclusion? If so, what means the Old Testament by all those promises, to some of which we have referred? What means the commission to the apostles? Have the inspired men of both Testaments, and the great and good who have believed their teachings in all ages, indulged in a faith which is groundless? And cherished hopes which are to have no realization? If it is not so, whose fault is it that so few comparatively are being saved?

This seems to us the most ponderous question which can engage the minds of this generation; to its investigation, therefore, we now propose to direct

3

the attention of the reader. The apostles themselves, in the course of their ministry, encountered this gloomy difficulty. And, perhaps, if we attentively examine the reasons assigned by them why all were not converted to whom they preached, we shall obtain some assistance in finding the right solution.

The apostle Paul has left on record the inspired account, which he rendered to himself and the world, of the rejection of the gospel by the two classes of men to whom he preached it. We cannot think that such a record was made without a special design, or that it was intended for only the age in which it was written. In the first letter which he wrote to the Church at Corinth he makes the following statement: "For the Jews require a sign, and the Greeks seek after wisdom; but we preach Christ crucified, to the Jews a stumbling-block, and to the Greeks foolishness." These are the causes which prevented the Jews and the Greeks from receiving the preaching of the cross. The devotion of the Greek to the pursuits of philosophy, and his proud confidence in those systems which the surpassing intelligence of the great thinkers of his nation had produced, was that which made the promise of life through a crucified Messiah seem to him foolishness. The Jewish scribe also had his eye fixed upon a system of life derived from the study of the law and the traditions of the elders, and in it his confidence was so great that he demanded both from the Saviour and his apostles a sign from heaven before he would consent to hear them, and when the cross of the Crucified was placed in the pathway of his self-righteousness he stumbled and fell. It is not without special significance that the spirit of inspiration has pointed out these two great divisions of mankind, and fixed the attention of the reader of the New Testament upon the central point in the life of each as the reason of their rejection of Christianity.

Nations do not come into being by accident, nor is the part performed by each one in placing its link in the chain of universal history a mere fortuity. There is a divine plot in the great drama of the world's national life. Each nation has its part to perform, some the great principle to illustrate before the eyes of humanity, which is necessary to make up and bring out the final *denouement*. Now here are two nations that have performed their parts and have passed away. The curtain has fallen behind them ages ago. What were they here for? In the great plan of God's providence, what principles have they illustrated and given to the world?

To understand this question, let us first place before our minds the two great departments of human nature, namely, the intellectual and moral; then let us glance the eye along the line of human history, and behold humanity struggling to comprehend itself, and to work out its destiny at one time on the ground of its *intellectual strength*, and at another on that of the force of its *moral integrity*. Then let us look at the two great divisions of the human race mentioned by the apostle Paul, each representing its side of human nature, and throwing its light on the solution of the vast problem of humanity.

In reference, then, to what the civilization and national life of Greece meant for the world, while the politician seeks his solution in her forms of society, in the annals of her struggles and her failures, her triumphs and her defeats, in the examples of her statesmen, in the genius and heroism of her generals, and in the eloquence and patriotism of her orators,— while the philosopher finds his in the achievements of her transcendent intellects, the teachings of Socrates, the dreams of Plato, the reasonings of Aristotle, Zeno, Pythagoras, and their successors,— and while the poet and the artist has each his department in the matchless beauty of her literature and ruins of her imperishable art,—let us, as Christian philosophers, while conceding that the remains of that marvelous people have been precious to the world in all these respects, maintain the higher stand-point given by the apostle to the nations. Instead of regarding either of these departments as a life within itself, let us contemplate the meaning of the whole problem of Greek life in its relation to the redemption and destiny of man in the book of revelation.

Man has ever been saying, especially among cultivated nations, that he can rely upon the achievements of reason to discover the truth which he needs, to find a remedy for his evils and sorrows, and the source whence to supply all the wants of the soul.

Knowing that this perverted confidence is so deeply imbedded in his nature that nothing but experience can detach him from it, the Author of his being, in wisdom and kindness, has permitted him to make the experiment. For that purpose he gave the Greek mind, invested it with powers such as he has bestowed upon no other people, and these he touched with a perfection of finish never equalled since that nation perished. With such intellects, in the midst of circumstances most favorable for their full development and free exercise for a period of more than 500 years, or, if we estimate the whole time which measures the history of Grecian literature as necessary to the culmination of their intellectual perfection, more than 1,000 years, was the experiment being made. When the apostle was at Athens and Corinth it was complete. The immovable superstition which he found in the former, and the moral corruption in the latter, proclaim the result. The conclusion is palpable. *No intellectual endowments*, no effort of human reason, however stupendous and far-reaching it may be, has any power to lift the burden of guilt and sorrow from the heart of man, or, in the summary of the apostle, the "wisdom and righteousness, and sanctification, and redemption" needed by him is utterly and forever unattainable by any system of human philosophy. But if man has become vain in his reasonings, his foolish heart, by its proud confidence in the strength of its virtue, has been darkened; hence, as a warning against this universal danger, another people, with a different cast of mind and another form of civilization, has left him its history and the lesson which it teaches. If in Greek civilization the intellect always and everywhere predominates, in the Jewish the moral nature is developed to an extent never found in the history of any other people. In Greek literature, the order, symmetry, and beauty which intellect creates reigns supreme in poetry, history, philosophy, and the arts. In Hebrew we have the instincts of the heart, the longings of the soul for the unseen and the infinite, the movements of which are too sublime for the regular processes of logic. Hence, if in Hebrew we look in vain for the unity and harmony of Sophocles, the philosophical order and graceful arrangement of Thucydides and Xenophon, the always studied conciseness, grace, and energy of Demosthenes, and the perfect logic of Aristotle, still less shall we find in Greek the deep natural pathos of Job, the simple unapproachable sublimity of Moses, the heart-gushing lyrics of David, or the spontaneous and never-wearied flight of Isaiah. The natural orbit of the soul described by the movement of such spirits as have given us our Hebrew Bible may be irregular, yet it is inconceivably above that of Greek intellect.

With a people thus constituted and exactly adapted to it, was the experiment made for the moral nature of man. That it might be perfect, they were transferred to a country isolated from all others by its natural boundaries; the mountains of Lebanon on the north, the Desert of Arabia on the east and south, and the Mediterranean Sea on the west. To make the isolation more perfect, the rite of circumcision was given them, which separated each individual from all other peoples. Then, to test the moral strength of human nature, there was given them a law, holy, just and good, which they were exhorted to keep, by the promise of every material and moral good, and against the breaking of which were threatened the severest penalties. They were commanded to teach it to their children on all occasions. It was illustrated daily in the Temple worship, and afterward read in their synagogues on the Sabbath day. They were allowed fifteen centuries to make the necessary trial, and when Christ, "the end of the law," was in Jerusalem, her moral condition was almost, if not quite, as sad as that of Athens and Corinth. The highest classes of her people, Scribes, Pharisees, and lawyers, he likens to whited sepulchres. The Temple itself was made a den of thieves. The testimony of Josephus, their own historian, in innumerable passages reveals the melancholy fact that the nation was a moral wreck without the hope of recovery. The conclusion becomes inevitable, that man has as little power in his moral nature to save himself as was shown to be in his intellectual.

When this great argument of God with man, one of whose premises was fifteen hundred years being formed, and the other more than a thousand, was

complete, these civilizations began to pass away.
There was nothing more that they could do for the
human race. They had taught all that they were
sent to teach. The national life of the Greek and of
the Jew was done forever. They had revealed the
utter helplessness of man on both sides of his nature,
and made known the mournful fact, that there was
no remedy either in the one or the other that could
reach his condition. Then it was time for Peter to
appear in Jerusalem, and Paul at Athens, preaching
Christ and him crucified; though to the Jew a
stumbling-block, and to the Greek foolishness, yet,
to them that believed, the power of God and the
wisdom of God.

By the light of this great demonstration, we may
now return to the question: Why are so few of the
earth's unsaved millions being converted to Christ?
We are now prepared to affirm that the greatest of all
reasons—that which has stood in the way of the
world's conversion for ages, is the fact, that *the
warning of these departing nations has been un-
heeded*. The apostles, and those who immediately
succeeded them, by preaching the cross of Christ
proved, by the successes which attended their efforts,
that the gospel has life and power in it enough to
save the world. But a little more than two centuries
after the last apostle was dead, the Church began to
try to improve on the apostolic method. It was
determined to put Christianity into what is now
termed a scientific form—to convert it into a sys-

tem of doctrines, which could be stated in logical propositions. Each of these was made an article of faith. The seat of Christianity was removed from the heart to the head. These systems, and the intellectual conflicts which forever spring from them as inevitably as leaves and blossoms from buds, took the place of the simple, living, loving trust of the soul in the person of Christ. The old Greek life which had engulfed in moral ruin, not only themselves, but all nations which had derived their civilization from them, began to be repeated in principle, and then began that tremendous apostasy which culminated in the dark ages, and left the world Romanish as the final result. This failure, more appalling in the moral depravity which it produced than both the others, was the result of an experiment made from the union of Greek philosophy and Jewish legalism.

When human nature was so deeply outraged by the dreadful corruptions, cruelties, and abominations into which it had been dragged by this perverted system, that it could no longer tolerate it in silence, began those indignant protests, called reformations, from which have grown up the Protestant denominations of Christendom. Each one of these in its turn, noble in its origin, and great in its first progress, promised to realize the hopes of that kingdom of truth and love which the hearts of men have cherished in spite of all failures, which the deepest abysses of darkness and woe into which they have fallen could never entirely wrest from them. But so

71

deeply rooted in our fallen nature is the old vanity of *the intellect* and the pride of *the heart* that every sect in the world has fallen into the same fatal error, is repeating the same sad experiment, and is promising to mankind the same *mournful failure*.

Without regard to chronological order, we select one of these systems, which, in respect to the point to be proved, represents all. The history of the Presbyterian Confession of Faith is as well known as that of any denomination. It was produced by a body of men possessed of as much ability, piety, and learning as could at the time it was made have been collected on the globe. It is the result of deliberations and discussions of more than a hundred ministers, besides distinguished laymen, continued, without intermission, for a period of five years—from 1643 to 1648. It is not necessary to our purpose to discuss the truth or falsity of its doctrines; so far as the argument is concerned, we might assume them all to be true, the simple fact that we want to use is this: That it consists of a set of abstract propositions, supposed to contain, in a scientific form, the teaching of Christ and the apostles.

Now suppose we grant that these propositions were formed by men of the greatest minds and the most profound learning then on the globe; of course, the greater the mind and the deeper the learning, the more abstruse will be the propositions in which they affirm their conclusions. It is notoriously so in this case. It requires more study and time to master the

Assembly's Confession and catechism than to become well acquainted with the life of Christ. But the argument is especially concerned with the nature of the process. When you put the Confession of Faith into the hands of a child, you have given him a set of abstract propositions to study which it required men of mature minds, some of them of immense learning, years of profound thought to produce. Now the faculties which he exercises in obtaining a knowledge of those propositions are the same that he would employ in studying a problem in algebra or geometry, and the process is precisely that by which the mind acquires a knowledge of the abstractions of Plato or Pythagoras. It is simply the exercise of the intellectual powers.

The same can be truthfully affirmed of every Protestant sect. The Episcopalians have thirty-nine of these abstract propositions; the Methodists, Baptists, Unitarians, etc., many. Every sect has its view of Christianity made into a scientific form, logically stated, in propositions, which, when taken together, make up its denominational system. Each system has for its object to convince the intellect that it is true and all others false; and in this conviction there is no religious element whatever.

The result is as patent as it is mournful. Among the thousands claimed to be under the influence of these systems, a large proportion have intellects thoroughly convinced—are intense partisans of some religious philosophy, while their hearts have no

73

living faith in the living Christ, and they do not even profess to be Christians.

But it will be said that a certain proportion of the adherents of these theories do confide in Christ crucified. This is freely admitted; we are thankful for all the faith that any human heart reposes in the Messiah, and pray that it may abound more and more; but this does not change the historical fact that there is even among those who so believe an element in that every belief which has for its object the intellectual system which each has embraced, and to this element is attached the chief importance.

It is a fact that the chief labor in denominational seminaries is bestowed in the preparation of young men for making proselytes to these theories, and, as a necessary consequence, a large amount of the talent, the learning, and labor of the whole protestant pulpit is expanded for the same purpose. Hence out of the whole number converted to these systems only a comparatively few are converted to Christ. Here, then, we find the answer to the question: Whose fault is it that so few of our race are being saved?

Jewish legalism tried for fifteen centuries on the side of man's moral nature to accomplish the salvation of the race, and ended, as we have seen, in a mournful failure. Human reason for more than a thousand years held the brilliant torch of Greek philosophy over the pathway of humanity, and then threw it down in grief and despair. Romanism, combining both of these, with some of the elements

74

of Christianity, tried for a period of 1,200 years to save the human race, and plunged both the intellect and the heart into an abyss of darkness.

Protestantism has had nearly 400 years to test its power in the conversion of the world, and its failure is becoming painfully intelligible to the best minds in both the Old World and the New. The world has already obtained from it what good there was in it. There is but little more that it can do. And yet those prophecies that have planted in the human heart a deathless faith in the universal dominion of Christ seem as far from fulfillment as ever.

If, now, from this position we turn our eyes toward the future, and inquire what must be the next great movement that may affect the destiny of our earth's population, there seems to be, from the whole premises now before us, but three things possible: The mind of humanity may return along one of the two great routes over which it has traveled to its present position, or it may find some other way in which to move forward; that is to say, the human race may return to Romanism, which has absorbed into itself the experiment of Jewish legalism; or it may fall back into rationalistic infidelity, which is only a new version of Greek philosophy; or it must move forward, walking by faith in Christ. The moral condition of the human race at the time when Christianity was first introduced reveals the possibility that under the perversion of false systems a large proportion of mankind may become infidel.

The condition of Christendom before the birth of Protestantism proves that a large part of the human race may become Roman Catholic; and the condition of the civilized world before Christianity was corrupted, by being converted into a mixture of false philosophy, religion, and superstition, shows that the whole world may become largely Christian. Leaving out the question which is the most probable, these three things alone seem possible; for with the history of Protestantism before us, and its present condition, to believe that any greater proportion of the human race will ever become Episcopalian, Presbyterian, Baptist, or Methodist is now simply impossible. Intelligent men in these denominations may hope that their churches may increase in numbers in some particular localities as the population of the earth grows; but that any intelligent man can seriously imagine that Protestantism can ever gain on that population we can not believe for one moment.

Another consideration already hinted at may be mentioned confirmatory of this position. If there is to be any further progress of the human race at all, it must be along some line not described by the movement of either Romanism or Protestantism. From created fountains the streams all flow down, never up; so of all systems created or arranged by the human mind; the forms of life which have flowed from them have ever tended downward. Even Judaism produced its best fruits soon after its establishment; after that it degenerated to its close, as a civilization. Greek philosophy exhibited some splendid examples of manhood at its beginning, and then sank lower and lower to the end. So of Romanism; we must go back more than 1,000 years, to find those men who were termed the fathers of the church. Lutheranism too; think of the characters it produced in the sixteenth century, and then of what it is doing now. Episcopalianism, Presbyterianism, Baptistism, Methodism have all done their best work long since. In the fruits which they may continue to produce they can never ascend. It belongs to uncreated, infinite, and eternal truth to move in lines ascending forever. If, then, there is ever to be any coming, in the unity of faith and of the knowledge of the Son of God, to a perfect man, it must be in a way marked out by something else than these systems.

If, then, the present religious organizations of Christendom are to continue, the conversion of the world is an absurdity, and the millenium a dream; no conclusion, it seems to us, can rest on a more solid foundation than this. But the Scriptures tell us that "the kingdoms of this world are to become the kingdom of our Lord and His anointed." Now the only power which Christ has, in this dispensation, of winning for himself the empire promised Him is by gaining the faith and love of the human heart. It is only through these that he can exercise dominion over the souls of men. It was in view of this fact, and the great failures of human nature to which He alludes, that the apostle Paul so earnestly affirmed that the only thing left for man was "to preach Christ and him crucified; to plant the faith of mankind, not in wisdom of men, but in the power of God." He knew that the diseases of human nature were too deeply seated to be removed by any system of philosophy or of law-keeping morality. They require a person, a living being; hence he brought no persuasive words of human wisdom, but the Healer of the woes of the human heart—Jesus the Christ. The world had said to him, when He came to bind up the broken-hearted: "Physician, heal thyself;" and having shown them that he was a man of sorrows like themselves, suffering before them even unto death, He came back from the grave the Great Physician, healed, able now to help all who were tempted. It is no abstract proposition, no doctrine, no process of logic, that men need; but the Almighty hand of this living and ever-present Helper, and this hand is laid hold of by faith, not in a *system,* but in *Him.*

When the soul is alarmed by its guilt and torn by remorse, its agony is too awfully real to be reached by any proposition stated in human speech. It never calls for a creed at such a time, but for an Almighty living friend who can take that guilt away. When we feel the ties that bind us to life giving way, and see the grave opening beneath us with no power on earth that can keep us from sinking into its darkness, it is not a theory bound up in a creed that we want, but One who has been in the grave and come out of it again; the hand that has burst the bars of death,

78

that it might deliver them who through fear of death were all their lifetime subject to bondage. Whoever heard a dying man ask for a doctrine or system? Again: When we follow to the grave a father or mother, a husband, wife, or child, and see the body let down into its vault, and the earth begin to close over it, to whom does the whole heart turn in that awful moment? Can imagination conceive a more hollow and heartless mockery, than to speak to it then of "the doctrines of our church?" If the soul's deepest longing at such a time could express itself in words, it would contain the question: Who will give me back my dead? And who can answer this tremendous question, daily and hourly crushed out of the heart of humanity? Neither Moses nor Plato ever mentioned it. Belief in systems of doctrine has nothing to do with it. But there does come One, not a creed, but a living person, in that dreadful hour, holding in his hands the keys of the unseen world and of death, and laying his right hand upon us, He says: "Fear not, I am the first and the last. I am He that liveth and was dead; and, behold I am alive forevermore." "All that are in their graves shall hear His voice and shall come forth." You shall have your dead again. Neither the law nor philosophy can say this. Of all that have lived on this globe, Jesus alone could speak thus to a broken heart. God has literally shut up the soul of man to faith in Christ, and obedience to him as its last and only hope.

Men only call for a creed when they wish to wrangle with and hate their fellow-men. To be indoctrinated into the abstractions of any system of church doctrine is to shut up the heart and embitter it against all who, by their training or mental constitution, are compelled to think differently. It is impossible to think of a kingdom of Christ in which there shall dwell a universal brotherhood, heirs of a common inheritance, without for the time losing sight of these systems, and falling back on the broad ground of simple faith in Christ and conformity to His will.

One feels tempted to exclaim: How long have these vain systems, born of the pride of reason and of the heart, yet to trifle and to mock the great wants and woes of the world? How long shall the souls of the dying millions of our race cry out against those who, with these obsolete systems, stand in the way of the world's redemption?

The premises before us are now wide enough to indicate the highest duty of the true men of this generation. It is to call men from these dumb idols to serve the living God; to work and pray for the annihilation of every system which stands in the way of the world's conversion to Christ. The position which we have taken as a people, involves nothing less than this. Our antagonism is not to men, but to systems as such. With these there can be no compromise. If there is a man among us who thinks of the possibility of such a thing, he understands neither the principles which he represents nor the people with whom he is identified. If God has given us as a people any mission in the world, it is to turn men from systems—which can not convert any large part of mankind, but which only make religious partisans—to Jesus the Christ, who can and will save to the uttermost all who come to God by him. It therefore behooves every true-hearted man to gird himself for the work, to put on the whole armor of God, and enter the contest as if the salvation of the world depended upon his personal success.

REBUILDING JERUSALEM

By F. G. ALLEN

"I am doing a great work, so that I can not come down;
why should the work cease, whilst I leave it, and come down
to you?"—Nehemiah vi:3.

THIS is the language of Nehemiah, the servant of
God, to the delegation sent to him by Sanballat
and Geshem, asking him to meet them in some one of
the villages in the plain of Ono, to hold a council together with reference to the rebuilding of the walls of
Jerusalem. In order that we may understand the
force and significance of this language, it is necessary
that we understand something of the circumstances
under which it is spoken. It has an interesting and
important history underlying it; and to this your
attention is first directed. It is the history of the

REBUILDING OF JERUSALEM BY NEHEMIAH.

Those of you who are Bible readers, and I presume that most of this intelligent audience are, remember that when the Jews were carried away into
Babylonian captivity, some of the poorest of the land
were left for vine dressers and husbandmen. These
continued, with their posterity, in the land of their

fathers. During the whole of the captivity, therefore, there were some Jews in and around Jerusalem.

It will be also remembered that during the captivity, a Jew might, by the special favor and providence of God, obtain a high position of trust and honor in the Persian government, such as we find in the case of Daniel, and that of Nehemiah.

Now it came to pass that during the latter part of the captivity, Nehemiah, a man of whose previous history we know nothing, obtained great favor in the eyes of the king, Artazerxes; so that he enjoyed one of the positions of confidence and honor in his government—that of cup-bearer to the King. While occupying this position, he came into the presence of the King on one occasion with a sad countenance. This was both unbecoming in the King's court, and dangerous; hence we infer that his grief was too intense to be hid. The King saw at once that he had some great sorrow at heart, and immediately asked him the cause. Nehemiah told him that one of his brothers and other Jews had come down from Jerusalem, and he had inquired of them the condition of the Jews that had escaped, who were left of the captivity, and of the condition of the city of Jerusalem.

From these he had learned that the remnant that were left of the captivity were in great affliction and reproach, and that the walls of Jerusalem were broken down, and her gates consumed with fire. Consequently he said: "Let the King live forever; why should not my countenance be sad, when the city, the place of my fathers' sepulchers, lieth waste, and the gates thereof are consumed with fire?'' In the kindness of his heart, the King asked Nehemiah what he could do to alleviate his distress. Then Nehemiah, forgetting all selfish considerations, and prompted by the holy patriotism of his heart, having previously taken the whole matter to God in prayer, in answer to which this favor was granted, asked permission to go over into the land of Judea and rebuild the walls of Jerusalem. This was granted, and Nehemiah had placed under his command a small force for the accomplishment of the work. With this little band, he came over to the city of Jerusalem. Nehemiah kept his own counsel. He told no man of the purpose that God had put into his heart. He selected a few reliable men, and with these he went by night and took a survey of the city. The moon must have been riding high in the heavens, and pouring the light of her full-orbed splendor upon the ruins of the ''City of the great King,'' as Nehemiah beheld and described them. The city was in silent slumber; fit emblem of the slumber of the glory of Israel. As an indication of the utter ruin of the city, when Nehemiah came to the gate of the fountain, and to the King's pool, the beast on which he rode could not pass for the *debris* that filled the way. Having thus made himself thoroughly acquainted with the condition of the city, he matured his plans, and immediately set to work to rebuild the walls, and restore the place of his fathers' sepulchers to its former grandeur and glory. He then revealed to his men the purpose of his heart, and how, through the Divine favor, he had obtained a commission from the King to accomplish the work. The grand ideal of restoring from ruin the city of their fathers, and wresting it from the reproach of their enemies, filled their souls with a holy enthusiasm, so that with one voice they said: "Let us rise up and build the walls."

But no sooner was the work of rebuilding the walls known to the Samaritans and other surrounding tribes, than it met with a united opposition. At first it was to them a source of merriment. They sharpened the shafts of their ridicule, and hurled them at it with fiendish delight. As a sample of their sarcasm, Tobiah, one of the leaders of the opposition, said: "They talk about rebuilding the walls of Jerusalem! The walls that they would build, even if a fox were to go up, he would break down *their* stone wall!" But Nehemiah was not to be turned from his purpose by this kind of warfare. His heart was set upon his work, and he was taking counsel with God, not with men.

But when the opposition saw that this kind of warfare was unavailing, like the farmer who could not bring the boy down from his apple-tree with tufts of grass, tried what virtue there was in stones, they resorted to a severer kind of weapons. They now brought the force of their united armies to bear against the work. When they saw that the walls were going to be built, and that a fox would not be likely to push them down, then the Arabians and the Ammonites and the Ashdodites, were exceedingly wroth, and conspired all of them together to fight against Jerusalem, and to prevent the accomplishment of the work.

When this emergency arose, Nehemiah placed some of his men on guard, fully armed and equipped, and every man of his working force had his sword girded by his side, and with one hand held a weapon while he wrought upon the wall with the other. The enthusiasm with which the nobility of their work inspired them was manifest in that they worked upon the walls from the "rising of the morning" till the stars appeared at evening, and then slept by their work at night, so as to be a perpetual guard to it; and none of them put off his clothing, save that every one put them off for washing. Catching the spirit of their leader, the unanimity of the entire force is thus expressed: "The people had a mind to work."

It was also the purpose of Nehemiah to bring up the walls in uniformity, not one part to the neglect of another. This being the case, and the walls being "great and large," his men were "separated upon the wall one far from another," consequently they were few and weak at any given point. Therefore Nehemiah, issued an order that at the sound of the trumpet, which was kept near him, they should all rally to the point of attack. Whenever an attack was made, the bugle sounded, the forces rallied, the enemy was driven back, and never was there a breach made in the wall.

Now, that the walls are completed, and the ponderous gates are ready to be set up, there comes a change in the tactics of the opposition. Sanballat and Geshem, two of the principal leaders, send a delegation to Nehemiah, requesting that he meet them in some one of the villages of the plain of Ono, to hold a counsel together with reference to the rebuilding of Jerusalem. This is the coolest specimen of impudence in the inspired record. The devil himself never surpassed it. They had opposed the work from its incipiency; first by ridicule, then by force of arms. But now that they see it is to be a grand success in spite of all their opposition, they want to hold a counsel about it, as if it was any of their business. But Nehemiah knew their purpose. He was too old a bird to be caught with chaff. He knew that they sought to do him mischief. And well might one less wise than he know that when such diplomacy follows the unsuccessful force of arms, mischief is always brewing. Nehemiah had no respect for such trickery; consequently he had no time for a council with such men in the plain of Ono, or anywhere else. He therefore responded in the language of the text: "I am doing a great work, and can not come down; why should the work cease while I leave it and come down to you?"

But perhaps, some one is ready to say: "All this is a very interesting lesson in Jewish history, but

87

what is there in it for us? What bearing has it on the religion of Christ?'' Much in several respects. I think it contains a very important lesson for us in our plea for the restoration of New Testament Christianity. For, be it remembered, much of Jewish history was typical of a diviner substance in the Church of Christ, and especially was this true of that part that pertained to the temple and to the Holy City. But even if we should waive the typical character of the lesson, we are enabled, by analogy, to get a clearer conception of our work as a religious people, than we could perhaps otherwise get. Hence, to this analogy your attention is now invited. It is found in the

HISTORY OF THE CHURCH.

When Christ established His Church on the earth, it continued for about three hundred years in one united body. During this time, while it had its troubles without, and its imperfections within, it was not troubled with the divisions now produced by sects and denominations. This was before denominationalism was born, or sectarianism became respectable. The followers of Christ were simply disciples, or Christians. They belonged simply to the Church of Christ, or, which is the same, to the Church of God. They wore no human names, nor did they belong to any sect or denomination, such as are now claimed to be within the pale of the Church of God. This everybody knows who knows anything of the New

Testament. But finally the "man of sin," whom Paul describes, began to be manifest. One corruption followed another, till the Church was led away into a dark night of captivity, strikingly typified by the Babylonian captivity of the Jews. The Church was in Babylon, and, like the Jews, the devoted friends of the Master, hung their harps on the willows, and mourned over the desolation of Zion. The Great apostasy predicted by Paul was upon the Church, and her few uncorrupted children sat in sack-cloth and ashes. Be it remembered that this great apostasy originated and developed *within* the Church, not without. Brethren, allow me to suggest a gentle warning just at this point.

The night of the Church's captivity grew darker as it grew longer, till twelve hundred years lay like a pall of death upon her prostrate form. During the greater part of this time the Bible was virtually a sealed book, just as the Church of Rome would like to have it sealed today. The priest-ridden people were kept in ignorance of the Word of God; indulgences were sold as cattle in the market, to meet the extravagances of the papal court, and the temples dedicated to the service of Jehovah became but whitened sepulchers, full of the corruption of death.

In the sixteenth century that grand man of God, Martin Luther, awoke the world, as it were, from a slumber of ages, and gave the Bible to the people. By exposing the corruptions of the Church of Rome, and giving the Bible to the people to read for themselves, he gave the ''man of sin,'' a blow from which he has never recovered and never will.

Luther attempted to reform the Church of Rome. In this he failed. That Church is as corrupt to-day except so far as it has been influenced externally by its contact with Protestantism, as it was in the days of Luther. But while Luther failed, signally, to reform the Church of Rome, he succeeded in building up a mighty power in the earth, protesting against these corruptions, and hence called Protestantism.

But while Luther accomplished a great work in the world, for which we delight to honor his memory, it never entered into his mind to cease his fruitless efforts at reforming a corrupt and apostate Church —a thing which, as yet, has never been accomplished —and going back over all the dark and corrupt ages of the Church's history, and taking the divine model which God has left us in the days of its primitive purity, and reconstruct the Church as it was at the beginning. At least, if such a thought ever entered his mind, he never acted upon it; hence it has never come down to us.

Contemporary wih Luther, and co-operating with him in his grand work, were other great reformers; such as Zwingle, Knox, and Calvin. Of all these, Zwingle alone seemed to have a correct conception of such a reformation as the age demanded. These are the different lights in which he and Luther viewed the same subject: ''Luther was desirous of retaining in the Church all that was not expressly contradicted by Scripture, while Zwingle was intent on abolishing all that could not be proved by Scripture. The German Reformer wished to remain united to the Church of all preceding ages (that is, the Roman Catholic Church), and sought only to purify it from everything that was repugnant to the word of God. The Reformer of Zurich passed back over every intervening age till he reached the times of the Apostles; and, subjecting the Church to an entire transformation, labored to restore it to its primitive condition.''—*D'Aubigne's History of the Reformation.* But while Zwingle had this just conception of a true reformation his influence was overshadowed by that of Luther; hence his principles never obtained in what is known as the Reformation of the sixteenth century.

Following this, in the eighteenth century, was the Reformation of John Wesley. Wesley's work was, in some respects, similar to that of Luther. He labored to reform the Church of England, of which he lived and died a member. But in this, like Luther trying to reform the Church of Rome, he made a signal failure. His efforts resulted, however, in the building up of another denomination characterized largely by those principles which he tried to infuse into the Church of England. But great as was the work of Mr. Wesley, for which we delight to do him honor, it seems never to have entered into his mind to leave the Church with which he stood identified, whose corruptions he was powerless to correct, and, going back over all the intervening ages to the days of the Apostles, reconstruct the Church of Christ as it was at the beginning. None of the Reformations of the past, therefore, were based upon this principle. It is chiefly in this respect that the Reformation with which we to-day stand identified differs from all others. Hence it is in strict propriety called

THE RESTORATION.

The current Reformation, inaugurated by the Campbells and their co-laborers, was not an effort to reform some existing church or denomination, as such. Evidently the correction of the unscriptural abuses in all the denominations was one purpose for which these godly men labored, yet it was not the fundamental principle on which their Reformation was based, nor the leading object for which it was inaugurated.

Neither was it the purpose of these Reformers to establish a new church, or to build up another sect or denomination in the world. They believed that already the world was cursed with too many; hence, to add another to the number was the farthest thing from their purpose.

Since their leading object was not to reform churches or denominations as such, nor to establish another, the question arises, what was the specific

OBJECT OF THIS REFORMATION.

I shall attempt briefly to answer this question.

About the beginning of the second quarter of the nineteenth century there seemed to be, in the special providence of God, a turning of many minds, wholly disassociated and unknown to one another, to the Word of God as the only authority in religion. There seemed to be almost a simultaneous longing in many hearts to throw off the yoke of human bondage in religion, and form their faith and practice simply and purely by the Holy Scriptures. Chief among these were Thomas and Alexander Campbell.

In contemplating the Word of God as our only authority in religion, these men saw the wonderful reformation that it involved as a consequence. They saw that the Church, as it was at first established, when it knew no other authority but that of divine inspiration, had fallen under the apostasy predicted by Paul.

It was led away into its Babylonish captivity by the "man of sin;" and from this bondage it had never been liberated. Luther had broken the fetters with which Rome had for ages manacled the people of God; but instead of bidding the captives go free, and return to their native land, he strove only to mitigate their bondage. Consequently the Church was yet in Babylon. It had long been her privilege to go out, but as yet she had no one to lead the way.

This was what the Church of God needed above all things else—to be taken out of Babylon; and this, by the help of God, they resolved to attempt,

They resolved to go back over all the dark and polluted pages of the Church's history, disregarding all authority that had been usurped during the long centuries of her captivity, until the golden age of her virgin purity was found, before the polluting touch of human hands was laid upon her, or the perfume of her garments defiled by the foul breath of the apostasy, and restore her to the world in all the divine perfection that characterized her when she emanated from Him who said: ''On this rock I will build my Church.'' Or, in other words, it was their purpose, like that of Nehemiah, to go up out of the land of captivity and rebuild the walls of the spiritual Jerusalem. Those walls had been broken down. Those gates had been consumed. The city of our fathers lay in ruins. Its principal highways were blockaded with rubbish. Even the sepulchers of those dearest to our hearts were dishonored. Laying aside the figure, it was their purpose to go back to the beginning, and, taking the Church as it is revealed to us in all its characteristics in the New Testament, restore it to the world precisely as it was at first. Their work, then, was really a work of *restoration*.

Every one must admit that the Church of God, during the first age of its history, when everything, both in faith and practice, organically, was given it by the inspiration of the Holy Spirit, was just such a Church as God would have. Had He desired it otherwise, He would have ordered it otherwise.

Not only was this true for that age, but for all ages. He who saw the end from the beginning, constituted His Church to meet the wants of His cause in all times and in all countries. This being true, it follows that the restoration of that Church in all respects as it was at the beginning, is the thing above all others that God in His providence would have accomplished. If He does not look upon a work of this kind with special favor, then we are without evidence that He looks with favor upon the observance of any divine precept or example. That which was well pleasing to the divine Father in the establishing and perfecting of the Church, must be well pleasing to Him now. If this be not true, then we are left in this age without a criterion of truth. It seems to us, therefore, that this work, when properly understood, must meet the approbation of all good men. While it lays the ax at the root of all sects and parties in religion, it lifts us infinitely above them. Since the Church of God at the beginning was purely a divine institution, its restoration is a divine work. Such a work is as far above that of laboring to build up a mere sect or party in the world, as the divine is above the human. This work is not in the spirit of sect. It is wholly

UNDENOMINATIONAL.

Since the Church of God in the apostolic age did not contain sects and denominations such as now claim to be identical with that institution, it follows that whenever the Church is restored as it was in that age, it will be divested of all these denominational peculiarities. Whether the Church restored shall eventually cover the whole earth, and destroy all denominationalism, or whether it shall obtain only in part, the principle is the same—it will be wholly undenominational.

The world is exceedingly slow to learn that Christianity may be purely undenominational. I do not mean in the sense in which Moody and that class of sensationalists use the word, and even in which some brethren are now using it—that is, laboring in the interests of *all* denominations. But I mean it in its true sense—that is, standing identified with *no* denomination.

When you talk to men about being a Christian, they want to know what *kind* of a Christian. Or in other words they want to know what you are in addition to being a Christian. When you tell them that you are simply a Christian; that you decline to be anything else, they know not where to place you. When you tell them that you belong to the Church of God, or, which is the same, the Church of Christ, they want to know to which branch of the Church, or to what denomination you belong. When you tell them that you don't belong to any denomination, but simply to the Church of Christ, they are unable to give you a "local habitation and a name." Yet this is one of the simplest things in all the world. This was precisely the position of the first Christians. They were Christians, or disciples of Christ, and they were not anything else. They belonged to the Church of Christ, and they did not belong to anything else. In this consisted their unity.

The undenominational attitude of New Testament Christianity may be clearly perceived by the aid of a simple illustration. It is said that during the late war a circumstance of this kind occurred in Northern Kentucky. Two preachers of different denominations who were quite friendly, as all preachers would be if it were not for these unscriptural divisions, concluded to hold a meeting together. The understanding was that each was to lay aside his denominational peculiarities, and they would labor together to bring sinners to Christ, without reference to denomination. Then, at the conclusion of the meeting, their converts, if they should have any, should be left free to identify themselves with either denomination, as they preferred. As well as I remember, and it was where I lived, they had about twenty converts. Assuming that they were truly converted, they were converts to Christ, not to party. They were all brought to faith in Christ, and to repentance of sins, and were buried with Christ in baptism. Now, before these converts are divided, and take their denominational stand, while on the seat before us, I want to ask with reference to them, a few questions.

1. What are they? They are Christians. This

every one must admit. For if they are not Christians, then believing in Christ and obeying the Gospel do not make one a Christian. But what else are they? Nothing. Not yet; as yet they have taken no other name. They are simply Christians; nothing more; nothing less.

2. To what church do they belong? To the Church of Christ. If not, then becoming a Christian does not make one a member of the church of Christ. They have believed in Christ, been baptized into His death, and become members of His body. They, therefore, belong to the Church of God. But to what denomination do they belong? They do not belong to any. As yet they have taken no denominational stand. They belong simply to the Church of Christ; nothing more; nothing less. They now occupy a position in which all Protestants, at least, admit them to be Christians and members of the Church of Christ.

3. Now suppose that, perceiving this, and seeing that they occupy the most popular and "orthodox" position possible, they conclude to continue in that position, and refuse, therefore, to go with either of the preachers. On the contrary, they continue to meet and edify one another, and to keep the ordinances as they were observed by the first Christians. Then what are they? The world must answer: They are Christians. What more than Christians? Nothing more. To what church do they belong? To the Church of Christ. To what denomination do they

now belong? To none. They stand precisely where the first Christians stood in all these respects; and they constitute just such a congregation as those engaged in this work of restoration have been constituting all over the land for the last half a century.

I know it is sometimes thought presumptuous to speak of belonging to the same Church to which Paul and Peter belonged. But I must be allowed to say, that if I could not belong to the same Church to which they belonged, I would not belong to any. If I could not stand where the Apostles stood, I would stand nowhere. Every one admits that Paul belonged to the Church of Christ. But to what denomination did he belong? Every one knows that he did not belong to any. Therefore, there is such a thing as belonging to the Church of Christ without belonging to any denomination; and, in so doing, standing precisely where the Apostle stood, and occupying the position of all the primitive Christians and thus presenting the only Scripture ground of

CHRISTIAN UNION.

The leaders of the Reformation saw very clearly that the Church thus restored would enable all God's people, who love truth more than party, to unite on the ground on which the first Christians were united during the golden age of the Church's purity. The Church as it was, without any human legislation, furnished the ground of Christian union then, and that alone can furnish a basis of Christian union now. Consequently the union of all God's people on the Bible as our only authority in religion was the ultimate object to be accomplished by the restoration of the Church. Grand conception! Glorious execution! The very thought never ceases to thrill me! I desire no higher honor on earth than to give all the powers of my life to the advancement of such a work, nor any greater glory in heaven than that which God has in reservation for those who are true to Him in this the divinest and holiest work ever committed to uninspired men.

That we occupy the only ground on which Protestantism can unite against its common and relentless foe—Catholicism—is simply conceded by those who have the freedom to impartially think, and the courage to fearlessly speak. Of this we had, but a few years ago, a striking illustration. During the excitement in the city of Cincinnati over the exclusion of the Bible from the public schools in the interests of Roman Catholicism, a public meeting was held at some point that I do not now remember, in the state of Indiana, of various denominations, to express their sentiments with reference to the introductory step in a mighty contest between the enemies and the friends of the Bible—a contest between the authority of ''the Church'' on the one hand, and that of the Book on the other. During the meeting, a minister of high standing in one of the most influential denominations in the world, speaking of the conflict which must inevitably come between Catholicism and Protestantism, and how Protestantism must be united in order to meet it, turned to one of our preachers who was occupying the stand with him, and, taking him by the hand, said: *"When it comes to this, my brother, then we will meet you on* "THE BIBLE AND THE BIBLE ALONE!' "

The inference from this is clear. As the exponent of the sentiments of that meeting, and of the Protestantism which it represented, that speaker virtually said: "We will maintain our partyism, and keep up our divisions till in the providence of God we are *driven* together; then we will come to that position to which you have for half a century been inviting us in harmony with the intercessory prayer of Jesus! Your position is right, and the only Scriptural and possible ground of union, but we will not come to it as long as we can help it! When forced from our sectarian position we will go to yours!" How wondrous are God's ways in making wrath of man to praise Him!

Since "it is glorious to create, but more glorious to redeem," the redemption of the Church of God from its captivity and apostasy, is the most glorious work that ever thrilled the human heart, or nerved the human will. My faith is that God's benediction will ever rest on the man who is faithful to this work, and that His curse will ever follow him who abandons it, or understandingly opposes it. But that the work of restoring the Church was to be opposed, is clearly indicated in several places in the Bible,

101

and typified, perhaps, in the opposition experienced by Nehemiah. Hence a few words with reference to the

OPPOSITION TO THE WORK.

The ridicule and contempt heaped upon the work of Nehemiah in rebuilding the walls of Jerusalem, have been more than reproduced by those who have set themselves in opposition to the work of rebuilding the walls of the spiritual Jerusalem of which that was a type. Especially have the fathers in this Restoration experienced this in a high degree. "These people talk about restoring the Church as it was in the beginning! Why the church that they would restore, even the bats and owls would hardly deign to occupy in twenty years!"

Forty years ago, such prophetic sarcasm was common as household words, not only in the family, and the irresponsible neighborhood gossip, but in the pulpit and the public prints. But there were false prophets in those days, even as there are false prophets now. These sect-inspired seers were estimated at their proper value; hence those grand men of God were not to be turned from their heaven-born purpose by the sneers and scoffs of a people who did not comprehend, and consequently did not appreciate, their work.

But this was not the only kind of opposition which the work was destined to meet. The united force of arms brought to bear against this work, like that against the work of Nehemiah, has made this country resound with their clash for half a century. Where is there a grand old hero in this contest for things as they were at the beginning, who has not felt the blows of the enemy, thick and heavy, from every quarter, and smiled as he heard their harmless ring upon his armor? Ah! my brethren, the man whose spirit is not stirred within him, whose best mettle is not aroused, who is not inspired with no mean kind of inspiration, as he stands in the thickest of such a fight for such a cause, clad in an armor of divine truth as impenetrable as the shield of Achilles, is a stranger to the spirit of genuine, sanctified chivalry! But, soul-inspiring as is this plea, and the labor for its accomplishment, there have ever been those who object, and I wish to notice the grounds of their

OBJECTIONS TO THE WORK.

"The idea of reconstructing the Church of God after the divine model, and on this confessedly ortho-dox ground unite God's people as they were at the beginning, I grant," said one of the leading men of Kentucky to me, "to be a grand conception of spirit-ual work in this age, and worthy of all acceptation; but I have serious objections to some of your methods of accomplishing the work."

"*First.* I think your people are too fond of con-troversy. You are too pugnacious. You delight too much in theological warfare."

Now, in this, I frankly confess there may be some truth. It may be that we are just a trifle more pugnacious than necessary. People are liable at times to overestimate the importance of opposition, and do more in meeting it than it really deserves. But if, in our work of restoration, we have occupied a war-like attitude, the question arises, who is to blame for it? If there has been too much theological warfare over this work of restoration, blame certainly attaches somewhere; then let us see who is responsible, and let the blame rest where it belongs.

When Nehemiah's men went forth on the wall day after day, each one with a sword girded by his side, and holding a weapon in one hand while he worked upon the wall with the other, what did it mean? Why were they thus armed? Were their arms any advantage to them in their work? Were they wearing them simply as ornaments, in whose glitter they took more delight than in their work? To ask these questions is to answer them. Nehemiah's work was opposed by the force of arms. He was, therefore, left to the alternative of arming his men, and defending his work while he prosecuted it, or, in craven cowardice, to abandon the enterprise. In the fear of God, and the love of his work, he chose the former; and his name is enrolled high upon the scroll of God's grandest heroes. The arming in his case was a necessity; and it has been none the less so in ours. Our work has been opposed; opposed by theological arms; opposed by the united forces of Christendom, because it means death to their party divisions; consequently we had to arm ourselves, stand upon those walls, repulse the enemy as the work progressed, or, in the contemptible fear of human opposition against a divine work, ignobly abandon it. In the fear of God, and the love of truth, we chose to stand upon those walls, and by the help of God we expect to stand there till He shall say, "Well done! good and faithful soldiers!" It is not our purpose to leave these walls and draw a sword or poise a lance outside of their limits; but woe be unto him who assaults the work! The objection, then, to our warlike attitude is not well founded. It is based on a misconception of our relation to the work. The blame attaches to the opposition; and there let it rest.

"*Secondly,*" says the objector, "you lay too much stress upon some parts of your work, and not enough upon other parts. For instance, you attach too much importance to baptism. You preach too much about it; write too much about it; debate too much about it. You seem to lay more stress on baptism than on any other part of your work. Instead of advancing your work, I think you retard it by this everlasting harping on baptism."

Now, that all of this may contain some truth I have no disposition to deny. I think it is at least probable that we have given just a little more attention to baptism than the strength of the opposition has demanded. Indeed, it would have required wisdom more than human to have determined at all times just the amount of force necessary to protect any part of the work from the opposition that sought its destruction. That man is a skillful gunner who never uses shot too numerous nor too heavy for the game.

But if we have given more attention to baptism than to some other parts of our work, the question again arises: Who is responsible for this? Remember that when Nehemiah was rebuilding those walls, he labored to bring them all up in uniformity—not one part to the neglect of another. Consequently he said, "The work is great and large, and we are separated upon the wall, one far from another. In what place, therefore ye hear the sound of the trumpet, resort ye thither unto us; our God shall fight for us." Now, imagine yourself standing on one of the mountains overlooking the city. You are watching the men as they quietly perform their work on all parts of the walls. Every man has his sword girded by his side, and holds a weapon in one hand while he works on the wall with the other. You discover, however, that their minds are not on their weapons, but on their *work*. You look down one of the valleys and you see the "army of Samaria" stealthily approaching the city. It is unobserved by the workmen. It selects its point of attack, and rushes to make a breach in the wall. Instantly the trumpet sounds, instantly the forces rally—*to the other side of the city!* What would you think of it? What would the world think of it? Those workmen would be held in everlasting contempt.

When did Nehemiah's trumpet sound? When an

106

attack was made. *When* did the workmen rally?
When the trumpet sounded. *Where* did they rally?
*To the point of attack—the place where the enemy
was.* Therefore, if they rallied to one place more
frequently than to another, it was not because they
valued this part of the wall more highly than any
other part, but because the enemy had selected that
part for its attack. Precisely so with the workmen
on the spiritual walls of the city of our God.

If we have had much controversy over baptism,
it is not because we value it more highly than any
other part of the work of restoration. It has been
our purpose to bring this work up in uniformity, and
hence to guard with equal care every part of it.
What would baptism without faith be worth? Just
as much as the sprinkling of an infant. And yet we
have had comparatively little controversy over faith.
Occasionally we are called to meet an infidel at this
point, and fight the battles of our religious neighbors,
as well as our own. Who met, in the city of Cincinnati, in 1829, the boastful champion of infidelity, who
had come from the far-off shores of Scotland, and,
Goliath-like, had challenged to deadly combat the
"clergy" of our land, from New Orleans to Boston?
Was it a man who lightly estimated faith in Christ,
and made baptism the center of a religious system?
The believing world, whose battle was there fought
and gloriously won, know better. Who fought the
battle of Protestantism in the same city, in 1837,
against a power that would nullify the Word of God,

107

and subvert our pure faith in Jesus Christ into the veriest idolatry? Was it one who held as efficacious mere external forms, regardless of the spirituality for which Protestantism has ever contended? I envy not the head nor the heart of him who so contends.

We have had little or no controversy with our religious neighbors over the divinity of Christ, prayer, repentance, godliness and the like. Not because we do not value these things as highly as it is possible to value anything else, but because they have not been assailed. Let one of them be attacked, and the trumpet will sound, the forces will rally, and the clash of arms over that hitherto quiet point will awaken the sleeping energies of Zion! The controversy over baptism, then, depends wholly on the movements of the opposition. So long as they see proper to attack that point, we are prepared to defend it. And equally so of every other part of the work.

NO COMPROMISE.

When the opposition saw that the walls of Jerusalem were to be completed in spite of their efforts to prevent it, they changed their tactics. They tried to induce Nehemiah to leave the work and counsel with them with reference to its completion. But he saw that this was only another trick to accomplish that which they had failed to accomplish by the force of arms. And just here, dear brethren, is our greatest danger. While we remain true to the principles on which we started out, there is no earthly power that can impede our progress. But the day we leave these walls and go out to take counsel with the world, will mark the day of our decline. We have nothing to fear from without. Our only danger is from within. This danger lies in the direction of indifference and compromise. While we are true to God in the maintenance of these principles, the divine blessing will rest upon our work. But should they ever be surrendered, ruin will as certainly follow as that the Bible is true.

When God dipped His hand in chaos and bespangled the universe with worlds He impressed upon them His divine will, and they rejoiced in that impression. In this impression they received the laws regulating their existence, and the moment one of those laws is resisted, disaster follows. When shining ranks of angels leaped forth from His open hand, they received a knowledge of His will, and they delighted in that knowledge; but the day that some disregarded it, they fell eternally under the divine wrath. When man issued from the plastic fingers of the Almighty, reflecting the Divine Image, the crowning work of His hands, he received a law of life unto life, or of death unto death. While he rejoiced in that law God was his companion and friend, but the day he compromised it with Satan, he fell from the favor of God, and went out under the curse of the Almighty. When God established

109

His Church on the divinity of Jesus, and under the authority of His Son, He developed that Church under His fostering care till it rejoiced in a full-grown manhood in Christ. But when that Church forgot the lessons of its development, it went into apostasy and bondage. When God put it into the hearts of our fathers to restore that Church according to its divine model, their souls were thrilled with the thought, and they rejoiced in the privilege. While they have builded according to the model, as Moses built the Tabernacle, they have received unsurpassed tokens of God's approbation; but the day that their posterity depart from that model and begin to build after the wisdom of the world, that day will God's presence and glory depart from them! Would to God I had the power to express this thought with angelic force, and burn it into the memory of our young preachers with a tongue of fire!

Never did a people have greater encouragement to hold fast their fundamental principles than do we. Their growth in the world has been unprecedented. The growth of Methodism has been regarded as one of the wonders of the world; and yet, when Mr. Wesley's plea for reformation had been earnestly pressed for nearly forty years, its adherents in Great Britain and Ireland numbered only 150 preachers and 35,000 members. At Mr. Wesley's death, when the principles of his Reformation had been proclaimed for about half a century, they were accepted

110

in Europe, America and the West India Islands, by a membership of only 80,000.

In estimating the numbers throughout the world that have accepted the principles of Restoration in half a century, would it be far from correct to multiply these figures by ten? The growth of Methodism was after the first half century of its existence. Our growth in the past has been unprecedented, and we have only to be true to God in the work He has assigned us, to see results in the next half century that will amaze the world.

But in estimating the influence of our plea for Restoration, we are not to look simply to the numbers that have publicly taken their stand on this ground. The influence of these principles on the denominational world in the correction of excesses and abuses, has been one of its marked results. The religious thought of the world to-day drifting more in the direction of the supreme authority of the one Book, and the union of God's people on that Book, than ever before since the apostacy of the church. We have, then, but to remain true to our principles— a "thus sayeth the Lord," in matters of faith; the largest liberty in matters of opinion. Uucompromising in essentials; relenting in incidentals. As unchangeable as the divine decrees, where God has bound us; as yielding as a mother's love, where He has left us free—and erelong they will prevail from pole to pole, and from the rivers to the ends of the earth.

111

In conclusion, let us not forget an important fact in the history of Nehemiah's work. The secret of his grand success is thus expressed: "We made our prayer unto our God, and set a watch day and night." Brethren, while eternal vigilance is the price of an uncorrupted religion, eternal prayfulness is its life. Therefore, while we set a watch day and night over the faith of the Church, let us not forget to make our prayer unto our God for its purity. While we gird on our sword and sleep by our work, "that we may be a guard to it by night, and labor on the day," let us not forget that "our sufficiency is of God."

One by one we will lay our armor down at the feet of the Captain of our salvation. One by one we will be laid away by tender hands and aching hearts to rest on the bosom of Jesus. One by one will our ranks be thus thinned, till erelong we shall all pass over to the other side. But our cause will live. Eternal truth can never perish. God will look down from His habitation on high, watch over it in His providence, and encircle it in the arms of His love. God will raise up others to take our places; and may we transmit the cause to them in its purity! Though dead, we shall thus speak for generations yet to come, and God grant that we shall give forth no uncertain sound! Then may we from our blissful home on high, watch the growth of the cause we love, till it shall cover the whole earth as the waters cover the face of the great deep.

ORDINANCES OF THE LORD

By J. Z. TYLER

And they were both righteous before God, walking in all the commandments and ordinances of the Lord blameless.— Luke i:6.

THE commendation was written of Zacharias and Elizabeth, the parents of John the Baptist. Its value lies chiefly in the fact that it is divine. The approving words of good men, however, precious, may hardly be compared with the approbation of God. Every reverent spirit desires to know what the Lord commands, and to do it. In this case he commends their righteousness, as shown in their walking in all his commandments and ordinances blameless.

There are some features in this text which I think it important for us to fix in our minds in the very beginning. One is that the ordinances which Zacharias and Elizabeth observed were ordinances *of the Lord.* Had they been the ordinances of men, having nothing more than human authority, I am sure this commendation would not have been written of them. The Lord condemns, with clear and solemn condemnation, the religious observance of all such ordin-

113

ances. They may be beautiful and elaborate, and impressive, yet he does not approve their observance as a part of religious duty. "In vain do you worship me, teaching for doctrine the commandments of men." Note this, too, that these aged servants of God did not make a division of the ordinances of the Lord, and observe some while they neglected others, but they walked in *all* the commandments and ordinances of the Lord. They had not adopted the theory of essentials and non-essentials. They observed all. Then, too, the manner and spirit in which this was done is worthy of notice. It is expressed by the word *blameless*.

There are those in our day who would scarcely have praised them for these things. They have such a distaste for ordinances that they would not think of making the observance of even divine ordinances any ground of praise. Although many of them are very good people, yet even to listen with respectful attention to a sermon on these subjects is a heavy tax on their toleration. And this distaste—or prejudice, I would better call it—arises from several causes. Let me mention a few.

The bitter controversies which have been waged over ordinances is one cause. For, it must be confessed, that some of the most bitter and disgraceful controversies which have convulsed the Church have been about these matters. Another cause is found, I think, in the extreme and unwarranted value which some have attached to ordinances. One extreme

114

begets another. Some overvalue ordinances, practically making all religion consist in their observance, and, quite naturally, others go to the opposite extreme and practically ignore them. And still another cause is found in the supposed antagonism between the observance of these ordinances and a spiritual religion: They seek to be spiritual; they desire a heart-felt religion; they look upon ordinances as carnal and ceremonial and cold, and so, for this reason, ignore them. And still another cause is found in the misapplication of certain Scriptures which speak of ordinances as having been abolished. (Eph. ii:15; Col. ii:14-20.) These are some of the causes which have produced a very positive distaste for ordinances and especially a dislike for even Christian discussion of them.

We should avoid extremes. While we may have a very wholesome distaste for controversy, yet it is unwise to seek the peace we covet by casting aside what God has enjoined. Nor should we allow any extreme position taken by others to force us to the opposite extreme. The best way to correct any extreme is to stand firmly on the golden mean where truth is found. Nor should cold formalism lead us to conclude that every observance of forms in religion must of necessity be empty formality. The proper observance of ordinances cannot exist without spirituality. We should obey from the heart. And when Paul, or other inspired men, write of the abrogation of the ceremonial law of the Jews, let us not be so unwise as to apply what is said of these Jewish ordinances, to the ordinances of the Lord enjoined in the gospel. Let us seek to know the truth in reference to all matters connected with our holy religion, and to enjoy peace and avoid all extremes.

My purpose this morning is to present briefly something of the functions of ordinances, and to estimate as near as we can their real value. I speak only of ordinances of the Lord.

1. *They are divinely appointed teachers.* They are not idle, meaningless ceremonies. They are stereotyped lessons. They are pillars erected by the divine hand on which the finger of God has written inscriptions for the passing generations of men. Take the oldest of all, the Sabbath. It tells of the Creator, of his word, of his rest, and of a rest that remains for his people. Then, too, what records and lessons were written all over the Passover. It was full of meaning. It told of bondage and deliverance; of the slaying of the Egyptian first-born, and of the sparing of the first-born in the homes of Israel; of hasty flight, of the opened sea; of the engulfed army in pursuit; of all that was thrilling and precious in the events that clustered about the birth of the Jewish nation. The day of atonement furnishes another illustration. It stood as a marble shaft written over with many of the profoundest problems that belong to the redemption of fallen man. It told of sin and helplessness and forgiveness. It cast its rays of promise on the future, and these finally

painted the rainbow over the cross. Baptism also is significant. It speaks of the facts on which our religion rests. It is radiant with the divine promise of forgiveness. It tells of death, it is a burial, it points triumphantly to a resurrection. It is a parable in action. So, again, of the Lord's Supper. How sweet and how tender are the lessons of love which make even these emblems of death beautiful. With his own hand, so soon to be nailed to the cross, our Saviour inscribes in letters of heavenly light over this table, "Do this in remembrance of me." This ordinance tells of sin and danger, and divine solicitude, and atoning love, and stern justice, and pleading mercy, and divine wrath, and inflexible law, and forgiving grace, and an open heaven and rejoicing ranks of ransomed souls, and all that salvation means and salvation costs. Ordinances are not empty ceremonies. They are significant. They are divinely appointed as teachers and helpers of men.

2. *In the second place they are a part of God's method of righteousness.* I ask attention to a single passage of Scripture and then to an illustration of it. This is the passage: "Brethren, my heart's desire and prayer to God for Israel is, that they might be saved. For I bear them record that they have the zeal of God, but not according to knowledge. For they, being ignorant of God's righteousness, and going about to establish their own righteousness, have not submitted themselves unto the righteousness of God." (Rom. x:1-3.) What is here meant by the

117

righteousness of God? Evidently, not the attribute of God which bears that name. For they were not ignorant of God's righteousness in that sense. They knew that he was righteous. Moreover, Paul cannot here be speaking of the attribute, for he says, they had not submitted themselves to it and it is not possible for men to submit themselves to an attribute. Nor can we suppose that when he places their righteousness in antithesis with what he here calls the righteousness of God he meant to say they were opposing their character to the character of God.

What, then, is his meaning? I answer, that by righteousness he means the plan or method by which they are made righteous. The context points to this. The word which Paul uses cannot be fully represented by any one word in English. By the substitution of a phrase we have his meaning in our own tongue. They were ignorant of God's method of constituting men righteous; they go about to establish their own method of constituting men righteous; and so they did not submit themselves to God's method of constituting men righteous.

The illustration to which I refer is found in the incidents of Christ's baptism. You remember that when he asked to be baptized, John said, ''I have need to be baptized of thee, and comest thou to me?'' And Jesus' reply was, ''Thus it becometh us to fulfill all righteousness.'' That is, thus it becometh us to observe all God's methods of constituting men righteous. Baptism is *a part* of the divine method

118

or plan of constituting us righteous. Since, then, ordinances are a part of the divine method of constituting men righteous, and if Christ could say that for this reason it was becoming in him to submit to them, certainly it is not becoming in us to condemn or ignore them.

3. Still further, *our treatment of ordinances is esteemed as our treatment of their author.* This is reasonable. An ordinance is an observance established by authority, and to despise it and trample it under foot is to despise and trample under foot that authority. And so Paul says, in the lesson which I read, in speaking of the Lord's Supper, "Whosoever shall eat of this bread and drink of this cup unworthily *shall be guilty of the body and blood of the Lord.*" That is, the way in which they treat this ordinance of the Lord is regarded as the way in which they treat the Lord himself. If we are indifferent when he has said, "Do this in remembrance of me," it is regarded as indifference not simply in reference to an institution of the Lord's house, but as indifference toward the Lord himself. If you profane this ordinance, if you turn it into a drunken revel, if you make of it only a feast to satisfy animal hunger, if you pervert it and prostitute it, the matter does not end there, but is reckoned as an indignity toward Christ. So of baptism. In speaking to the Jews, of John and his baptism, Jesus said: "And all the people that heard him, and the publicans justified God, being baptized with the baptism of

119

John; but the Pharisees and lawyers rejected the counsel of God against themselves, being not baptized of him.'' (Luke vii:29, 30.) And, on another occasion when he asked them concerning the baptism of John, whether it was from heaven, we are told that they reasoned with themselves, saying, ''If we say from heaven, he will say, why then believed ye him not! And if we say, of men, the people will stone us, for they be persuaded that John was a prophet.'' (Luke xx:4-6.) They easily saw that if they admitted its divine origin they would condemn themselves as guilty of rejecting divine authority, and this was so plain and conclusive that they deliberately agreed to return a falsehood for an answer to Christ's question. In fact, all the force and authority of an ordinance is found in its origin. We should stand by every ecclesiastical ordinance with the question, ''Is it from heaven or is it of men?'' If of men we may reject it, but if from heaven we cannot, without setting at defiance the authority of heaven. And this leads me to say, in the fourth place that:

4. *Obedience to ordinances is a test of loyalty.* All commands *may* be tests of loyalty. Christ says, ''Ye are my friends if ye do *whatsoever* I command you.'' And again, it is written, ''If you love me, you will keep my commandments.'' The Scriptures are full of this test of love and loyalty. But some things commanded are more decisive tests of loyalty than others. Among things enjoined upon us by divine

120

authority are some so manifestly right and in such perfect accord with our inclination that we may observe and do them with no regard for the authority which enjoins them. Marital love, parental love, filial love, obedience to civil rulers, truthfulness, fidelity, honesty and many other things commanded of God may be obeyed with no thought of the command or its authority. Some things are commanded because they are right, while others are right only because they are commanded. When the candidate for baptism this morning humbles herself to submit to this ordinance, what reason can she have for this act save the all-sufficient one, the Lord has commanded it. It will be bowing down to take his yoke. It is an open and public acknowledgement of his authority. In this view of the case it seems to me there is a manifestation of wisdom in placing at the very threshold of the Christian life an ordinance that is inconvenient, distasteful and humbling. It makes it only a more efficient test. So when I hear it reviled and ridiculed it confirms my conviction that it must be of God. He tries us, He tests our loyalty. But if others revile there is a brighter side which presents itself when we remember that,

5. *God has seen fit to join special blessings to obedience to this ordinance.* When Jesus came up out of the waters of baptism and paused on the bank of the Jordan to lift his heart to God in prayer, the heavens were opened and the voice of the Father was

heard confessing his Son. The Holy Spirit, like a dove in visible form, descended and abode upon him. This event stands at the opening of his ministry. After that ministry had been fulfilled—after his example had been placed before men, after his words of life had been committed to chosen ambassadors, after the agony of the garden, the bloody-sweat, had been endured, after his blood had been shed upon the cross and death had been conquered by his resurrection and he was ready to be received back to the Father, in his own name he commanded his apostles to "Go into all the world, and preach the gospel to every creature," adding the promise, "he that *believeth and is baptized shall be saved,* but he that believeth not, shall be damned." And when we come to the time, in the unfoldings of the divine plan, that these commissioned ones are to enter upon the work committed to them we hear them give answer to the agonizing cry, "Men and brethren, what must we do? They promptly reply in the words of Peter, "Repent and be baptized every one of you in the name of Jesus Christ, for the remission of sins, and ye shall receive the gift of the Holy Spirit." God meets obedience with blessings. The promise of God joined to an ordinance gives to it a significance and value not its own.

Let us here pause a moment while we glance back over what has been said. We have learned that the ordinances of the Lord are divinely appointed teachers; that they belong to God's method of constituting men righteous; that the treatment of an ordinance is esteemed as if we so treated its author; that they are tests of loyalty, and that God has seen fit to join special promises to their proper observance. With these facts before you I leave it with each of you to form your own conclusions as to the way you will bear yourself toward the ordinances of our Lord. I will detain you to add only one other thought, and that is, that,

6. *Obedience to ordinances should always be from the heart*. There are no empty forms and idle ceremonies in the gospel. It is a spiritual religion. It deals always with the heart. In writing to the church in Rome, Paul thanks God that, though they had been servants of sin, yet they had *obeyed from the heart* that form of doctrine which had been delivered unto them; being *then* made free from sin they became the servants of righteousness. Their obedience was a voice of the heart. Had it not been, had they obeyed the form of doctrine as a mere form, this blessing would not have been theirs. As we go down into the waters to be buried with our dear Saviour, it should be with a heart contrite and penitent, for we have sinned; meek and humble, for we are unworthy; loving and trustful, for the Lord has spoken in mercy, and his promises are sure. It is the sealing of the soul's vows. It is the public declaration of its sacred covenant with God. It is the open, and formal, and solemn renunciation of the sinful past. It is the entrance upon a new life. Over

123

the baptismal grave is the rainbow of promise, placed
there by the pierced hand of Christ. "He that
believeth and is baptized shall be saved."

POSITIVE DIVINE LAW

By BENJAMIN FRANKLIN

IN THE Bible we have what has been designated positive divine law. On the other hand, we have what is called moral law. We have also positive divine institutions, positive appointments and positive commandments. We have also moral institutions, moral appointments and moral commandments. In positive law there are positive institutions, positive requirements or commandments. Moral law relates to that which is right in itself, always was right, and requires things to be done because *they are right*. The things it requires can be seen to be right in the reason and fitness of things, and will be readily admitted to be right—not because any authority requires them, but because they can be seen to be right in the nature of things. It always was right to speak the truth, and wrong to speak a lie; and moral law requires the former, because it is right, and forbids the latter because it is wrong. The same is true of all moral requirements. They are all required because *they are right*.

But positive divine law is of a higher order than this. It has the force to make that right which is not right intrinsically in itself, and is the highest test of respect for divine authority known to man. It is also the greatest trial of faith ever applied to man. It is intended to penetrate down into the heart, and try the heart, the piety, the devotion to God. The very acts that some men have irreverently styled, "mere outward acts," "mere external performances," are the Lord's tests of the state of the heart, intended to penetrate deep down into the inmost depths of the soul, try the heart, the piety, the devotion to God. *They try the faith.* The man that will obey a commandment, when he can not see that the thing commanded can do any good, or, it may be, that he can see pretty clearly that it can not do any good in itself, does it through respect to divine authority; does it solely to please God; does it solely because God commands it. This has no reference to popularity, pleasing men, or to the will of man, but it is purely in reference to the will of God. This is of faith; it is piety, devotion to God. It rises above mere morality, philosophy, or the pleasure of man, into the pure region of faith, confidence in the wisdom of God, and in submission to the supreme authority—yields to it reverently when no other reason can be seen for it is only that the divine will requires it. The man in his heart says, "It must be done, because the absolute authority requires it."

There are three degrees in this before it can reach the highest test, the greatest trial of faith. 1. To obey when we can not see that the thing commanded can do any good in itself. 2. To obey when we can

126

see pretty clearly that the thing commanded can *not* do any good in itself. 3. To obey when we can see that the thing commanded is clearly *wrong* in itself, morally speaking. It tries the state of heart, the faith, the devotion to Him who commanded, to obey a command when we can not see that the thing commanded can do any good in itself. The test is greater, and the trial more severe, when we can see *clearly* that the thing commanded can not do any good in itself. The test is greatest, and the trial of faith most severe, when we can see that the thing commanded is clearly wrong in itself, but only *made right* by the arbitrary force of the absolute authority. This will all appear presently.

The first Scripture adduced is found in Exodus xii.1-13, and is intended as an illustration of the principle involved in the theme of the present discourse. A lamb was required to be slain, and the blood sprinkled on the door-posts of all the houses in which the Israelites were dwelling while they were yet in Egypt. The promise was, that when the Lord should pass through, destroying the first-born, he would pass over every house where the blood was sprinkled on the door-post, and leave the first-born alive. But in every house where the blood was not sprinkled on the door-posts, the first-born should be destroyed. No man could see any philosophical connection between the thing commanded to be *done* and the *end* had in view. What an opening there was here for a modern doctor, who talks of essen-

5

tials, and non-essentials, outward ceremonies, external rites, etc., to have puzzled Moses! How many
pert questions he could have propounded! He
could have inquired of Moses, ''Do you think there
is any saving efficacy in the blood of a lamb to save
the life of the first-born? Why apply the blood to
the door-post? Could not the Lord see which houses
the Israelites were in without the blood on the door-
post? Why must it be a lamb without blemish?
Could not the Lord save the first-born in Israel
without this *outward ceremony?*''

Unbelieving and hard-hearted, as many of the
Jews were, it does not appear from the history that
there was a man among them sufficiently skeptical
to come before Moses with any such rebellious talk
as this. Moses and Aaron were not men of this type.
They gave heed to no such irreverent and unworthy
talk. They believed God, regarded his wisdom, and
did what he commanded, without inquiring what
good it would do, or anything about the efficacy of
the blood of a lamb, or what power it would have,
sprinkled on the door-post, to save the first-born in
the house. They believed God, and had all confidence in his wisdom and goodness—that he was wise
enough to know what to command, and good enough
to command that which ought to be done. They
never inquired, when he commanded a thing, why
he commanded it, or why he did not require something else; but took it for granted that the very circumstance that he commanded it was sufficient for

them; and they obeyed because he commanded it, and not because they could see why he commanded it. How did it turn out in the end? It turned out that in one hour, the hour of midnight, the first-born in every house where the blood was not sprinkled on the door-posts was dead! The first-born in every house where the blood was sprinkled on the door-post was saved alive! Precisely as far as obedience went life was preserved, or salvation was enjoyed; precisely as far as disobedience prevailed, death spread—there was no salvation. This is an awful warning to all who inquire, "What good will it do?" when God commands. Men talk of "the spirit of obedience!" This is precisely the thing wanting. "The spirit of obedience" will do what the Lord commands, *because he commands it;* but the *spirit of disobedience* will cavil at the Lord's commandments, and inquire, "What good will it do?" This comes of unbelief.

There is a statute in the law of Moses that forbids that any man, except a Levite, shall touch the ark of the covenant. The penalty for the violation of this law is death. No man could see that it was any harm, in itself, for any man to touch the ark any more than for a Levite to do it. No man could see why it should not be touched, in anything, *only* that the Lord forbid it, and declared that he who did it should die. Here again is a test of respect for divine authority, a trial of faith. It can not be seen to be wrong to touch the ark, in itself. Why may

129

none but a priest touch it? No man can tell why, only that the Lord says *he shall not.* The commandment of God forbids it. This is enough for the man of faith. Faith requires this to be observed; unbelief inquires, "What harm is it to touch it?" Will not "the spirit of obedience" do, without the *outward act?* To touch the ark is a mere *external performance,* and has nothing to do with the heart? If a man is sincere, will he not be accepted of the Lord without doing the precise thing commanded? See 2 Samuel vi:7;1 Chronicles xiii:11, and see how it turned out. What does the result show? A man, who appears to have been friendly to the ark, as it was borne along on the new cart, saw it shaking, and in danger of falling, and, though not a priest, put his hand against the ark to keep it from falling, and the moment he touched it he fell dead! What a warning in reference to *good intentions,* in doing what God forbids! It availed nothing that he was friendly to the ark; that he was honest; that he meant it all well; that he aimed to save the ark from falling! He was taking charge of the ark, caring for it, but not minding the commandment of the Lord. His *good intentions,* in *doing what God forbid,* led him to ruin and made him an example to warn all others to let their *good intentions* lead them to do *what the Lord has commanded.* He followed his own wisdom, not the wisdom of God.

The first commandment God ever gave to the human being was of the kind here introduced. It was in these words: "Of every tree of the garden thou mayest freely eat; but of the tree of the knowledge of good and evil, thou shalt not eat of it: for in the day that thou eatest thereof thou shalt surely die."—Genesis ii:16,17. No man can see any reason for interdicting that tree any more than any other tree in the garden. This case staggers unbelief. Paine, in his "Age of Reason," falsely so-called, inquired, "What harm was there in eating an apple?" In itself, no man can see that there was any harm in it. No one can see any reason for refraining from eating it, in the fruit itself, no matter whether an apple or other fruit; nor in anything connected with it, except that the Lord said: *"Thou shalt not eat of it."* The reason, and the only reason, for refusing to eat was that the supreme authority *forbid it.* It is not human reason, nor human wisdom, nor philosophy, nor science, that forbids it, but the *absolute authority.* Here comes a test. Will man obey when he can see no reason for doing so, only to *please God?* His appetite is against obedience. The trial is now to be made; the matter is to be tested. There is but one thing in favor of obedience —that is, the *positive divine commandment.* Will that prevail, or will it be set aside?

The first preacher that makes his appearance after the law was given was a *false one.* He was no *legalist;* he was not particular on the *letter of the law.* He obtained the most sacred audience on earth. Eve heard him. We have no full report of

131

his sermon. He had some method, and was a little of the modern Universalist type. His leading position was in these words: "God knows that you shall not surely die."

This point he undertook to carry by three appeals, as follows:

1. To the human appetite. "That tree in the midst of the garden is good for food." No doubt he discoursed upon it beautifully, sweetly and lovingly, and made his appeal to the appetite in a most telling manner. Before we become harsh in our judgment in regard to Eve sinning, we ought to stop and consider how far we withstand appeals to the appetite. Please consider a case or two, and see how far the appetite prevails, and how far the judgment governs us. Go to that young friend, whom you love dearly, but who is falling into the habit of intoxication, and reason the case with him. Inquire of him, "Do you not know that this besetment will ruin you as a business man?" He will likely respond: "I do; I have already felt the sting of it." "Are you not aware that it will destroy your standing in society, and that moral, civil and pure people will shun your society?" He will answer you candidly: "I am aware of this also, and have already suffered from it." "Are you not sensible that it will destroy your constitution and ruin your health?" "I am," he cheerfully responds, "Do you not see that it will destroy your estate?" "I do; I have lost heavily by it already." "And do you not see that it will

132

destroy your family?" He replies, "I do; I have thought of all this." After he concedes all this, you make your appeal to him: "My dear sir, why do you not quit it?" Now comes the answer: "I have acquired *an appetite* almost insatiable and irresistible, and find no power to resist it!" Or, take a case more common, and one in which more men have had experience. Go to a man some forty-five years of age, and inquire of him, "What do you think of this popular habit of chewing, smoking and snuffing tobacco?" He candidly replies, "I think it is a filthy habit. I contracted it when I was a boy, and thought I could not be a man till I could chew tobacco; but I am sorry I ever contracted the habit." When he makes such a candid concession, you appeal to him: "Why, then, my dear sir, do you not quit it?" "Quit it!" he replies. "I have acquired the *appetite*, and it demands it, and I find no power to resist it." Yet you talk about Eve partaking of the forbidden fruit.

2. The appeal to the appetite did not succeed with Eve, and the preacher proceeded to his second head, which consisted of an appeal to the lust of the eye. That tree is *pleasant to the eye.* We all know something of the lust of the eye, or ought to, when about one-third of all our hard earnings go for no purpose only for the gratification of the lust of the eye, and that, too, not our own eyes, but the eyes of other people. But this appeal to the lust of the eye did not succeed with Eve.

133

3. The preacher proceeded to his third head, and made his final appeal to the wicked desire of the human heart for unlawful knowledge. That tree in the midst of the garden is the tree of knowledge of good and evil. It is good to make one wise. Eat of that and you shall be *as gods,* knowing good and evil. But you say you did not know there was any unlawful knowledge! Moses says, "Secret things belong to God, but revealed things to us and to our children forever." Man has an orbit as certainly as the earth, or any of the heavenly bodies. Inside of that orbit all is free to him; outside of it he may not go. One of the most sensible books that has appeared in the past twenty years is styled, "Limitations of Human Thought." It maintains rightly that God has set limits to human thought, as certainly as he has to the waters of the ocean. Beyond these we can not in safety go. What mean all those poor degraded creatures, styled "fortune tellers?" They mean that they unfold the future, and reveal to you your fortune in time to come. What mean those poor deluded creatures, styled "spirit rappers," "spirit mediums," "table tippers?" They profess to give intelligence from the dead! What mean all those idle people who go to and consult these? They want the vail pulled aside, that they may see the future, and see what is coming to them, or to receive intelligence from the dead. Suppose the Lord would remove the vail, and let them see all that lies before them for the next ten or twenty

years! Would it add anything to their happiness? Surely not!

But this final appeal to the desire for unlawful knowledge did not succeed with Eve. What was the resort then? The preacher then assumed all the arrogance and importance possible, and made a most impudent and defiant assertion: "*God knows* you shall not surely die." This assertion did what all his appeals had failed to do. It *deceived Eve.* Woman should be thankful for the relief afforded in this matter by a brief statement made by Paul, 1 Timothy ii.: "The woman being deceived was in the transgression." She did not sin *knowingly.* But in the same sentence Paul says, "Adam was not deceived." It may be, though it certainly can not be proved, that when Adam saw what was done—that Eve had sinned and was separated from God—that he looked at her, as she stood by his side, and reflected that she was the dearest object to him on earth, made for an helpmeet for him, "bone of his bone, and flesh of his flesh," and decided that if he stood with God he would be separated from her, and that he deliberately decided to go with her in the transgression, and be with her in suffering the penalty, and lay side by side in the grave. Be this as it may, Adam was not deceived. He sinned with his eyes wide open. Many a man has done the same thing since then.

But now for the consequences. What followed the "outward act," the "external performance?"

135

God had said: "Thou shalt not eat of it." "Thou shalt surely die." Here was the point in dispute. The tempter said, "You shall not surely die." The trial comes. "By sin came death." "Death entered into the world." For six thousand years the results have been spreading, in mourning, grief, suffering and death; and man will not learn obedience.

But now for a hard question. What would you do if you should come to a positive commandment that would come in direct collision with moral law? Do you say that such a thing can never occur? But such a thing did occur. The question is not whether it occurred, or can occur, but what would you do in a case of that kind? Do you say that you would obey the *moral* law, and let the *positive* go? But you say, "Where did a case of that kind occur?" It occurred when God commanded Abraham to offer Isaac. It was wrong to kill, and worse to kill a child, and worst to kill an *only child*. The Lord called "Abraham!" The venerable patriarch and servant of God, never ashamed, but always ready, responded, "Here am I." The Lord proceeded, "Take thy son," and, as if to give it force and penetrate into the depths of his soul, he added: "Thine only son Isaac, whom thou lovest, and get thee into the land of Moriah; and offer him there for a burnt-offering upon one of the mountains which I will tell thee of."

Remember, this man was no hardened Pagan, trained to human sacrifices; but a man whose whole training was averse to anything of this kind. What does he do in the premises? What an opening was here for talk about *essentials* and *non-essentials!* for talk about "the spirit of obedience," without obedience itself! What a plausible speech might have been made, excusing himself from doing what was commanded! He might have urged that to execute this commandment will frustrate the *promise of God,* that "in his seed all nations shall be blessed." Then, it is contrary to the moral law. It is wrong to kill. Not only so, but the sentiments of filial affection, which God has implanted in his own breast, forbids that this thing shall be done; and even the common sentiments of humanity forbid it. Did Abraham institute any such reasoning? Not a word of it! No such unbelieving talk falls from his lips. God has spoken! The Jehovah has commanded! The Supreme Majesty of heaven and earth has commanded! There is but one way of it. That which has been commanded *must be done.*

We have no account of his consulting his wife, to ascertain what she thought of it. He listens to but one thing—that is, the voice of God. There is no equivocation, no inquiring whether some other way will not do as well. He calls Isaac to his side. No doubt Isaac appeared dearer to him than ever; but he falters not. He calls the servants, and bids them to prepare the wood for an offering and bring the beasts. All things are ready; the procession moves off. As they pass on, profound meditation is in the mind of the patriarch; his eye many times rests upon the child; the solemn scene of offering his son, comes before him; the tears trace down his furrowed face. Silently he moves on till the evening of the first day. They stop and worship God. They rise and worship on the morning of the second day, and pursue their journey. Oh, you of little faith, look at this man and you have before you an example of *faith;* not that caviling, carping and evasive thing that some style faith, that *will not obey God;* but the living, active and glorious faith that moves right on as the Lord commands.

On the evening of the second day the venerable man of God worships again. On the morning of the third day, the day the great trial is to come, he worships again. This day is to be one of trial; a trial of faith, of loyalty to God, of integrity, that is to go before all nations. "God tried Abraham!" The solemn little company proceed on till about noon, when, at a distance, they see the Mount Moriah. The patriarch turns to the servants, and bids them to remain there while he and the lad would "go yonder and worship." He and Isaac proceed up the mount till they reach the appointed place. An altar is prepared. When all was ready, Isaac, in the simplicity and innocence of a child, said: "My father, behold the fire and the wood: but where is the lamb for a burnt-offering?" He had seen his father worship, no doubt, many a time, and knew what was necessary, but saw no lamb as usual. How his question must have pierced the heart of Abraham! He

138

answered, "My son, God will provide himself a lamb for a burnt-offering." This he no doubt uttered by inspiration, but did not himself know how it would be fulfilled.

He now probably explained to Isaac what was to be done. He had never told him anything that was not true; never deceived him in anything; and Isaac believed that God had commanded it, and voluntarily yielded to it. This is most probably so from two considerations. 1. Abraham was from one hundred and twenty to one hundred and twenty-five years old, and Isaac from twenty to twenty-five years old, and that aged man could not have bound that strong young man, contrary to his will. 2. It adumbrated the offering to Christ, and *he* voluntarily offered himself when he had power to call twelve legions of angels to his assistance. The most reliable conclusion, therefore, is that when Isaac heard that God had commanded his father to offer him, he submissively yielded to it and voluntarily gave himself up to be offered. His father bound him and laid him on the altar, and, standing over him, lifted his hand with the deadly knife, and was calling up his energies to execute the commandment of God, and just before the fatal blow would have fallen God called out, "Abraham!" He promptly answered, "Here am I." God said, "Stay thy hand." He had gone so far that he had received Isaac from the dead in a figure. He had, in his mind, seen him struggling in death; his blood running down upon

139

the altar, and the flames devouring his flesh! But
the scene is changed; Isaac is alive; and the words
he had just uttered, probably without understanding their meaning, are literally fulfilled. God had
"provided himself a lamb for a burnt-offering." He
looked behind him and saw a lamb caught in a
thicket; released Isaac; took that lamb and offered
it. How he and Isaac must have praised God, as they
stood and saw the smoke of that offering ascend to
heaven as a sweet incense!

That lamb pointed to the Lamb of God that takes
away the sin of the world; and that transaction
honored God, and Abraham was styled "the friend
of God," and "the father of the children of God by
faith." The Lord Jesus honored Abraham; the
apostles honored him, and his name has gone down
through the ages in honor, and will continue to do
so, in view of that transaction, till the end of time;
nor will time end the honor God has conferred on
him, in view of his wonderful devotion to God, in
withholding not his only son. Men talk of "Abraham's faith," who never *walk in the steps* of our
father Abraham. When God commanded, his faith
did not inquire, "What good will it do?" He has
this put down to his credit—that he obeyed God.
So much for this "outward performance;" this
"external rite!"

In 2 Kings, chapter v., there is a case that sets
forth the principle involved in this discourse. There
was a captain, or more than is meant by a captain

in our day—a *chieftain*—a man in great power and wealth, whose worldly surroundings were favorable; but he was a leper. This was a drawback to all his fine worldly prospects. He had in his family a little captive maid, and she told her mistress that there was a prophet in Israel that could heal Naaman, her master. Naaman's wife informed him of this, and the captain determined to find this prophet. He went to the King of Syria and obtained a letter to the King of Israel and presented the letter. When the King of Israel read the letter he was excited, rent his clothes; thinking that he was required to heal the leper, and said: "Am I God, to kill and to make alive, that this man doth send unto me to recover a man of his leprosy?" He thought that he was seeking a quarrel with him, and aimed to involve him in war. "When Elisha the man of God had heard that the King of Israel had rent his clothes, he sent to the king, saying, "Wherefore hast thou rent thy clothes? let him come now to me, and he shall know that there is a prophet in Israel." Accordingly Naaman was sent and stood before the door of the prophet in Israel. The prophet never went out. He was a different style of prophet from many in our day, or he would have gone out, and been seen bowing and scraping before the captain, and planning to get a big pile of his money. He sent a messenger out and told him to "Go and wash in Jordan seven times, and thy flesh shall come again to thee, and thou shalt be clean."

141

The captain was insulted at this! "Naaman was wroth, and went away, and said, Behold, I thought, He will surely come out to me, and stand, and call on the name of the Lord his God, and strike his hand over the place, and recover the leper." He was indignant at such treatment, and said, "Are not Abana and Pharpar, rivers of Damascus, better than all the waters of Israel?" He had not been brought up in that way. It was not according to his *way of thinking*. He "went away in a rage." His servants saw the madness and folly of the captain, and preached to him a short but excellent sermon, as follows: "My father, if the prophet had bid thee do some great thing, wouldest thou not have done it? how much rather then, when he saith to thee, Wash, and be clean?" This simple-hearted reasoning overcame him. He yielded the point, went down and dipped himself seven times in Jordan, and was made whole.

Never did any commandment have the appearance of a non-essential more than this one. No man could see how dipping in Jordan could heal leprosy, nor why he must *dip seven times*. He was not to be healed when he dipped once, nor twice, but *seven times*. When the Lord requires certain steps to be taken to obtain an object, the object, or end, is never obtained till the last step is taken, or the last item in the programme is performed. The prophet of God had something in view more than simply to heal a leper. He intended that Naaman should "know

142

that there was a prophet in Israel." This he made him know; for after he had healed him, Naaman said: "Now I know that there is no God in all the earth, but in Israel." He did not, by this transaction, show him that there was great efficacy in the water of Jordan, or in dipping in Jordan, but that there was a great God in Israel—above all gods—a God that could heal leprosy; and thus glorified the God of Israel. Naaman carried the name of the God of Israel home with him, and honored that name among his people.

While the Israelites were in the wilderness, they spake against God and against Moses, inquiring, "Wherefore have ye brought us up out of Egypt to die in the wilderness? for there is no bread, neither is there any water; and our soul loatheth this light bread. And the Lord sent fiery serpents among the people, and they bit the people; "and much people of Israel died." The people came to Moses, making confession. They said: "We have sinned, for we have spoken against the Lord, and against thee; pray unto the Lord, that he take away the serpents from us." The wickedest and hardest-hearted people will repent when a calamity comes, war, or pestilence, and desire prayers. Moses listened to them and prayed for them. See Numbers xxi:7. "And the Lord said unto Moses, Make thee a fiery serpent, and set it on a pole: and it shall come to pass, that every one that is bitten, when he looketh upon it, shall live."

Moses made the serpent of brass and put it upon a pole. What think you of this for an "outward performance," an "external rite?" etc. What think you many preachers in our day would have said of this pole and serpent? They would want to know whether there was virtue in the pole, in the brass, in looking, etc., etc., and whether they could not be saved *some other way*. Could not God save a man without looking? What good could it do to look at the brazen serpent? The wisdom of God was in this appointment. He intended that all men should know that there was nothing in the pole, the serpent, or looking, in itself, to save them. He intended that all men should see that it was not *that they did* that saved them, but that *God saved them*. Yet he did not please to save them without the pole, the serpent and the looking. He required them to submit to this appointment, as a test of their faith, a trial of their loyalty, in an act of submission that had *nothing in it but submission to him.* When they *submitted,* he demonstrated his approval by *healing them.*

Suppose Moses had prepared a liniment, and it would have healed every bitten Israelite, what would have been the result? Would it have given God the glory? Not at all! They would not have looked beyond the liniment, and nothing would have been heard of but the *liniment,* the *liniment*—the grand *panacea!* But no man thought the serpent healed any one, but that God healed them, and they gave

144

the glory to God. Joshua ii:1-30 we have more positive divine law. Joshua appears, connected with an
army, in a siege against Jericho—though it is not
now recollected that he is anywhere styled *General
Joshua*. Jericho was like some places we have read
about within the past fifteen years—it was *not easy
to take!* They had tried their battering rams, and
all the other engines they had for breaking down
strong walls, and had utterly failed. Joshua went
to the Lord for a war programme, and the Lord
commanded him to march the army around the city
once every day, for seven days, and on the seventh
day to march round seven times; then to blow the
trumpet and tell the men to shout. What a set of
"outward performances" there was in this! What
an amount of "external ceremony!" What an
array of "non-essentials!" We have heard much
of *pious* generals, *praying* generals, and the like,
within the past few years; but how many of them
had faith enough to have carried out this programme? Many of them, doubtless, would have
preferred trusting to shells and solid shot. Modern
chaplains, many of them, would have argued that
marching round the walls was not essential; that
blowing trumpets could avail nothing, and the shout
of men could not break down the formidable walls
of Jericho.

But Joshua was a man of *faith*. He did not expect the marching round the walls to throw them
down, nor the blowing of the trumpet, nor the shout

of the men; but he believed the Lord would throw down the walls and give them the victory; and what they had to do was to *obey him*. All men can see that what they were commanded to do could not, in itself, accomplish the object, or have any tendency to do it. God could have thrown down the walls without their doing anything, just as well as with it, so far as we can see. Why, then did he command the marching round, the blowing of the trumpet, and the shout of the men? Because *so it pleased him to do*. They had no reason for doing what he commanded, only that *it was commanded*. They could not see that it could do any good. On the first day they marched round once. In the evening there stood the wall, apparently as invulnerable as ever! On the second day they went round again—no sign of the wall giving way. Thus they continued to go round day after day, till they had gone round seven times. There stood the wall, as formidable as ever. On the seventh day they started and completed the seven rounds. Not a break in the wall yet! All they had done did not appear to do any good. This was trying faith! Two items in the programme are lacking, and they certainly appear as much like non-essentials as anything the Lord ever commanded. Yet, if they are left off, all that has been done will be lost. No matter if they have marched round many times, and done it all right, if they stop now they will not receive the promised benefit.

The command is given to blow the trumpet. The

146

trumpet is blown; but the wall moves not. Only one item remains in all the items commanded, and that was for the men to shout. All eyes are turned to the wall, not believing that the shouts would bring it down, but that *God would bring it down.* The men shouted; the wall fell, and Jericho was made an easy prey. No man gave the glory to the marching round the wall, to the blast of the trumpet, or the shout of the men; for all knew that these did not overthrow those strong walls—but the glory was given to the God of Israel, who is mighty in battle, and whose strong arm gave them the victory.

In all these transactions there is reason for following the instruction of the God of Israel, in full confidence that whatever he promises he will most certainly perform. One more positive institution will be sufficient, and will end the present discourse. To find one without delay, and in the shortest possible time, turn to Mark xvi:16: "He that believeth, and is immersed, shall be saved." "Saved," here, is *saved from sins, or pardoned.* But no man can see any power in immersing a man in water to save his soul from sins. Immersing the body in water certainly can not cleanse the soul from sin. There is no efficacy in water to take away sin; no virtue, or power, of any sort in it to cleanse from sin, either soul or body. All men can see satisfactorily that immersing a man in water can not take away sin. It is not going too far to say that the Lord designed that all men should be able to see that there is no

147

virtue in the things commanded, either the faith or
the baptism, to take away sins. It is as certain that
believing can not take away sin, as that immersion
can not, and it is equally as certain that the two
together can not take away sins, as that either one
alone can not.

Why, then, must a man *believe* and be *immersed?*
Man may see why he must believe, as the belief
changes the heart, and prepares him in heart for
pardon. But then, the belief can not take away sin,
any more than the immersion. But who can see why
any man should be immersed? No man can see that
it can do any man good, in a religious, or a spiritual
sense, to immerse him. What, then, is there to impel
a man to be immersed? Nothing to the rationalist.
He can see nothing in it, *in itself,* to lead him to be
immersed. Indeed, he can see pretty clearly that
there is nothing in it, in itself, for soul or body;
that, in itself, it can have no tendency to produce
or bring what the sinner is seeking—the salvation
of his soul, or the remission of sins. Yet there stand
the words of the Great Teacher: ''He that believeth,
and is immersed shall be saved.'' There is the
promise, the other side of baptism—''Shall be
saved.'' Does the sinner desire what is promised?
If he does, there lies before him the commandment,
''Be baptized.'' Why must the sinner be immersed?
Not because he can see any virtue in water, immersing a man in water, or in all of it together; but
because the supreme and absolute authority has
148

appointed it as the initiatory rite of the new institution; has ordained that men and women shall be
"immersed into the name of the Father, and of the
Son, and of the Holy Spirit;" that they shall "believe and be immersed," in order to come to the
promise, "shall be saved;" that they shall "repent,
and be immersed, every one of them, in the name of
Jesus Christ, for the remission of sins;" that "so
many of us as have been immersed into Jesus Christ
have put on Christ;" that all shall be "immersed
into one body;" that, "except a man be born of
water and of the Spirit, he can not enter into the
kingdom of God."

There is but one institution in the law of God
that has "the name of the Father, and of the Son,
and of the Holy Spirit" connected with it. That is
the *one immersion* "into the one body." In this
institution, in one formal and voluntary act, the believing penitent accepts the name of the Father, and
the Son, and the Holy Spirit; accepts and enters the
new institution; the new and better covenant, upon
better promises; formally and voluntarily yields
himself to Christ as his new Sovereign. Baptism is
the test of his belief in Christ—the trial of his
loyalty to the King. Here, at the entrance of the
kingdom, the question comes before him of *obedience*
in a matter of the most trying nature—*obedience* to
a commandment, where he can see no reason for the
obedience, only that *the King requires it.* If he
stops at the first formal act required of him, and

149

refuses to *obey,* what may we expect of him at any subsequent time? If the very appointment intended to test his loyalty, try his faith, and develop the spirit of obedience in him, shall be set aside by him, what ground have we for expecting obedience of him in the future?

In this view of it, any one can see the wisdom of God in placing such an appointment as immersion at the entrance into the new covenant. In the first place, he can not see that the thing commanded, in itself, can do any good to soul or body. In the second place, he can see pretty clearly that the thing commanded can not, in itself, do any good, in any philosophical way, to soul or body. In the third place, it appears as if it might do the body injury. Then, it is humiliating to the last degree. Still further, as any one can see, the Lord *could* save a sinner without it as well as with it. Why, then, must it be done? The wisdom and goodness of the Supreme Majesty of heaven and earth require it. The absolute authority commands it. Shall this authority control? or shall poor mortal man decide that it is not essential?

Here is the issue, between the supreme authority which commands it and the human will. Either the supreme authority must be *set aside,* or the human will *must submit.* The issue has the salvation of the sinner in it. God has sent Christ crucified to the sinner, with salvation for him; he has graciously sent him the gospel of salvation, proposing repentance and remission of sins in the name of Christ; he has ordained one positive institution, in which he offers the sinner Christ, his blood, his grace, remission of sins, the impartation of the Holy Spirit, and the hope of everlasting life. Will the sinner come to this institution, in faith, penitence and love, and receive all this in *submitting* to the appointment of God; in *obeying* this commandment? If he will, he can thus yield himself to become a servant of God, and have the assurance of the promise of God, confirmed by an oath, of acceptance with God. As he yields he can in heart say, "Here, Lord, I give *myself away;* 'tis all that I can do." He may then sing such words as: "Through floods and flames, if Jesus lead, I'll follow where he goes." Rising from this obedience, he can sing, "How happy are they who their Saviour *obey.*"

How noble it is to thus acquiesce in the divine will; to let our will be swallowed up in the will of God! Then, when the soul is in the "spirit of obedience," and in a condition to inquire in the word of the Lord, for instruction, it is easy to find the right way and walk in it. May we, in humility, love, and submission to our Heavenly King, find and walk in the right way of the Lord, and finally be brought to the enjoyment of his everlasting kingdom!

THE UNIFYING POWER OF THE CROSS

By J. Z. TYLER

And I, if I be lifted up from the earth, will draw all men unto me. This he said, signifying what death he should die. —John xii:32,33.

THE "if" in this text is not to be taken as expressive of doubt. Christ knew from the beginning of his ministry that he would be crucified. In his conversation with Nicodemus, which occurred in the early part of his ministry, you remember he said, "As Moses lifted up the serpent in the wilderness, even so must the Son of man be lifted up." In the latter part of his ministry he spoke plainly and repeatedly to his disciples of his death by violence, saying, "The Son of man shall be betrayed unto the chief priests and unto the scribes, and they shall condemn him to death, and shall deliver him to the Gentiles to mock, and to scourge, and to crucify him." And not only did he foreknow the nature of his death, but he understood beforehand its profound significance as a fact in the government of God, and its essential worth in the solution of the problem of man's redemption. To Nicodemus he explained that he should be lifted up so "that whosoever believed on him should not perish, but have eternal life."

When he uttered the language of the text he was near the time of his crucifixion, and the shadow of the cross which had rested upon his heart all the while, now casts a deeper gloom. It was Tuesday; on Friday he must die. The context reveals in some degree the sorrow which even then he felt flooding his heart, "Now is my soul troubled; and what shall I say? Father, save me from this hour? but for this cause came I unto this hour." He had already entered upon his great baptism of suffering. To me there is a sacredness in any great sorrow, and especially in the great sorrow of our Saviour and this sacredness attaches itself to this text. With tender touch and loving hearts let us seek to unfold its meaning—for I feel it is full of meaning and redolent of love.

1. Jesus herein declares his purpose to *unite* men of every race and rank into one harmonious and fraternal bond, by drawing them to one common center. "I will draw *all* men," not in the sense that each one of the entire race will actually be drawn to him, but that from all classes, and conditions, and nations I will draw.

It was the request of the Greeks to see him that called forth the response of the text. For "there were certain Greeks among them that came up to worship at the feast; the same came therefore to

Philip, saying, 'Sir, we would see Jesus.' " As Philip was the only one among the twelve who had a pure Greek name, it is supposed that he was of that blood, and that this was probably the reason they approached him with their request to see the new teacher, now attracting so much attention. This request was presented to the Master by Philip and Andrew, and it awoke within him thoughts of his atoning death upon the cross and the world-wide provisions of his grace. I will be lifted up, but not for the Jew alone. This uplifting will be the widening of my work and mission. It will possess an attraction over the wide world—to civilized and savage, learned and illiterate, Greek and Jew alike. It will break down opposition, and form out of the most heterogeneous and discordant materials a kingdom of surpassing glory.

This purpose marks the opening of a new era in the religious history of the world. Not only was the purpose unparalleled, but the thought was new. No religious teacher prior to this had even suggested such a thing. All other religions were ethnical. Each nation had its gods and its system of religion, as it had its laws and its system of government. Even the divinely-given religion of the Jew was never intended for any other than the chosen nation. It was limited in its provisions, its application and its territory. But the religion to be established by Jesus was designed for the whole world. Its author proposed it as the religion for the race. It is catholic

154

in spirit, its provisions are universal, its field is the world. Nor was this an ambition kindled within it after its splendid victories made universal dominion appear possible, but in the hour of comparative obscurity did its founder entertain and declare this great purpose!

It was so new, so unlike anything the world had ever known or heard before, that his immediate disciples and their early converts were slow to apprehend and understand it. They seemed to regard it as a revision and enlargement of Judaism. The story of Peter's vision on the housetop in Joppa, and of the commotion and controversy occasioned by his visit to the house of Cornelius, and the history of the Jerusalem council, reveal to us how slowly the light dawned upon their minds. The development of his catholic purpose met with very strong opposition from his own followers then; and, sad to say, in different ways it has experienced the same opposition from his professed followers since. And even now we are slow to understand the riches of his grace, the wideness of his mercy, and the catholicity of his purpose. The narrowness and bigotry of man is like the little land-locked sea of Galilee, which is shut in from all the world, and its waves wash the shores of no land but its own; while divine mercy is like the Great Sea, bearing upon its bosom the commerce of the world, and with its blue waves it washes the shores of all the nations.

There's a wideness in God's mercy,
  Like the wideness of the sea;
There's a kindness in his justice,
  Which is more than Liberty.
For the love of God is broader
  Than the measures of man's mind;
And the heart of the Eternal
  Is most wonderfully kind.

In the broad philanthropy of Christ is an argument for his divinity. Whence came this gracious, catholic purpose, set forth in the text? We know that the age, the country, the education, the society of early years exert a wonderful moulding influence over every one. The seeds of that definite form and character which we eventually assume will be found to lie within our early history. But Jesus was born and reared in the midst of a nation and at a time proverbial for religious bigotry. By natural birth a Jew, trained from infancy by a Jewess, a regular attendant of their synagogues and their temple service, how came he to be the founder of a religion so broad in its philanthropy, so catholic in its spirit? His gracious purposes strongly suggest, if they do not fully demonstrate, that he came forth from the bosom of the universal Father. The Father of our race, must be the Father of Christ, its lover and Saviour.

The nature of his kingdom is new. He forms it into a perfect union by drawing each one to a common center. It was formed and is governed by the power of attraction. There had been universal

156

dominions before his day, but they were formed and sustained by the force of arms. That which he proposes to establish is, like our solar system, to be held in unity and harmony by a hidden power which holds each part to a common center. Nor does he propose to destroy all individual peculiarities. Mercury and Venus and Mars and Jupiter and Saturn retain their features of individuality, and yet they harmoniously combine to form one system. Then, too, some are much nearer their central sun than others. And, yet, each fills its appropriate place. It is a grave mistake to suppose that the union which should characterize the kingdom of Christ among men is a dead, a slavish uniformity. Great variety is consistent with perfect unity.

It is important for us to know, since this is the character of his kingdom, exactly what that center is toward which all are drawn and around which each revolves along his appointed course. Should we suppose that to be this center which is not the center, confusion must appear even though harmony prevails. So it was with the old astronomers. They supposed the earth was the center of the system to which it belongs. Upon this supposition other parts appeared to be deranged. When, however, they found the sun to be the common center perfect harmony appeared. So, should we suppose any creed or doctrine or ordinance or theory of church organization, or a special interpretation of any passage of Scripture, to be the center, when, in fact, it is not, all would appear to be in fearful discord. We are not left, however, to grope in a vain search for this center of gravitation and government in the spiritual kingdom on earth. The text states it—"And I, if I be lifted up, will draw all men to *me*."

2. Jesus Christ is himself the center, and personal, heart-felt attachment to him is the controlling principle in the life, as it is also the final test of Christian character. The basis of Christianity is not a theory, nor a system of formulated doctrines, but it is a person. In Christianity, Christ is the Alpha and the Omega, the beginning and the end, the first and the last. Its two great questions are, "What think you of Christ?" and "What, then, shall I do with Jesus?" He who in heart and life gives the true answer to these questions is a Christian. He has been drawn to Christ and is obedient to him as the planets are obedient to the sun.

A study of the historical development of the church as recorded in the New Testament will serve to illustrate and demonstrate this. If we go back to the time of the personal ministry of our Lord, before the existence of the New Testament Scriptures, we see him gathering, chiefly from the fishermen of Galilee, the nucleus of the church. He does not propound to them a system of abstract truth, as the Greek philosophers did, to which he demands their assent; nor does he present for their acceptance a plan or constitution for the organization of societies to be called churches, and call upon them to adopt it and aid him in putting it into practical operation, but his simple request was, Follow me. He makes himself the center of a group of personal friends, and he is the bond by which they are held together in the fellowship of a fraternal love. They loved him, they followed him. Their confidence in him was the cord by which they were held. They willingly left all for his sake. Persecutions could not drive them away from one so dear to their hearts. This devotion to him was the central principle of character in each, and the vital point around which their lives developed into spiritual strength and moral beauty. They could not, even after three years of discipleship under him, have passed an examination in a modern theological seminary. Yet during all this time he had been preparing them to evangelize the world! He had not been drilling them in dogmatic theology, and the science of church government, so much as he had been binding them with multitudinous cords to himself.

At a later period, when they had fully entered upon this world-wide mission, we find that everywhere they went they preached Jesus. They told the story of his gracious life and his sacrificial death over again and again and *again,* and sought to win and to bind the hearts of the people in loving devotion to *him.* In him they saw all fulness dwelling. Their converts were not converted to doctrines, to churches or to men. They were converted to *Christ.* All faith, all obedience, all hope had value only as they centered in his person and work. He was the object of saving faith as he was the substance of their simple confession of faith. He was held before the people as their only teacher and guide, and as the one who alone could give rest to their weary souls. They were to wear no yoke but his. Above all other love should be their love for *him*. He was the living vine into which believers were engrafted, and from him they drew the vital current which sustained their spiritual life. Paul's experience was also the experience of the whole body of believers, "I am crucified with Christ; nevertheless I live; yet not I, but Christ liveth in me; and the life which I now live in the flesh I live by the faith of the Son of God, who loved me, and gave himself for me." Christ was their life.

It is to be feared that controversy over many other things has perverted this simple faith of the early Christians. These controversies have lifted minor points into undue prominence. Questions concerning divine sovereignty, human agency, Christian ordinances, spiritual influence, church government, and many other matters have grown, through controversy, to occupy controlling positions in many ecclesiastical organizations. The result has been to displace, in a greater or less degree, the simple heart-trust in Christ which made the early Christians what they were. It is to be feared that most of that which now passes for religion is little more than ecclesiastical morality. It is practically Christless. His loving

160

presence, his sympathetic mediation, his kingly authority are obscured by the clouds of religious conflict.

Then, too, may not *we* be making a mistake in the method of our labors for Christian union? Do we not need to make a more practical use of the fact that the only union worthy the name is union in Christ? Is it strictly true that the Bible is the basis upon which we are to unite? Would it not be much nearer the truth, yea, would it not be the exact truth, were we to say that we are to unite *around* Christ and *in* him? And does not the New Testament teach that in this union there may still be harmonious variety? As when from the circumference of a circle we advance along its radii toward its center, we must come nearer and nearer together, so must we, as Christians, come nearer each other, as, from our remote positions, we come nearer and nearer to Christ, the center of the spiritual kingdom. "I will draw all men to *me*." It was in this way that the most discordant elements in society were harmonized in the first churches. They became one in Christ. The Jews and the Gentiles were as far from each other as pole from pole, and yet Paul could say, in writing to the Ephesians, "But now, in Christ Jesus, ye who sometimes were afar off, are made nigh by the blood of Christ. For he is our peace, who hath made both one." From each extreme they drew near to Christ, until they became one in him. His attraction was so strong that it broke down the middle wall of partition between them. If, therefore, we are to succeed in our labor for union we must rely upon this same attraction. Turn individual hearts, with their deepest devotion, to *Christ*. Let his magnetic power sway our own hearts—

> As still to the star of its worship, though clouded,
> The needle points faithfully o'er the dim sea,
> So, dark as I roam through this wintry world shrouded,
> The hope of my spirit turns trembling to thee.

In his church, Christ himself is the center, and personal, heartfelt devotion to him is the controlling principle in Christian life, as it is also the final test of Christian character.

3. In his atoning death upon the cross, we find the magic power which draws the hearts of men, which reconciles discordant elements and moulds believers into one fraternal band. "And I, if I be lifted up from the earth, will draw all men to me. This he said, *signifying what death he should die.*" Paul finds this attracting power in the bloody tree, saying, "Ye who were sometime afar off are made nigh by the blood of Christ." The history of preaching demonstrates the fact that the power which wins men to Christ is focalized in the cross. German theology is practically without the cross and so is shorn of its power. Unitarianism is weak from the same cause. Never has there been a preacher, from Paul's day to this, who has done much for the conversion of souls, who has not made much of the cross. To the Jews it was a stumbling-block; to the

162

Greeks it was foolishness, but unto them who are called, Christ crucified is the wisdom of God, and the power of God. It is wonderful power. No analysis can fully reveal its hidden potency, and yet it may be a delight and a help if we hold before us for a while this morning a few of its prominent features.

1. In its revelation of divine love I find power. Love draws. Herein is love. God commendeth His love towards us in that while we were yet sinners Christ died for us. In the cross I find the genesis of our love for God. For we love him, because He first loved us. There are problems which have been solved by the cross too profound for my comprehension. I do not undertake to explain the deep philosophy of the atonement. But one thing I do understand, although its fullness passeth knowledge. I know that the cross is radiant with love. While all that Jesus did was but the unfolding and expression of his love, yet chiefly in the cross of Calvary do I see this love displayed. In the manger at Bethlehem is love incarnate; in the ministry of Jesus is love working; in the scene at the grave of Lazarus is love weeping tears of sympathy; in the garden of Gethsemane is love sweating, as it were, great drops of blood; but on the cross is love enduring the agonies of a fearful death and swelling with a strength and fulness that breaks the heart. Here is love that has height without top, depth without bottom, length without end, breadth without limit. Let us seek with all saints to comprehend its fulness. Let us

163

believe in its genuineness and reality. It is love that draws us with its silken cords and binds us to the cross.

2. In its revelation of danger and of safety I find power. Is there anything in God to fear? I answer yes, and point to the cross. That is a revelation of the danger of sin, and a fearful demonstration of the divine wrath against it. He was made sin for us. Every pang he felt was a pang of suffering for sin. He suffers upon the cross as our substitute. The cross stands before the world as God's warning.

At the same time it is a place of security for us. We flee to it for refuge, and are safe. Its blood saves us. As the blood that was sprinkled upon the doorposts of the Israelites in Egypt preserved from danger all within, on that dreadful night when the firstborn of the Egyptians were smitten by the angel of death, so the sprinkling of this blood is our defense and shield. Under the seal of Christ's blood we are safe. I have been told that out upon those vast prairies of our Western frontiers, where the grass grows rank and high, there are often in the autumn great sweeping fires. The leaping flames fly with a swiftness greater than that of the fleetest horse. And it is said that, when the frontiersmen see the approaching hurricane of flame, they quickly set fire to the grass on the leeward side and then take their stand in the place thus burned bare, and await in safety the approaching storm. Though it sweeps about them they are safe. The place where they stand has already been burned bare. So there is one place already burned bare for us. It is Calvary. Standing by the cross, when the world shall be wrapped in its winding sheet of flame, we shall be safe—perfectly safe. There is safety here; there is safety nowhere else. Many have fled to it because of its revelation of danger and of safety. Will you? It seems to me that when anyone comes to understand its revelations of love, of danger, and of safety they must feel so driven and drawn to it that they cannot withstand its power.

> In the cross of Christ I glory,
>   Towering o'er the wrecks of time;
> All the light of sacred story
>   Gathers round its head sublime.
>
> When the woes of life o'ertake me,
>   Hopes deceive and fears annoy,
> Never shall the cross forsake me;
>   Lo! it glows with peace and joy.
>
> When the sun of life is beaming
>   Light and love upon my way,
> From the cross a radiance, streaming,
>   Adds more lustre to the day.
>
> Bane and blessing, pain and pleasure,
>   By the cross are sanctified;
> Peace is there beyond all measure,
>   Joys that through all time abide.

THE PEARL OF GREAT PRICE

By J. S. LAMAR

"Again, the kingdom of heaven is like unto a merchant-man seeking goodly pearls, who, when he has found one of great price, went and sold all that he had and bougt it."— Matt. xiii:45, 46.

I COME now to speak of the text which I have read in your hearing—the parable of the merchantman seeking goodly pearls. In the treatment of this Scripture, two courses are open to me: Either, first, to consider it in what I may call its personal sense, in which it is applicable to individual men in every age of the Church and in every condition of religious society; or, second, to view it in its historical sense, which I regard as descriptive of the age in which we live, and indicative of the special work desiderated by this age. I shall pursue, as being more appropriate to the occasion which has brought us together, the latter of these courses.

The thirteenth chapter of Matthew contains a series of seven parables, in each of which, save, perhaps, the last, I recognize this double sense. I am aware that the second—that is, the prophetic or historical sense of these Scriptures—though advocated by eminent theologians, has never been popularized; and it may be, therefore, that you have not been accustomed to entertain it. Still, if you will remember that not only the principles and characteristics, but also the various phases and fortunes of His kingdom, were distinctly before the mind of the Saviour, you will have no difficulty in believing that these latter were also embraced by him in his beautiful descriptions. The difficulty would lie in not believing it; that is, in believing that he beheld all these, and yet said nothing about them. And I am persuaded that your admiration of his wisdom will be sensibly increased, when you perceive that these simple pictures, which exhibit with so much beauty and propriety the nature, the genius, the soul, the spirit, the life of His Church, portray at the same time and with wonderful accuracy, the successive stages through which that Church was to pass. In this view, each of these seven parables will have a period peculiarly its own—a period in which the state of things indicated by it will predominate—a period specially described and characterized by it. Features and conditions described by the other parables may not be absent from this period, but they will subordinate it.

If you will allow me, I will briefly indicate, as I understand them, the periods or ages respectively covered by these different parables; ages which, of course, are not separated by distinct lines, but shade into each other like the colors of the spectrum. The parable of the sower, which stands first in order, makes known for all times, in its personal sense, the reason why in so many cases the gospel is inefficacious; and yet it is manifest that the first age of the church was peculiarly and characteristically the *seed-sowing* age. This was the work specially demanded, and necessarily it took precedence of every other. The seed was the Word, and the apostles and their co-laborers went into all the world, scattering it broadcast—preaching the gospel to every creature, and preaching *it only*.

Subsequently, after churches had been planted; after the seed sown had sprung up and brought forth fruit, it is perceived that a state of things had supervened of which the first parable takes no notice. Error, corruption, heresy manifest themselves; or, in the language of the second parable, "there appeared the tares also." Now, the culture and conservation of the church is the work demanded. Error must be pointed out and opposed, truth must be elaborated and confirmed; and so, when the primitive age had passed there stand the wheat and the tares growing together, but discriminated by apostolic insight; and further, as they are destined to "grow together until the harvest," they are discriminated *in writing* for all future ages.

In process of time—it was a long time—but the very next thing which *distinguished* the Church was its attainment of great eminence and power. Paganism was suppressed; the Emperor and the court were converted; the religion of Jesus became the recognized religion of the civilized world—so that the Church, no longer feeble and struggling, and seeming to need support, had itself become the shelter and refuge of mankind. How like the mustard-seed in the third parable, "which indeed is the least of all seeds, but when it is grown it is the greatest among herbs, and becometh a tree, so that the birds of the air come and lodge in the branches thereof."

What is the next period? Without searching for it; without any theory to guide you to it; just follow the stream of history, and you will find that before long the sun of the church's glory begins to decline. Faithfulness and purity are supplanted by pride, and pomp and lust of power, with their train of falsehood and corruption. You see reflected more and more of this world and less and less of Heaven, until at last, amid forebodings of an awful future, the sun goes down. Twilight comes on, the shadows deepen, the last lingering rays disappear from the horizon, and night, with sable mantle, covers the whole earth. We are in the gloom, the awful gloom of "the dark ages," and are bewildered by the glare and the glamour of superstition's lurid lights. But, during this long night, where was the truth? It was not lost, it was simply buried out of sight. It was like the leaven which a woman took and *hid* in three measures of meal. And there in the dark, removed from the gaze of men, unseen and unknown, it was working—slowly working, but ever working,

until at last "the whole was leavened." Not the
whole world, nor even the whole nominal church, but
the whole of the definite quantity, the "three-meas-
ures of meal," which had come into contact with
the leaven. Hence the fact, which, but for the light
of this parable, would be so surprising and unac-
countable—the spontaneous outburst of the Reformation. Where it succeeded at all, it succeeded promptly, as in a day, because men were "leavened"—
prepared for it; and where it failed at first, it has
continued to fail till now. It is a remarkable fact
that, with all the missionary zeal, intelligence, enterprise, wealth, and power of Protestantism, nothing,
or next to nothing, has been accomplished by aggressive work against Roman Catholicism since the very
first age of the Reformation—certainly not until
quite recent times.

Let it be noticed now that, while the origin and
remarkable success of early Protestantism are *ac-
counted* for by the parable of the leaven, the dis-
tinguishing *work* of this period is not *described* and
characterized by it. *That* is covered by the next
parable; and the very nature and construction of this
point to a brief historical period. There is no process of gradual work; no seed growing to maturity;
no leaven working long and slowly to results; but
the simple and, as it were, accidental, *finding* of a
hidden treasure. In a very short time steps are
taken to appropriate it—and the parable is fulfilled.
Now we may call it chance, or we may call it Provi-

dence, but certainly it is remarkable that the characteristic *man* of this period should, in his own personal history, have so wonderfully and almost literally illustrated this parable. You remember the account of Luther casually and carelessly glancing over the library of Erfurt *stumbling* upon a Bible. He was not *looking* for it; he was not *thinking* about it—but he *found* it. Permit me to quote the exact language of history. It says: "About this time he *discovered,* in the library of the university, a Latin Bible, and *found,* to his no small delight, that it contained more than the excerpts in common use."

In other words, he recognized it as a priceless treasure. The more he examined it the richer and more valuable it seemed. But it was not his. The ecclesiasticism claimed the proprietorship of the Bible. And what was he to do? I will tell you what he did. He gave up the ecclesiasticism; he went and sold honor and place and reputation and the hope of Ecclesiastical preferment—all that he had—and bought this treasure for his own and asserted and maintained his right to possess it.

As with Luther, so with his contemporary reformers; the Bible, in its integrity and completeness, so long lost to the Church and the world, was found by them, and, at whatever cost or sacrifice, was bought and retained. They translated it into vernacular tongues; they printed it, circulated it, and so enabled thousands and hundreds of thousands to come into possession, not only of the Book, but of the hitherto hidden treasure contained in the Book. This it was which distinguished the Lutheran period of the Reformation; and nothing could describe it more accurately or happily than the parable of the hidden treasure.

This first period of Protestantism gradually shades into that which follows it; the latter becoming more and more distinct until, at length, but at what precise period we cannot say, the age becomes marked and characterized as that of the merchantman seeking the goodly pearls. And this brings us to the consideration of the text.

The "spirit of the age," of which we hear so much—what is it? What single word would most aptly describe and characterize it? The word is upon every tongue. It springs unbidden from every heart. And it is the identical word used in the parable—*seeking*. Distinctly and pre-eminently, this is the age of investigation. I claim this as no discovery of mine; everybody sees it, everybody recognizes it, everybody speaks of it. The fact is so prominent that it has impressed itself upon the universal mind. The truth is that men seem to be everywhere *looking* for something. Turn where we will, examine whatever department of knowledge we may, and we find minds busily engaged in seeking, searching, investigating, exploring. Men are going down into the bowels of the earth to seek out and decipher the imperishable records of unnumbered ages past—searching in the rocks of hoary antiquity for goodly pearls of truth; aye, and finding them, too—"Sermons in stones and good in everything." They are sending dumb messengers down into the voiceless deep of the ocean, and are bringing up from that eternal silence eloquent messages of truth—revelations of mysteries which have been hid from the generations and the ages. With eyes of supernatural power they are peering into the depths of infinite space, where stars have their birth, and are bringing down from those heavenly mansions pearls, "goodly pearls."

So it is everywhere. In chemistry and botany, in physics and metaphysics, in geography and history, in law and medicine, in government and sociology, in every realm of matter and every department of mind, investigation is going on; and men are seeking, searching, toiling, to find truth. And from my heart I bid them Godspeed, every one. There is not a feeling in my soul, as there is not a principle in the Christian religion, which does not prompt me to welcome, embrace and appropriate as from God, every truth under Heaven.

> "On Christian or on heathen ground,
> The pearl's divine where'er 'tis found."

As might be supposed, the Protestantism which gave birth to the spirit of the age has itself been characterized by it. Religious men have been searching the Scriptures, seeking for goodly pearls. The Bible was never so profoundly studied, nor its meaning so patiently and carefully sought after as in these last days. It is the book of the age, and is read and studied more than all other books together. Men, women, and children own it and read it; own it all and read it all, not only without danger to their souls, but with unspeakable profit and blessing.

It is to be regretted that just as scientific men go astray by too hasty generalization, and have been forced time and again to abandon theories and positions once regarded as impregnable, so theologians have been too ready to postulate as certain truths, their hasty inferences and imperfect deductions.

The scientific theory which happens to prevail at any given time is regarded as the standard of scientific orthodoxy, and opposition to this on the part of the Church is paraded as opposition to science itself. In like manner theologians have misused their human creeds and articles of religion. A simple publication of these, to show what men at any given time *do* believe to be truth, would be right and innocent; but when erected as standards, and made authoritatively to declare what men *must* believe in order to Christian fellowship, we regard them as pernicious in influence and non-Protestant in principle. I am happy to say that, little by little, the age is becoming a unit with us on this point. Speculative questions have lost their hold on the popular heart. The world is not interested in them; and churches themselves have outgrown their old creeds, and are attaching

174

less and less importance to their denominational differences. As the poet laureate says:

"Our little systems have their day;
They have their day and cease to be;
They are but broken lights of Thee,
And Thou, O Lord, art more than they."

As an evidence of the change that is taking place, I noticed that a few months ago there was published in one of the daily papers of Louisville an old-fashioned Calvanistic sermon. It was by a theological professor, and was very able and logical. I read it with pleasure—and *forgot it*. The public, no doubt, did the same, and that was the end of it. No enthusiasm was excited; no opposition was aroused. But forty years ago! I tremble to think of the confusion and disaster which the publication of such a sermon would have produced. A hundred knights, armed cap-a-pie, would have sprung into the arena to attack it. Half the pulpits in Louisville—and mine among the number—would have answered upon the spot. Countless pamphlets, full of sarcasm and theology, would have been circulated in opposition to it. challenges would have passed; debates would have been held; reputations have suffered; and the whole community, perhaps the whole State, if not the United States, have been agitated by that one little sermon. But, as it was, the Calvinists cared nothing about it; the Arminians cared nothing about it; nobody cared anything about it—and the same would have been true of any other sermon upon any speculative point.

Now, what is the reason of this striking change? I think our text will answer. It is because, in the earnest seeking after goodly pearls which is going on, men of all parties are beginning to find that there is just "one pearl of great price," and that *it* is worth all the rest.

What is it that touches the popular heart in any religious public assembly of the day? Is it philosophical theology? Is it the quodlibets and quidlibets of schoolmen? You know it is not. Do you not remember last winter, when Dr. Deems, in the Presbyterian church in this city, rasped and belittled and bemeaned the miserable denominational distinctions that are keeping us all apart; and when he brought out before our hearts the divine Saviour as the center of union, and the only object of faith and obedience—don't you remember how good we all felt?

And look at Moody and Sankey, and their work. A very important work it is, certainly—a building without a frame, that can only stand while it is propped and upheld from without. Serious, thoughtful Christians in all ages have known that Christianity lives in its ordinances and institutions. These are not its life, but they are the body that contains its life. Without these, religion is a mere sentimentalism; very delicious, it may be, but destined to evaporate and pass away. True philanthropy, therefore, and true fidelity to God, require that *the*

CHURCH, *with its divine ordinances, shall maintain, uphold and exhibit the religion of* JESUS. Moody and Sankey are not the church; they operate outside and independently of the Church as an institution, and their work is without ordinances. We know that while keeping back and ignoring a part of the commission, they can not teach men how to *possess* the pearl of great price; and yet, because they see and exhibit that pearl, and only that, to the exclusion of all sectarian differences, the popular heart is kindled wherever they go.

The Young Men's Christian Association, too—what an index to the future is that! I do earnestly hope that it may not commit itself unreservedly to the blunder which Moody and Sankey are making, that of assuming to do Church work without Church ordinances; for I regard its existence as one of the most promising signs of the times. It means dissatisfaction with denominationalism; it means the recognition of something better; and it means an earnest effort to attain unto something better.

I might speak of the Evangelical Alliance and its work; of the tone of its published addresses; and of the cordial reception given to its utterances. But I forbear. All these signs point in the same direction, and mean the same thing; and, if I read them aright, they signify that Jesus of Nazareth has come in sight, and that not much longer will the men of this age dwell among the tombs of the dead past. They have *found* the pearl of great price, and they

177

mean to possess it. But the mistake which they make, the mistake which the Evangelical Alliance makes, which the Young Men's Christian Association makes, which Moody and Sankey and their imitators and co-operants make, is, in supposing that they *can* possess this pearl without selling and parting with "all that they have." Hence, after finding it, they are still holding on to their past acquisitions and possessions. As individuals, multitudes, I grant, are making the sale and completing the purchase. But our Lord has something in store for us better than that. The time will come, and may God speed the day, when every true Christian—Greek, Roman and Protestant—shall do this; when the *whole "king-dom of Heaven* shall be like the merchantman;" when all the Church of God shall sell out its party names and creeds, and buy and be satisfied with the one pearl of great price.

It is for the attainment of this object that the Christian Church lives, and labors and prays. This is our divine mission. In the very beginning of our service the Great Captain sent us forward as sappers and miners of the grand army which is destined to come after us. With such faithfulness as we possessed we have been preparing the way, cutting down the hills and smoothing the valleys. In spite of many difficulties and much opposition, we have been able, by the grace of God, to reach, occupy and maintain the position to which he is now calling and leading all His people. "Step by step," says Tenny-son's Cranmer,

> "Step by step,
> With many voices crying right and left,
> Have I climbed back into the primal church,
> And stand within the porch, and *Christ is with me*."

So have we felt. We have demonstrated the practicability in the nineteenth, as in the first century, of church orginization and efficiency without a human creed or a sectarian name, and of Christian union and co-operation without a human standard or a human bond. The war, with its unholy bitterness, has come and gone; and while the ties that bound most other communities were severed like wax in the fierce heat, God, for some wise purpose, kept us together. A thousand questions of opinion, of policy, of expediency, are rife among us as among others, but they have not divided us. The Great Power that directs us unites us in the maintenance of this fundamental principle: That, without respect to differences of opinion, *the only test of fellowship is faith in the Lord Jesus Christ, and obedience to his holy commandments*. He is the "pearl of great price." He is all and in all; the fountain of order and government, of love and life, of truth and salvation. The ordinances, or sacraments, as they came from his mind and heart, are sacred and precious, and to be jealously preserved and guarded, just as *he delivered them*. In the abstract they would be nothing; and those who can bring themselves to think

179

of them in the abstract regard them as nothing; but in the concrete, as coming from Christ and connected with Christ, they are holy and efficacious, because he, *the All*, is in them all—filling them with his own divine grace and virtue. This is why we contend for apostolic ordinances. It is not that *this* is better in itself than *that;* for in themselves both are nothing; but it is that the false is disconnected with the Fountain — a dry channel — emptiness, vanity and delusion—while the true is full of the very Christ. This, then, I conceive to be our special, our divine mission as a people; and oh! brethren, let it be yours —unmoved by temporary excitements, unseduced by the hope of temporary success—to stand firmly on the rock, and *hold up the light* for those who are seeking to find it.

And now to conclude. When the favored period in which we live shall close, there is but one to succeed it. The net cast into the sea shall be drawn to the shore; for there *is* a shore beyond the billows of this troubled sea, where we shall surely rest. The Church of Christ, like a good old ship, is carrying us safely onward. She has passed, as we have seen today, through many a storm and tempest. Fierce waves have lashed her sides and strained her timbers. She has battered against the opposing currents and contrary winds; and sometimes the breezes which seemed most favorable have carried her into danger and disaster. She has seen awful, gloomy nights, and rough and roaring seas; but, blessed be God, she

180

has seen many a sunburst of joy, and many a starlit night of glory. But in them all, and through them all, her course has been onward, ever onward. And now her eager passengers begin to look and long for the land. "The morning cometh, and also the night;" but there is no land yet. A little longer to wait and watch and pray. A little longer to buffet the billows and contend with the storms. And after a while — it may be at some midnight hour — the watchman aloft shall see a light in the distance—a glorious heavenly light; and *then*, when the morning cometh, there, in all its rapturous loveliness, there at last is the land! Oh, beautiful land, bathed in the glory of divine light! Oh, beautiful city of God, radiant with beamings of the divine presence! Moor thee, good ship, moor thee forever; for this is Heaven, and this is Home!

And there shall be everlasting rest!

TWELVE REASONS WHY DISCIPLES OF CHRIST ARE RIGHT

By H. T. MORRISON

1. *They take the Bible alone* as their rule of faith and practice. Nearly all other religious bodies hold to human creeds or confessions of faith, in addition to the Bible, and require men to subscribe to them before becoming members of their respective churches; and in this way the Bible is, to some extent, kept in the background, and the members of the church hindered from exercising their God-given freedom in the study of it. The man who subscribes to a human creed must study the Bible, less or more, through that creed, and, like the colored glasses one wears, the creed will give coloring to what he sees. Among the Disciples, the members are urged to study the Bible with the utmost freedom; and if the humblest member can learn some truth that has not yet been known, all the rest are bound to receive it.

2. *They are the only people* I have ever met who could give me a clear and satisfactory understanding of the scriptures. Neither before nor since I identified myself with this people have I met a man,

belonging to another religious body, who was able to point out, in a clear and satisfactory manner, the essential difference between the Old and New Testament, or between the Law and the Gospel, or who understood the seven grand divisions of the Bible. I had been under the ministry in other churches until I was a man grown, and never knew that some things in the Bible were addressed to Christians alone, and that others were addressed to those who were not Christians. After hearing the Disciples preach on these subjects, the book I had been reading all my life seemed almost like a new book.

3. *They are the only people* that demand of the sinner just what Christ and his apostles did, or that answer the enquirer in the exact language of the apostles. Such men as Moody and Mills and Harrison and Jones, Billy Sunday and Gypsy Smith, and hundreds of other preachers, in the various denominations, never insisted, in their revival meetings, on the last commission given by the Saviour (Mark 16:16). Who ever heard a preacher, except those among the Disciples, answer enquiring sinners as did Peter on the day of Pentecost (Acts 2:38) or as Ananias did the penitent Saul, in Damascus (Acts 22:16)? These preachers seem to utterly ignore these Scriptures when they come in contact with men who want to know the way of life.

4. *They aim to wear the names given to God's people* in the Scriptures, and repudiate all sectarian names, believing them to be fruitful causes of the

divisions now existing among God's people. Such a rage has there been in modern times for human designations among God's people, that many are slow to see how a body of people, like the Disciples, can exist without some kind of human name; and have found much fault with us because we will not submit to be called Campbellites, or some other sectarian name.

5. *They make nothing a test of fellowship but faith in the divine Saviour*—true Scriptural faith that takes Christ at his word and *obeys* His commandments. One of the most vital mistakes ever made in the religious world, and that has done more to confuse and divide God's people than any one thing, was that of exalting human opinions, and making them tests of fellowship. The numerous creeds in the world are scarcely more than the *opinions* of uninspired men, and should not be dignified by the name creed, much less bound upon men as tests of their loyalty to the Head of the Church. The Christian system, strictly speaking, has but one article of faith in it, and that article relates to Jesus of Nazareth as a person and divine Saviour. He who believes with his heart so fully that Jesus is the Christ, the Son of the living God, that he is willing to come under his authority, *has the faith of the Gospel.* And to question him about much that is in the creeds would be to confuse him and make his way dark at a time when he needs the clearest light.

6. *They have always believed that the existing*

divisions among God's people were wrong, and are contending earnestly for the overthrow of denominationalism, and for the union of God's people. And a very different state of things is now found in the religious world from that which existed three-quarters of a century ago, when the restoration for which we plead took definite shape. Then the most bitter strife existed among the various denominations, and many people went so far as to contend that division was a good thing, and was intended by God as a means of grace. It is only within the last twenty-five years that any one, in any other religious body, could be found who had the hardihood to come out squarely and oppose denominationalism, and contend for the union of God's people on the one foundation upon which Christ said he would build his Church (Matt. 16:18). The union of God's people has been a part of our plea, and for this we have ever contended with a zeal and a constancy that ought to challenge the respect and admiration of all thinking people. We have done the pioneer work in turning the current of the Protestant world in favor of Christian union. We have borne the burden and heat of the day in this contest, but, thank God, the fruits of our labors in this hard-fought battle begin to appear on every hand. The union sentiment that lingered so long has come at last, and come to stay. It is taking deep root in the hearts of God's people everywhere. The signs of the times fully indicate that the long, dark night of the apostasy is drawing to a close, and that it will not be very long until God's people will be marching, as one army, to the conquest of the world.

7. *The Disciples have done more in public debate to stop the mouths of infidels than any other people.* Alexander Campbell, when comparatively a young man, stepped to the front and accepted the challenge of the bold infidel, Robert Owen, and triumphantly defended the Christian religion in public debate, when no other man in America was willing to undertake the task. And since that time our preachers have met in public debate more opposers of the Bible than all other preachers combined.

8. *They do not debar any one from the Lord's table who loves him and is trying to live a Christian life.* They look at the family of God as being much larger than the people they represent. They are not so narrow in their views as to think none can be saved but those who are identified with them. They are neither what are called close nor open communionists. They say the table is the Lord's and on that account all who are his children have a right there. They let a man examine himself.

9. I believe their position on Christian baptism to be more scriptural and reasonable than that of any other body of people. Baptism, with many, has been little more than a meaningless rite, in no way whatever connected with salvation. Many have claimed it to be "non-essential." To many it has seemed to be a stone without any particular place

in the great building of divine truth; and on this account some have gone so far as to entirely discard it. The Disciples believe that, to the proper subject, it is the initiatory rite into the kingdom of Christ; and that to such it holds the same relation as does the marriage rite to those who enter the marriage state. They do not believe there is any more *virtue* in the water or in the act than there was in the waters of Jordan, when the leper was commanded to go and wash seven times in that river. But they find it to be a positive command, coupled with faith in the last commission of our blessed Lord, and also found in every case of conversion that took place under the preaching of the inspired apostles. They believe the Saviour saw the necessity, before extending clemency to the penitent soul, of an outward and public surrender to him; and that, in making choice of an act for this purpose, baptism is one of the most expressive and appropriate he could have chosen. Why should it be thought a strange thing that Christ should demand some such test of his loyalty to him before accepting the penitent sinner? If for no other reason, the penitent himself needs it. In this act he reaches out his hand, as it were, and accepts the proffered mercy. In this act the believer knows he has met the requirements of his Lord, and has the assurance that he is accepted of him. In this act he claims as his the promise, ''He shall be saved.''

As to the form of baptism, they hold, in common with all other Christian bodies, that immersion is

187

baptism. It is true that many others hold that sprinkling and pouring will do, but none dispute immersion. It passes for baptism among all denominations, so that in this they stand upon common and undisputed ground.

10. *I believe them to be more fully united* in their belief on what may be called the essentials of religion, than any other people. It is true they have had some differences, as well as other people, but these have been about methods of work more than about matters of faith and doctrine. And these differences, too, are very largely things of the past. In our national conventions, where our people meet from almost all parts of the world, there is generally the utmost harmony. Our preachers, as a general rule, all speak the same things. Once in a while someone gets away from the clear light of truth into the fogs of speculation; but his case is soon disposed of, and he drops out of the ranks, giving us very little trouble. We have never had any case of discipline, like some of the older religious bodies, harassing the entire body for years, and finally causing a division.

11. *They have never aimed at starting a new religion,* or at simply adding another great denomination to the hundreds already in existence. What they have aimed at, is a complete overthrow of denominationalism, and the return of the order of things that existed in the apostolic church, not only in spirit, but in faith and practice. Christianity was then pure, and the Church undivided. But through

188

the great apostasy, which gradually grew up in the absence of the apostles, Christianity has been greatly corrupted, and the religious world "made drunk with the wine of her fornication." They consider that the efforts of such reformers as Luther and Calvin and Wesley, and others, have fallen short of what they had in view. The noble work that these men did has to a great extent been neutralized by the formation of human creeds, which virtually say, "Thus far shalt thou go, and no farther," and by the formation of warring sects, built upon these creeds. What the Disciples propose, as the way out of this modern Babel, is to lay aside all human creeds and doctrines of men, all party names and human designations, and go back beyond modern partyism; beyond the reformers; beyond synods and councils; beyond the dark ages, back to the Christianity of the New Testament, and make all things according to the pattern therein shown by Christ and his holy apostles.

12. *They have clearly shown the possibility of God's people uniting upon the Bible,* without the assistance of human creeds. Many churches, with the best creeds in Christendom, have split again and again, while the Disciples have never had what may be called a split. During the late war when men's souls were tried as never before, the Disciples, who were equally divided between the North and South, came out of that terrible ordeal an undivided people, something that could not be said of some of the older

189

religious bodies. In the beginning of our movement, many of our religious neighbors ridiculed the idea of uniting people upon the Bible, without an interpretation of it in the form of a creed, which men would be required to subscribe to. They predicted that we would soon have all sorts of men preaching all sorts of doctrines, and that the whole fabric would soon drop to pieces. But at the end of about three-quarters of a century, nearly a million of communicants from various sources have been gathered together, and are as firmly united as any body of people in Christendom.

ORTHODOXY IN THE CIVIL COURTS

THE Disciples of Christ enjoy the unique distinction of having been declared orthodox by a court decision. They were tried by a court in Northern Indiana and declared free from heresy. It is the only case of this kind in this country that is on record.

The following is the closing speech by the attorney for the defense.

ARGUMENT BY W. D. OWEN

Gentlemen—You have committed to your trust a case of uncommon importance. Never before in the history of juries has a panel been called upon to decide the orthodoxy or heterodoxy of a religious body of people. That such a thing is possible under the eaves of the Twentieth Century, confirms it that something is strangely wrong in the religious world. I believe you are possessed of religious prejudices. Most men are. But when you ascended those steps into that box, you took your seats above bias, in the realm of exact justice, and you will a true verdict give, in the fear of God, and in the love of his truth, according to the testimony rendered.

A Methodist Protestant body, known as the Salem

7
191

Church, in this county of Noble, and State of Indiana, and situated in the county, four miles from Ligonier, owned a church building that was rotting, and a membership that was dying. They resolved to build a new meeting-house. The membership being unable for the task, asked assistance of the community. Friends proffered to assist, provided the house be made free to other religious people. Whereupon it was inserted in the subscription papers for the house, as follows, to-wit: "When the said house is not in use by the Methodist Protestant congregation in its regular worship, then the said house shall be open and free to the services of all other orthodox denominations." Three thousand dollars was raised thereon, fourteen hundred dollars of which came from persons not members of the Methodist Protestant Church. Of themselves they raised by one hundred dollars over half.

The evidence shows that, after the house was built, J. H. Edwards, of Ligonier, pastor of the Christian Church, preached in it once a month for nearly a year; he occupied it on Sunday afternoons, at three o'clock, a most difficult hour to obtain a hearing; and that he always had good attention and fine audiences. It has also been disclosed that the audiences of the Rev. Mr. Post, the Salem pastor, were neither good nor fine, and that for the past year they have been working on the problem of a further reduction.

Last January the Trustees of Salem Chapel notified Mr. Edwards that he could no longer use "their" house, "except on funeral occasions." A member of the Protestant Church, and a gentleman not a member of any church, both, however, on the subscription paper, prayed the Court for a mandamus requiring the doors of Salem Chapel to be opened to J. H. Edwards and his congregation.

The Christian Church did not bring this action. Strangers brought it. We would not be known in this case, more than any other religious body, but the defense, in their answer to the complaint, charged that the Christian Church, the Church of Christ, of which J. H. Edwards is a member, was unorthodox in Christian religion, and preached and practiced things not lawful by the Word of God. Their answer makes the orthodoxy of the Christian Church the issue in action. This brings us to the lead in this trial, by casting the burden of proof on us. We are compelled to establish our orthodoxy. We take up the lead in this prosecution with considerable earnestness. We have much at stake. The verdict here rendered will not affect the Protestant Church to any great extent. They are a fragment that has flown off from the Methodist body in its natural revolutions. They have but seventy thousand members in the world, a less number than we have in this State of Indiana alone. They are reckoned as fractions in religious statistics. Under the present aggregating tendencies of religious bodies, they will be absorbed and taken finally out of existence by some larger party within a few years; which is as it should be, for they have never had the least excuse for an existence beyond their plea for lay representation. To us, however, your finding is a matter of large consequence. Our orthodoxy is on trial. Our seven hundred thousand members will go forth from this house "legally" orthodox, which will be a strength to the divine plea of the "Bible alone," so just in its character, and so valuable an ally in our mission that you will never be able to appreciate the good you have done for the story of the cross; or we shall go forth as heterodox, as unworthy of his high name whom we worship. The banefull shadow of such a verdict would not cease to the ends of the earth, and would hover about the doors of our houses of worship with awful significance.

As we assert the orthodoxy of the Christian Church, and the defense denies it, the burden of the proof rests with us. Where shall we find the true standard of church measurement? You are not to receive the testimony of Mr. Edwards as furnishing that standard. Highly as we may esteem him, his testimony must not be regarded as creating a standard for the church of the living God. We only ask that you accept his testimony as truly pointing out the faith and practice of the Christian Church. Likewise the utterances on the stand of Mr. Chapman, myself and Mr. Carpenter, were not made to erect an orthodox standard, but to establish clearly before your minds what this church does hold and do. You are to take this solemnly proven position of the plaintiff's church, and place it alongside the infallible standard of Christianity, and see wherein it may vary, or if it fits into its exact measurement without the stroke of a hammer. Neither will you permit this standard to be erected by the testimony of the Rev. Dr. Smith, who is the acknowledged head of the eleven witnesses called for the defense. His testimony that we are unorthodox and heretical, was doubtless the earnest conviction of that venerable gentleman. But this jury, in its justice, will not tie us to the convictions of this witness. He charged many things against us as heretical which it was his "understanding" that we practiced. If you find anything he charged against us as "heretical and unsound" forming a part of our position, then take it and try it by the standard.

The utterances of our leading writers and speakers, here introduced, do not establish the standard of orthodoxy. They are only corroborative evidence on our faith and practice.

Where then shall we find the desired standard? Dr. Smith testified that the great doctrinal points of theology upon which the orthodox churches were agreed, formed the test. And he asserted that differing from them was heresy. These agreed points are the atonement, depravity, impact of the Spirit, and the Trinity. A few of the Protestant churches have made a corner on these elements in transcendental theology, and won't let any one into their orthodox pool unless accepting their statements of these four cardinal points. Scarcely any matter what else be preached, the acceptance of these establishes your orthodoxy. These fundamental points of Messrs. Smith and Post constitute the popular orthodox standard. They have sworn it. Also, these must be received in the formulated statements given by the schools. But these are not the standard. They are not the test of Christian fellowship and character. No man has ever been commanded by divine authority to believe in or to obey either of these formulated statements. To enforce them on the soul is impious towards the Head of the church, and subversive of the plan of Divine government. They are the doctrines of scholastic divinity, the vapory fulminations of brains pregnant with the philosophies of theology, but barren of the simple story of him whose life has filled the nations with light, and whose love is bringing a weeping world to his cross. The acceptance of these formulated statements can never bring a soul to the presence of its God, nor forgive a single sin. They may be the test of recognition among numerous religious bodies, but they can not decide the fitness of a church to wear the name of the risen Christ.

By what authority has any school, or church, or set of churches ever set up a standard of orthodoxy? No competent authority has ever authorized it. It was a power unasked for in heaven, unassumed in hell, and only usurped among men when theologians were born. We repudiate these standards which the defense seeks to have accepted here. They are partial and sectarian. 'Tis ourselves who have affirmed our orthodoxy. Not against any other church, but before God. The word orthodoxy means the *true Christian faith*. We bring the book of the Christian faith and place it before you. You have heard our sworn witnesses on what we teach. Take our positions, measure them by the teachings in this Word of God. And if they lie four-square by the line herein given by the Spirit, justify us by your verdict; if they do not, cast us forth, as also shall the judgment of God at the last day.

Hence in our evidence we have known no standard but the Word of God. We lift it above the heads of all the theologies, assert that it is divine, and challenge the defense to refuse it as the final chamber of appeal in this action. Therefore have we introduced the Bible as the Christian's only standard of guidance. It says, "The entrance of thy word giveth light." It says, "The gospel is the power of God unto Salvation." That is all the power needed in the world. It says, "All scripture given by inspiration is profitable for reproof, for doctrine, for instruction in righteousness, that the man of God may be perfect, thoroughly furnished unto every good work." By inspiration it pronounces itself able to accomplish that for which it was given to man. We have appealed to this infallible and divinely true standard.

The defense has followed us up here, and say they place the Bible in all their creeds as the only correct test, but that we do not make acceptable interpretations of the great cardinal doctrines. Our witnesses have repudiated these interpretations from every source whatsoever. To stand over a church, or in a court of justice, and proclaim one a heretic for refusing to accept certain statements of divinity is the worst of heresies. This scholastic theology has desolated the house of God for fifteen hundred years. The crime of the church has been that it has assumed to know more than Christ and him crucified. One may comprehend all these doctrines, and never know a sin forgiven; he may have mastered all the complicated formulas of systematic divinity, and never had his heart touched by the love of God. But if one accepts the Gospel, he has been touched by the cross, he knows his sins forgiven, and has come to the salvation of God. If he be saved, Christ is for him, and who can be against him? The heretical maledictions of a doctor of divinity can not reach him there. If any man be in Christ Jesus, he is a new creature. His orthodoxy is established. What God has cleaned call not thou common or unclean.

The Word of God must decide all our controversies. The true Christian faith—real orthodoxy— is receiving the Bible alone, and obeying the commandments which take us from the world into Christ. Who have done this are orthodox. Who have not done so can not so claim. We claim to have done this.

Gentlemen, we accept the law's assertion that you are twelve men good and true, and with confidence we place this Word of God before you as "the divine path of salvation," of which path divinity has said, "It is so plain that the wayfaring man, though a fool, need not err therein." Our confidence in the integrity of God is such that we believe the path is just as plain. Although every one of you differ widely from us in your religious views, we believe you look down this book and see that path as it is. We have unrolled the history of our church before you, and with an unfaltering trust in your uprightness we boldly, confidently commit to your decision whether we have ever, by faiths taught or practices obeyed, stepped beyond these ordinances of the King.

Orthodoxy does not mean the formulated doctrines of the schools. It does not mean a peculiar and technical phraseology concerning the cardinal points of direct impact, depravity, atonement, and the Trinity. We have ascertained that it means the true Christian faith. Putting it into practical operation it signifies the Bible, the whole Bible, and simply the Bible. Being permissible, under the evidence, let us go back to the original time and take some observations along the line of operation when this standard was set up and its great principles were for the first time put in motion.

We are told in the divine testimony that the

doings of Israel were written for our ensample.
Israel, a nation of two million souls, was assembled
around Sinai—the pulpit of the Almighty—where
he gave them the law which formulated their religion, and created them a church. There had been
no church before this. There was no church in
Abraham's day. From Eden to Sinai the world was
churchless. All worship had been restricted to family lines. We now see the family lines enlarge until
they swell into a single circumference, and all Israel,
so far as worship is concerned, is melted into one
family before the Lord. Families and tribes sink
from sight, and the church in the wilderness stands
a single organization, with one tabernacle, one high
priest, one uniform and unchangeable order of worship and practice. If the Saviour built his house
after the pattern of the sample shown in the Mount,
he has one tabernacle, one high priest, one uniform
and unchangeable order of worship and practice.
But if the theory of the defense be correct, it is a
righteous thing to break up the circumference line
of this organization, and have a wilderness of lesser
lines; to dissolve the solitary house, to wreck the real
unified body, and let a house be built on Mount
Gerizim, or any other mount, and bear any other
name; to let the objects of faith be altered or increased at pleasure, and the practices be changed by
climate and observed according to individual caprice.
The defense is manifestly wrong. God never intended for His house to be desolated by such con-

fusion. His dealings with Israel, after this time, afford an incontrovertible ensample. That people were thrown into conflicts by the opinions of the rabble growing into the dignity of the law. They accepted doctrines that came from their great elders, and received traditions because they were venerable. A part of their tribes wandered from Palestine, and the remaining ones were divided in their worship, and split into sects. Rendered blind by their pride and the bitterness of their strifes, they knew not Christ when he came as the fulfillment of their law. Had they been living in the law, they would have known Him, and a united Israel would have speedily converted the world. But instead they were a divided house, with a disregarded law; and a world with a ransom was prostrate under sin. The indignant wrath of Almighty God was stirred against Israel, and for these eighteen hundred years she has been kingless and priestless; she has been a wanderer, with every man's hand raised against her, and finding no rest for her weary feet. Her presence today in every commercial center of the earth, persecuted, but "going on forever," forever expiring but never dead, is a living monument to the integrity of God. Men may, while professing to be his children, divide His house, and disregard His law, but His judgments shall not fail. On every public square you meet Israel with that curl of the hair and print of features stamped upon Abraham and Moses. Jehovah says, "My house is divided and my laws altered, but these wanderers shall be changeless forever.'' If this be true of the type, how much sorer shall be the punishment visited on those who distract the real house.

The interest of the kingdom of heaven in humanity is more universal and permanent than the interest of any earthly government can be; so the testimony offered by the records of the New Testament upon the establishment of its church and house of salvation is of primary value. Whatever it testifies was then done, must be accepted as the revealed purpose of Divinity. A law inaugurated, a commandment given, an ordinance established, an example recorded, or a suggestion offered, are all and severally to be viewed as revelations of the divine mind on human redemption. We accept and live by them, or reject and die from them. When God gives a commandment or form, it is to be obeyed. No substitution will answer. The thing given is what the Father intended. To say that it is not clothed with an imperial negative, a ''thou shalt not do otherwise,'' is trifling with the eternal character. Whatever is given has the royal stamp upon it. That, and that alone, that in its entirety, must be obeyed. A deviation from that precise thing is disobedience and heresy.

Mr. Edwards testified, and Mr. Carpenter corroborated him, that ''on such doctrines as the Trinity, predestination, original sin, the decrees, etc., we are content to allow men to hold such opinion as seems good to them without putting them under the ban of heterodoxy.'' On all these doctrines we leave the child of God to the same liberty Christ and the apostles extended him. No one of these doctrines is ever in the scriptures, by command, practice, or implication, connected with the conversion of the sinner or a righteous life. Any church that makes the formulated statements of these doctrines a test of fellowship has usurped authority in the house of God, and has added to the things herein written. The Christian Church does not make a test of these doctrines, it does not recognize orthodoxy as connected with them, it does not place them at the church door and say, ''You can not enter unless you bear them in with you.'' It says, ''On these profound and intricate subjects have correct views; you had better avoid constructions and stick to the test, speaking your faith in these things in the exact words of the scriptures.'' This is our practice. On all of these great dogmas we again present perfect fidelity to the divine standard.

Counsel was at a loss to understand how we determined the construction to be placed on any passage of the Scriptures. Mr. Carpenter replied to such a question that we settled differences as other churches. ''When they arraign a man and try him, they do it by their standard, the creed—as David Swing by the Presbyterians, and Dr. Thomas by the Methodists; and when we arraign a man and try him, we do it by our creed, but that is the Bible itself.''

Then it was asked, if the particular congregation where a difference arose was the ultimate judge in that case. He answered, ''Well, as we have never had any such case (and we are not likely to have), any answer I might give would only be an anticipation of it; but, to give my own opinion, I presume, as we have the congregational form of church government, that it would fall to the congregation where the difference should arise to handle it, either by its own membership, or by other brethren whom it might select to do so.''

Then came the question that was to produce a demonstration of the attorney's statement of the case, on the opening of the trial. He asserted that we were creedless, without helm or rudder in the religious world, and that our preachers taught all sorts of doctrine, and that we were destitute of any settled faith, or rules of interpretation. He contended that a church occupying our position would constantly be found in a wrangle of differences; that it was systemless and unorganized, and could never arrive at any uniform teaching or practice. With all the assurance of a lawyer that means to overwhelm a witness, the question was hurled at Mr. Carpenter, ''Do you know of any such thing as a serious difference in doctrine having arisen at any time?''

And to the confusion of the lawyer the answer was given, ''No, sir; we have never been troubled in that direction, and we are not likely to be. We take the Bible as our rule of faith and practice, and let it do its own teaching; we have never been troubled, to my knowledge, about the question of doctrine so-called.''

It was determined to risk another approach: ''Do you mean to say that in your church, there is no uniform opinion—that one may have his own opinion, no matter what it is?''

Now, the answer had no such meaning, for if we had had no serious differences, we had a pronounced uniformity of faith and practice, and presented to the world an unparalleled system in our organization. But let the witness answer: ''No sir. In matters essential to salvation there must be uniformity of opinion; in the things not necessary to salvation the widest latitude and freedom are granted; the whole thing hinges upon the relation these things sustain to salvation, whether they are necessary or not necessary thereto.''

The entire line of questioning on biblical interpretation was conducted on the presumption that the primitive church did not present a perfect model, and that the experience of the ages had enabled men to improve on the revealed plan. The defense evidently believes it a necessity for church existence, that articles of doctrine be drawn from the scriptures, and surrounded with a corresponding form of church organization. Hence they regard the divided condition of the religious household as a prudent

205

and economic measure that brought order out of chaos, and a definite plan out of a confused generalization; that there must ever be broad differences in the constructions placed upon much of the divine teaching; that each of these paths of construction grows its own peculiar church practices; that this affords a house or refuge for every shape of doctrine, and the harmony of a government that has naturally grown up under it; that thus, the gospel, to be a practical value, necessitates religious denominations. This position is right or wrong. If right, we are wrong. If wrong, then the whole fabric of denominationalism is insecure, and must eventually fall.

It has been twice demonstrated to be wrong. For sixty years we have existed as a people; our preachers and members have been scattered everywhere preaching the gospel; they have gone forth without any creed or "constructed doctrine," but with the gospel alone. We are today the third most numerous religious body on our continent, and we have never had any serious difference of doctrine at any time. We have demonstrated their theory to be wrong. The primitive church was without a creed or "constructed doctrine" for more than two hundred years. The apostles and early proclaimers bore to the world nothing but the gospel alone; false teachers came in, but they went out; it was the most harmonious, prosperous, and glorious era of the church, and they never had any serious difference of doctrine at any time. The primitive church demonstrated this theory to be false. Can the defense present such a record? In the whole array of denominations is there one but what has been torn and rived by "serious differences"? And these factions have again warred and separated, until there are now more than five hundred denominations. Mr. Chapman uttered a truth when he said that the scriptures were not susceptible of more interpretations than are put upon human creeds.

The primitive cause did not have its unity and prosperity distracted until men sought to enforce "constructed doctrine" upon the churches. Since that hour constructions have multiplied, and each new construction has brought a difference, and every difference has increased trouble in the house of God. Human creeds, composed of constructed doctrines, for the purpose of accommodating differing views, are pernicious in theory, and injurious to religion in practice. That part of the Bible that treats on the things necessary to salvation does not require a "construction." All the statements concerning the necessary matters in salvation are plain commandments of things to be done by the sinner. Personally, I feel that God would not be good in placing the words of eternal life in such a darkened way that interpretation of them would be necessary. If such be the fact, the apostle made a mistake when he spoke of the gospel as being God's revealed plan of salvation. Neither do I feel that he is all-wise, if a "construction" be required upon these essentials of salvation; because experience has shown that finite men have differed in the construction to be placed upon these things, and by the conflicts growing out of these different constructions the church has been desolated for fifteen centuries. On the matter of human depravity, the direct operation of the Spirit, the eternal decrees, the freedom of the will, and the whole array of intricate and profound theological problems, known as scholastic divinity, the Bible has not given a formulated statement, nor required a specific faith. The members of the primitive church, doubtless, differed upon these great questions. As they have no necessary connection with salvation, God has left us free to whatever opinion we may prefer. And all the statements concerning the necessary matters in salvation are plain commandments of things to be done by the sinner.

You, no doubt, were much interested in the testimony on baptism. We rejoice that you had the privilege of hearing our position upon this subject stated from the witness stand, and supported by all the solemnity of a judicial oath. I am glad we got into court, so our standing on the question may be established by operation of law. For more than half a century, every bigot that has assailed us, every unchristian feeling that has been aroused, every charge of heterodoxy, every prejudice agitated, every slander propagated, every malign influence exerted against us has been along the line of the baptismal lie. Here, now, in this evidence, you have seen what our teaching and practice is, and its conformity to the divine plan passes unquestioned.

Witness Carpenter was asked, ''Does the Church believe the teaching that immersion alone, immersion without faith, without repentance, without confession, avails anything to the salvation of the soul?''

Did the witness hesitate? Did he halt and explain? His answer forever settles whatever doubt you may have had on the question. His answer was, ''No sir, the church believes and teaches that such a baptism would be blasphemy before God.'' And the church everywhere lifts its voice and adds to that answer its indignant emphasis.

The witness was then asked about the necessity of baptism. He answered, ''It becomes necessary because it is one of the commandments of the Lord Jesus Christ; but the efficacy to save from sin is in the blood of Christ, which is appropriated and applied to the conscience by obedience to His commands.''

The witness read from Mr. Campbell's debate with Mr. Rice, p. 555, ''While we regard immersion, in Christian baptism, as a wise, benevolent, and useful institution, we neither disparage nor underestimate a new heart, repentance, or faith; nay, we teach with clearness and definiteness, that, unpreceded by faith and repentance, it is of no value whatever.'' And again, on p. 678, he says, ''You may have heard me say here (and the whole country may have read it many a time), that a seven-fold

209

immersion in the river Jordan, or any other water, *without a previous change of heart, will avail nothing,* without a genuine faith and repentance. Nor would the most strict conformity to all the forms and usages of the most perfect church order; the most exact observance of all the ordinances, without personal faith, and moral righteousness—without a new heart, hallowed lips, and a holy life, profit any man in reference to eternal salvation.''

Mr. Campbell believed this and taught it all his life. Mr. Carpenter believes it; and teaches it, as an evangelist in Indiana. Mr. Edwards believes it; and teaches it, as a preacher. The preachers of the church everywhere believe and teach it. There is not a member of the Christian Church anywhere but believes it with his whole heart, and teaches it with all his zeal.

When Mr. Carpenter retired from the stand, we rested. We had introduced Messrs. Edwards, Chapman, Owen, and Carpenter. Their evidence was clear, direct, and convincing.

Viewing the ''orthodox churches'' in the light of the spirit that animated these when they were established, our position is unique and consummating. Looking at these churches as organizations that have crystallized, and propose to stay permanently where they are, we have no particular apostasy of Romanism, and to seek for the primitive faith and practice, we have a very intimate relation. There is a great common purpose in our battle, and the glorious

210

object at which we aim, the restoration of primitive Christianity, is of infinite concern. Let us examine the Protestant bodies in their reformatory character. They were all a protest against Romanism. The protest created them. They were pro-test-ants. Men protested against what they conceived to be wrong in the mother church.

The primitive church had a clearly defined practice. We may enumerate, that Christ was preached, and never a doctrine as such; sinners obeyed from the heart, and gladly, whatever the apostles commanded them to do, and no service was accepted as obedience that differed from the exact divine requirement; this obedience was the vehicle that transported the sinner into the church; Christ's body was at a place, and the sinner, as to a domicile, must arise and go there, that he might enter in; those coming into Christ, Christians, continued steadfastly in the apostles' doctrine; they knew nothing else as doctrine. Now, this life of Christ, contained in Matthew, Mark, Luke and John—this preaching of Christ's gospel to sinners, and the practices connected therewith, contained in Acts of Apostles—the letters of instruction to those who had become Christians, contained in Romans, Corinthians, etc.—with Revelation, constitute the counsel and wisdom of God in the Church. Congregations established in Christ's body by this "royal law," were soon multiplied, enlarged and augmented throughout the civilized world.

211

When the Council of Nice organized a doctrine in the Trinity, which drove men from the church, and forbid others an entrance therein, a step was taken which departed from the clearly defined practice of the primitive church. These departing steps multiplied with increasing councils, until the church stood forth robed in complete apostasy. It was now Romanism, and no longer *The Church*. Men sometimes wonder at the Dark Ages, and inquire the cause. There is no wonder here. When the light that lighteth every man that cometh into the world, is put out, darkness must come. In one sense, his light was yet in the world; "but if the light in thee be darkness, how great is that darkness!" In proportion as men retire from the divine likeness, in just that proportion do they retire from a prosperous dominion over the earth. When God created man in his image and likeness, he *gave* him dominion over the earth; and as man restores that marred likeness, he regains earthly dominion. Great and beneficial results to humanity are not possible in heathen lands. Railroads, telegraphs, telephones, the application of steam and electricity, are not possible among the heathen. So among a continent of people, when the restored likeness is debased, advancement halts, and prosperity turns back on its axis. From Nice to Worms, the likeness largely restored was prostituted, and the world of growth was worse than standing still.

We locate the organization of the Roman Catholic

212

Church in the Council of Nice. It was a new establishment in the religious world. Its councils decreed its articles of faith, prescribed its practice, and defined heresy. The Bible was always theoretically upheld; but in the course of years a creed grew up, which was consulted by every inquirer, which was the standard in every appeal, and which controlled every movement of the church. The church was founded on the creed.

The important doctrines of Christianity were perverted in the most wretched manner, and such primitive purity as remained was obscured with extravagant opinions and idle fancies. The essence of religion was placed in the worship of images and departed saints. The fears of purgatory exceeded the apprehension of the eternal torments. The latter they expected to avoid through the intercession of the saints, but none dared to hope for heaven without the pains of purgatory first. The people were not privileged to read the gospel; it was a sealed book, and given out only by priestly interpreters. A long series of reprobate practices and apostate faiths poured a current of calamitous events about the church, until Zion, on the beacon hill of the world, became black as sackcloth of hair, and the sweet waters from her fountain of salvation and peace had turned to wormwood and gall.

It was necessary that a reformation should come. God had said it would come. But for nearly twelve hundred years it did not come. It required more than a thousand years for the Church of Christ to reach the depths of complete apostasy. But having turned from the simplicity of the divine establishment, there was no halting grounds until the depths were reached. Then a reaction began. One man alone could not produce a reformation. Reformations are not created single-handed, neither do they come forth in a day. They are an influence that moves forth unseen and unappreciated, an unformed sentiment, sweeping over a vast area of territory, and occupying much time, and finally converging at some center, and pouring into one man as through a funnel. He becomes the embodiment of the principle. It is personified in him. He is all afire with its integrity. He moves forth to its organization, and its consequent victory. So Luther became the incarnation of the faith and protest that had been growing in Germany for half a century. He flashed the sword of the Spirit before the dazed vision of the Pope, and at Augsburg organized the great return to the old paths of the apostles. The Lutheran Church, founded on the Augsburg Confession of Faith, did not reach the old paths, but it went as far as one generation could march. What the world had been growing into for a thousand years, could not be outgrown in one generation.

Far be it from me to criticise this stalwart son of the faith. He did the grandest work of any man of his time. His mission was single. No man ever has more. His work was to arrest the career of universal apostasy. He did it. He built his church on the Augsburg Confession, which was a protest against Romanism; but must needs leave the consummation of his holy purpose—the restoring of the simple primitive church—to the ages after him.

The spirit of protest moved in England, where Henry VIII organized a revolt, and established the Church of England, the Episcopal Church. The king was moved against the Mother Church by his unrighteous desire to put away his wife, and marry Anne Boleyn; but God may cause the wickedness of man to glorify his cause. Out of the baseness of Henry's adultery, England, with her vast influence, took up her march from Rome. The Church of England was founded on what we may term the Episcopalian creed. It did not pass over all the creeds and councils, and take its stand on the ground its movement embodied. This was not possible, but England's coming made the reformation a certainty.

Next came the Presbyterian Church. The spirit of reform was abroad in the world, and could not down. Bold spirits were hurrying in every direction, to find the church from which the fathers had wandered. As men surrounded by a fog in an untraveled and dangerous valley, seek to escape and find safety, all alike interested, but each distrusting the other's way, and with a confidence in his own that was born only of necessity, so did scores of reformers toil, through this age, to rid themselves from the warp of judgment which twelve centuries of apostasy had thrown about the church, and come to know the truth as the early Christians knew it, and stand where they stood. In Geneva, John Calvin gave to the world his singular and wonderful doctrine of the Eternal Decrees. A hundred years after Luther they crystalized into the Westminster Confession of Faith, and gave us the Presbyterian Church. This Confession was not the story of the cross simply, as it was preached by Peter and John. It was a feeling through the fog, if haply they might find the house which they sought.

Out of this same spirit came the Baptist Church, and built itself on the Philadelphia Confession. In that they expressed what *they* believed to be the right road to the grounds of common interest. But the way was so beclouded they could not venture yet into the Bible alone, but must have a creed as a staff to guide and protect them. Religious thought was steadily rising out of the valley. Men now needed but little of councils, conventions and creeds to help them. They were now beginning to see each other face to face. The Bible itself was begun to be read. It had become a sign-board, on which the hurriers by could read the way.

This same spirit brought forth the Methodist Church. John Wesley never intended to establish the Methodist Church. But the tendency of worldliness in the churches was paralyzing all that had been gained by the reformation in other respects,

216

and a path of real piety must be sought out. The methods employed by Wesley to infuse spiritual life into the people, were original and peculiar. In the course of time they assumed a system, and took on the machinery necessary to continue the movement. Out of this an organization grew, that ripened into the Methodist Church. It took on itself a name indicative of its peculiarity, method-ist, and consigned itself thereto by establishing the Discipline, a creed conforming therewith, which was to control all its actions. The religious world has progressed so far into the light, that there was little need of longer resorting to experiments. There was small use for any discipline coined to assist a Christian. I have always thought that John Wesley ought to have protested against the hierarchy of the Church of England, and against all human appliances and church creeds, and with his devout nature and splendid powers, called believers to the simple word of God, and it alone. It may be that I am wrong, that the fullness of time had not yet come, and that the mission of this saintly man lay along the path of a restoration of personal piety. The world was not prepared for a restoration of piety when Luther came, or Henry, or Calvin; their movements gave that which the times required. But there was a hungering and thirsting after righteousness when Wesley came. He filled the want of the soul. God appears to have assigned one task to each of these reformers, even as he gave one task to Moses and another to Joshua. Wesley was a glorious herald— an unconscious John the Baptist, setting in order the last work for the restored kingdom.

The spirit that had worked among men for three hundred years brought forth the movement in which we are engaged, and resulted in the prophecy of Worms. Mr. Campbell was the leader of the special movement now known as the Current Reformation. He did not seek a new church, and earnestly protested against the formation of another sect. No sect was created, no church was organized. But a religious body was presented to the world, whose existence was not a purposed protest against Romanism. It had moved from a protest to an affirmative plea. It was not founded on a creed. Its faith was not defined by formulated articles, and the edicts of councils did not give it shape. It rested on the word of God. It rested on the word of God only. Every practice which the primitive church practiced, it put into practice; every person or doctrine which the primitive church required a faith in, it required a faith in. Whatever practice the primitive church did not operate, or faith not required, it made no movement in. It stood where the primitive church stood. The grand march began at Augsburg, and extending over three hundred years of toil and struggle, reached its blessed consummation when a handful of disciples, weary with the way and bruised in the conflict, cast themselves upon the word of

God alone. Up out of the valley, the "Old Paths" had been reached.

Primitive Christianity was restored. God had built the house, and it was appointed with every appliance to move its vast interests in His service. Having reached the coveted ground, it only remained to operate the divine appliances, to make good the blood of the martyrs and the labors of the reformers. Has it been done? Have we only reached the goal to which the Lord's people started, or have we carried consummation to a fruition, and entered into the practice of the Israel of God?

This Church preaches the gospel to sinners as the power of God unto salvation, and never a doctrine as such. Is this heterodox? It is what the primitive church did; therefore it is apostolic. This Church teaches the sinner to have faith in Christ, repent of his sins, confess his Saviour, and be baptized into the name of the Father, Son and Holy Spirit, and he thereby becomes a child of God. Is this heterodox? It is what the primitive church did; therefore it is apostolic. It never requires faith in any formulated statements of doctrinal divinity, leaving each person free to his own honest convictions thereon. Is this heterodox? It is what the primitive church did; therefore it is apostolic. This Church teaches those in Christ to add the Christian graces, and continue in the apostles' teaching. Is this heterodox? It is what the primitive church did; therefore it is apostolic. This Church calls itself by the name of Christ, by the divine names, and rejects all other names. Is this heterodox? Is it what the primitive church did; therefore it is apostolic. This Church excludes all confessions, disciplines and creeds, and takes the word of God alone as its rule and guide. Is this heterodox? It is what the primitive church did; therefore it is apostolic. This Church practices or excludes, respectively, everything here enumerated. Mr. Edwards, Mr. Carpenter, Mr. Chapman, swore that we did so, and Rev. Mr. Post testified that this would make a man a child of God, and save his soul. This is not heterodox, for it is what the primitive church did, and is therefore apostolic.

The testimony of the witnesses reveals this Church as holding the exact faith of the early church, and using every form of its practice. It reveals that nothing is omitted that the early church operated, and not a name, or a ceremony, or a creed, or anything whatever, has been added thereto. It does as that church did. This is Christianity restored.

PAUL'S ANSWER TO KING AGRIPPA

By JOHN S. SWEENEY

"Then Agrippa said unto Paul, Almost thou persuadest me to be a Christian. And Paul said, I would to God, that not only thou, but all that hear me this day, were both almost, and altogether—such as I am except these bonds." Acts xxvi:28,29.

IT matters very little in what spirit or with what meaning King Agrippa said, "Almost thou persuadest me to be a Christian;" whether he was really almost so persuaded, and, therefore, gave an honest expression of his state of mind, as some suppose; or, as others suppose, in irony, meaning to belittle the apostle and his cause, and call attention to his own greatness—to minify the apostle's speech and magnify himself. Anyhow *the apostle* was in earnest. If, as a great man to start with, Paul was one thing more than another, he was an *earnest man*. Earnestness characterized his whole life from the first we hear of him to his last word and act. Such was the apostle's manifest earnestness in this answer before King Agrippa that the governor, who had heard him before, "Festus, said with a loud voice, Paul, thou art beside thyself; much learning doth make thee mad. But he said, I am not *mad*, most noble Festus; but speak forth the words of truth and *soberness.*'' Such was the soberness, the earnestness, with which the apostle spake that Festus thought he was mad.

We shall not concern ourselves then in this discourse with the language of Agrippa, but rather with the apostle's reply, in which he owned that it was his aim and his pleasure to persuade men to be Christians; not simply *one* king, but *all* who heard him: not to be *almost* but *altogether* Christians, such as he himself was, excepting his bonds.

The first thing suggested by his reply that we shall notice is that there is such a thing as being partly and yet not wholly a Christian.

1. Some persons are called Christians because they were born, and reared, and educated, and live, in a Christian country; because they have been used to Christian civilization, customs and usages; because they date their letters ''in the year of our Lord,'' and as Christians in this sense often do, swear by the name of Jesus instead of that of Mahomet, or Jupiter, or Buddha, or that of any other founder of a religion. That is, they are Christians only in the sense of historic or geographical classification; as one must be a Jew, or a Christian, or a Mohammedan, or a Pagan, or be left out entirely. There are more Christians in this sense than there are such as Paul was. Col. Ingersoll

222

would be called a Christian in Arabia! In this sense persons are called Christians without being Christians in any sense worth speaking of.

2. We have many persons in all Christian countries, and possibly in some others, who are Christians simply in judgment; that is, persons who in their own minds have decided in favor of Christianity as against all other religions; persons who even believe the Christian religion to be true, right, divine; who really believe it is right to be a Christian; who have promised themselves, time and again, when sick, or otherwise alarmed, that they would try to become such, and expect at some future day to do so, but have deferred a practical consideration of the matter. There are many such persons in all Christian countries; of good education and intelligence in secular matters, persons of high places who consider themselves too busy with matters of state, matters of commerce or trade, and of the general interest and welfare of the country, to give the matter of becoming Christians their personal attention; and many who seem willing to commit the interests of their souls to the priests, the preachers, or the churches, or to the Lord—anybody who will take it, so that they may be excused from a personal consideration of the matter. They send their children to Sunday school, and are glad even to see them join the church; pay their wives' church subscriptions, and even go with them to church on Sundays and holidays. But such persons lack a

good deal more than his "bonds" of being Christians such as Paul was.

3. Then, again, there are many persons who no doubt are Christians at heart, as we often say; that is, they are not only convinced in their minds that Jesus is the Christ the Son of God, and the Saviour, but they love him; their feelings and desires are all on the side of Christianity. They hear and think of the story of Jesus only with pleasureful interest. But they go no further. They have been mistaught, it may be; or they may not have been taught at all, as to their future duty. They have been taught, it may be, to look for something they have never been able to see, or to listen for something they have never been able to hear, or wait for some experience they have never had. They are waiting, in consequence of such teaching for some mysterious and wonderful change, more than faith in the Son of God and a sincere desire to be a Christian, that will be to them an evidence of sins forgiven and of their acceptance with God. They have not the imagination that some have, and cannot have the experience that some have supposed they had, and they suppose that they are not sufficiently converted to take any further step in the matter. And they are waiting for something they know not what; but something nevertheless. They may have been taught there is nothing they can do; that if they belong to the elect, God will make it known to them in his own good time, and if they are not of the elect, why, then they are not;

and they really fear to try to do anything lest they should be found fighting against God. And they wait. Many no doubt thus honestly wait all their lives, and die waiting, Christians at heart. No doubt it is better to be a Christian at heart than not to be. No doubt God will judge rightly all honestly misguided persons. But these honestly mistaken, misguided Christians at heart are not Christians such as Paul was.

Then, a great many people who are Christians at heart are confused by foolish preaching and the jargon of the creeds. The preachers instead of telling the simple story of Jesus of Nazareth and teaching the people the duty of faith, obedience and trust, have been preaching about the Godhead, the Holy Trinity, the fore-knowledge of God, the divine decrees, unconditional election and reprobation, etc., etc., and the people have failed to understand them. The fact is the preachers themselves have not understood them. They have been preaching these profound doctrines, as they doubtless suppose they are, because they are in the creeds of their churches, and because the preacher must believe and preach them in order to be orthodox, and because one who is not orthodox is heterodox, and it has always been and always will be a terrible thing to be heterodox. The consequence is that many honest souls, Christians at heart—made so by the simple story of Jesus, which they have gotten in spite of the creeds—are left in utter confusion upon the whole matter of further duty, and of becoming Christians, such as Paul was.

4. Then there is such a thing as being a Christian *in fact*. This is more than birth, education, country; more than the convictions of the mind and decision of the judgment; more than sympathies, desires, feelings, or a Christian at heart. One becomes a Christian formally and in fact by publicly confessing Jesus Christ as the Son of God, and by putting him on in his appointed way—the way he appointed when he committed the gospel to his disciples and sent them to all the nations to preach it. Let us see: "Go ye, and make disciples of all the nations, baptizing them into the name of the Father, and of the Son, and of the Holy Spirit. (Matt. xxviii:19.) "Go ye into all the world, and preach the gospel to every creature. He that believeth and is baptized shall be saved; but he that believeth not shall be damned." (Mark xvi:16.) This is the Lord's appointed way; and it's right or it's not right. Which shall we say?

Some persons have been taught that there is nothing in *forms*—and therefore there is nothing in becoming a Christian *formally*—that baptism is a *mere form,* and in no sense vitally connected with the matter of becoming a Christian. Well, it is true that baptism is a form—not a *"mere"* form, but a form—the baptizing of an infant is what might be called a *mere* form. It is true, also, that by being baptized the believer *formally* becomes a Christian, formally puts on Christ, is formally initiated into

226

the body of Christ. Who is authorized to say that there is nothing essential in *forms*? God did not leave the earth "without form and void," but he "*formed* the earth." Is there nothing essential to the earth in its form? God "*formed* man of the dust of the ground." Is his form essential? "God formed every beast." His "hand formed the crooked serpent." Yea; he "formed all things" that were made. Things are distinguished by their forms. Jesus "took upon him the form of a servant" and was in the fashion of a man. We have in the New Testament a "form of doctrine," a "form of sound words," a "form of godliness." True, a form without power, without life, without utility, without beauty, without anything but form would be only a form, "a mere form." But God has no such forms. Forms are necessary to power, and even to life itself. And so God has appointed that men shall be Christians in form—shall become Christians *formally*.

By the way, that is just what's the matter. Presumptuous and ignorant men have *deformed* Christianity. They have deformed the very simple God-appointed form of becoming a Christian; and with many the whole matter of becoming a Christian is "without form and void." Hence the confusion upon the subject, and the many Christians at heart who know not how to become Christians formally and in fact.

Yes. The confession of Christ, the good confession, is a form; and baptism is a form, too; and by making the confession and being baptized the believer formally becomes a Christian. That's exactly it. Nor is this form unnecessary simply because it is a form. Things are distinguished one from another by their forms. By this divinely appointed form we can see persons become Christians, and believers can see themselves become Christians. The Lord has made no unnecessary appointments. A form may be just as necessary as anything without a form. Baptism is associated with faith and repentance, and sustains the same kind of relation to the body of Christ and salvation that they do. Let us see: In the commission (Mark xvi:16.) "He that believeth and is baptized shall be saved." Belief and baptism are associated by "and," and alike related to salvation. Peter in answer to the inquirers on that noted Pentecost (Acts ii:28.) said, "Repent and be baptized every one of you in the name of Jesus Christ for the remission of sins." Here he associates repentance and baptism, and by the same word connects both with remission of sins. Again: Paul so associates faith and baptism (Gal. iii:26,27) in these words: "For ye are all the children of God by faith in Christ Jesus; for as many of you as have been baptized into Christ have put on Christ." And all this notwithstanding baptism is a form. Associated with belief, and put in the same relation with it to salvation; associated with repentance and put into the same relation with it to remission of sins; asso-

228

ciated with faith and made *initiative* to Christ, to His body, to His church; and still baptism is a form. The difference between it and "mere" forms, needless forms, non-essential forms, is that it is God's form, while all "mere" forms are men's forms. When the Lord prescribes a form and puts upon it the "name of the Father, and of the Son, and of the Holy Ghost," "mere," or "needless," or "nonessential," is no proper adjunct for it.

Some persons make much ado over the fact that in the Greek Scriptures persons are said to "believe *into* Christ"; and we are asked how that can be and yet persons be "baptized into Christ." Simple enough. Both expressions are scripture, are they not? that is, both "believe into Christ" and "baptized into Christ." And if we believe one because it is scripture we ought to believe the other for the same reason, ought we not? Both are true. I believe both. How can both be true? Are persons initiated into Christ twice? Once by belief and once by baptism? Certainly not. Well, then, are some persons initiated into Christ by faith and others by baptism? Certainly not. How, then, can both statements be true—"believe into Christ," and "baptized into Christ?" Why, because, as we have already seen, belief and baptism are associated in bringing sinners into Christ. The end, "into Christ," may be predicated of both; or it may be predicated of *either one,* when that one is the subject of the conversation, just as in case of the association of two or more

229

men in the accomplishing of a given work. A person may be brought into court by the sheriff, the jailor, and a guard. The bringing of the man may be predicated of either one of the officers named, if we are speaking of that officer and wish to magnify his office. Whether in strictness of speech it is correct or incorrect, it is a liberty taken by writers in all languages, and common-sense has no difficulty in the interpretation of it.

A believer, then, is made a Christian formally by the *divine form:* that is, by confessing Jesus Christ with the mouth, and being baptized in his name. People generally have no difficulty in understanding this, and the necessity of it, in reference to anything else than Christianity. Take Free Masonry, for instance: Is one a Mason simply because his father was? Is he already a Mason because he believes Masonry to be a good thing—becuse in his judgment he has decided in favor of it? Is he a Mason *in fact* simply because he is a Mason at heart? May not one be a Mason in judgment, and at heart, and yet not one in *fact?* And is it not true, that he is not a Mason in fact because he has not been *formally* made a Mason, because he has not taken the steps? because he has not been formally initiated?

People have no difficulty in understanding this matter in case of American citizenship. Is a man an American citizen in fact just because he is in judgment, or even at heart? Certainly not. We all understand that. A foreigner may be ever so thoroughly convinced of the greatness of America, of the advantages of American citizenship; and he may be an American at heart; but all this does not make him a citizen in *fact*. To be a citizen in fact he must be formally made one.

We all understand this matter as it relates to *contracts*. Is a man a husband in fact because he has contracted marriage with a certain woman? Certainly not. No matter how much he may love the woman, at heart; and how well suited to be his wife he may believe her to be, he is not her husband until he is formally married to her. And, as I have said, this is true of becoming anything, or a member of any order or association, or a citizen or any country, or subject of any government; and yet some people seem to think that one can become a Christian, a member of the body of Christ, a subject of his kingdom, *in fact* without any form; and this, too, notwithstanding the divine form taught through the New Testament, both by our Lord himself and by his apostles. One passage here from Paul, (Rom. vi:17), is too fitting to be passed: "Ye have obeyed from the heart that form of doctrine which was delivered you; *being then made free from sin* ye became the servants of righteousness." And it is almost impossible not to understand the apostle here by "that form of doctrine" to allude to what he has just before said: "So many of us as were baptized into Jesus Christ were baptized into his death. There we were buried with him by baptism into death;

231

that like as Christ was raised up from the dead by the glory of the Father, even so we also should walk in newness of life,'' (verses 3, 4). Dr. Macknight says in his comment on this 17th verse: ''The original word, (translated *form*) among other things, signifies *a mould* into which melted metals are poured, to receive the form of the mould. The apostle represents the gospel doctrine as a mould into which the Romans were put by their baptism, in order to their being fashioned anew. And he thanks God, that from the heart, that is most willingly and sincerely, they have yielded to the forming efficacy of that mould of doctrine, and were made new men, both in principle and in practice.''

But let us notice in the next place, ''Such as I am except these bonds.'' Paul was no mere Christian at heart—or in judgment and at heart. He was all that, and more. The point at issue, or point of difference, as to belief, between Paul prior to his conversion and the disciples of Jesus, was one as to the resurrection of Jesus from the dead. When the Lord appeared to him on the way from Jerusalem to Damascus and he believed that it was really Jesus of Nazareth risen from the dead and alive, the point of difference was decided against him at the bar of his own judgment; and just like the brave and honest man he always was, he surrendered. There is often the grandest heroism in surrender. Paul at once acknowledged Jesus as Lord, and asked what he would have him to do. Let him tell the story in his own style: "And I said, what shall I do, Lord? And the Lord said unto me, 'Arise and go into Damascus; and there it shall be told thee of all things which are appointed for thee to do.' And when I could not see for the glory of that light, being led by the hand of them that were with me, I came into Damascus. And one Ananias, a devout man according to the law, having a good report of all the Jews which dwelt there, came unto me, and stood, and said unto me, Brother Paul, receive thy sight; and the same hour I looked up upon him. And he said, the God of our fathers hath chosen thee, that thou shouldst know his will, and see that just one, and shouldst hear the voice of his mouth; for thou shalt be his witness unto all men of what thou hast seen and heard. And now why tarriest thou? Arise, and be baptized, and wash away thy sins, calling on the name of the Lord." (Acts xxii:10-16). And in another account of his conversion we learn that when Ananias had so instructed him as to the things "appointed" for him to do, Paul at once "arose and was baptized." (Acts ix:18). And thus, he, as he himself said, "put on Christ." (Gal. iii:27). He was not the kind of man to be satisfied with being "almost" a Christian, with being a Christian in judgment, and at heart merely, Paul was an "altogether" sort of man. Whatever he was, that he was "altogether." When he became a Christian he became "altogether" one. And when he persuaded men to become Christians he persuaded them to become not only almost, but altogether, such as he was, except his bonds. That is, he persuaded men to be Christians not merely in judgment and heart, but *in fact*—outwardly, openly, actually, formally, as well; and both in the profession and in the practice of Christianity.

"Persuadest me to be a Christian." Paul *persuaded* men to be Christians. This he confessed in his answer to the king; and this he taught elsewhere, both in his preachings to the sinner and in his epistles. He *persuaded* men. God doesn't persuade stones, rocks, or seas; worlds, suns or comets; but he persuades *men*. He governs the world of matter by sheer force, or power; but not so men. He reasons with men; persuades, exhorts, entreats and warns men. While he rules the material universe, all worlds and suns, by his own almighty power, he stops at the door of man's heart, and knocks for admission. He says (Rev. iii:20) "Behold I stand at the door and knock; if any man hear my voice, and open the door, I will come in to him, and will sup with him, and he with me." No divine violence here. God respects his own image in man. He will not break down the dignity of his own image even to save man from eternal ruin. Man is so wonderfully and fearfully made that he may choose sin and death here, and hell forever hereafter. If man's salvation were merely a question of divine power, or will, or sovereignty, as some suppose it is, there would be no sense in standing at the door of man's heart and knocking, or in reasoning with him. Persuading man would be mocking men. If man were the mere machine that popular theology would have us believe that he is, utterly unable to be or do otherwise than God has decreed from all eternity that he should do, then all talk about persuasion is nonsense. Why persuade men, if they indeed can do nothing but what God has foreordained from all eternity that they should do, and are compelled to do that, just as the world is to sweep round in circles? But God persuades men, notwithstanding the jargon of the creeds that have come down to us from the darker ages.

Again: Paul persuaded men to be *Christians*. Only Christians. His plea could be readily understood. The issue he made with men was single and simple. To be or not to be a Christian; that was it. I think it is to be regretted that it is not so now. There is some confusion about the issue we are making with men now. We have questions about churches, denominations, parties; about creeds and ecclesiastical politics. The priests and preachers now have to do a good deal of persuading, arguing, and debating about matters of difference in their creeds and churches; and when they get men persuaded to be Christians their work is only fairly begun. Many men are today standing out in the world, never having made any kind of public confession of Jesus, although entirely willing and anxious to be Christians—because they are confused by the many creeds and churches we have in the world, whose claims are being pressed upon people, more than the simple story of Jesus and his love. This ought not to be. There have been very grave mistakes made by somebody, since Paul's time; so that the simple issue he made with men has been almost lost sight of in the wars of churches and conflicts of creeds. If Paul was right we have gone wrong; and have brought upon ourselves unnecessary labor and trouble. How shall we go about getting right again? I can see but one way: Let the creeds and the parties they have made go. Let them go entirely. We shall not make the difficulties less by trying to alter and amend them, and adjust them to our advanced civilization. Let them go. Then let us persuade men to believe in Jesus, and confess Jesus, and put on Jesus in his own simple and appointed way, and to walk in Jesus; and be simply *Christians*. Men can be Christians without the creeds and parties of our day—Christians such as Paul was, except his "bonds." We have no need of the bonds with which man bound Paul; nor of the "bonds" with which men have sought to bind all the children of God. Let all the bonds go!

Finally. With Paul, it was not enough simply to become a Christian—a Christian in belief, in heart, and in fact—to be saved, and to feel happy, and be taken to heaven on flowery beds of ease. No, no! With him, to become a Christian was to become a soldier; and having enlisted, to fight the good fight of faith; to fight on until death should release him. Hear him: "So fight I, not as one that beateth the air; but I keep under my body, and bring it into subjection; lest that by any means, when I have preached to others, I myself should be a castaway'' (I Cor.ix:26,27). Again, near the close of his earthly career: "I have fought a good fight, I have finished my course, I have kept the faith; henceforth there is laid up for me a crown of righteousness, which the Lord the righteous judge shall give me at that day; and not to me only, but unto all them also which love his appearing'' (2 Tim. iv:7,8). And to those left behind he says: "Fight the good fight of faith, lay hold on eternal life, whereunto thou art called, and have professed a good profession before many witnesses." Let us try to be Christians such as Paul was.

"I would to God that not only thou, but also all that hear me this day, were both almost, and altogether such as I am, except these bonds."

OUR STRENGTH AND OUR WEAKNESS

By F. G. ALLEN

"Out of weakness were made strong."—Heb. xi:34.

THE religion of God has ever been a religion of faith. The faith of the Bible is a principle of action which governs the lives of men and brings them into submission to the divine will. A life of faith, therefore, is a life of growth. By faith men are out of weakness made strong. But this strength is not the work of a day. It is the result of a life. We are all babes before we are men.

In recording the many wonderful things which the ancients accomplished by faith, it is affirmed that out of weakness they were made strong. In noting the extreme weakness of some of the prominent characters of that age in the early stages of their life of faith, and the grand heroes which they finally became, we find much to encourage us in our struggles toward a higher life and a closer walk with God. We are thankful that God has given these examples for our imitation. Among these Abraham, Isaac and Jacob are prominent representatives. Abraham and Isaac were both so weak, even after they had been

238

in close communion with God, and had assurances of His protection, that they relied on human strategy rather than divine providence. They both prevaricated in regard to their wives. They made a deliberate effort to deceive. They seemed to think that their wives were too handsome to claim. The complaint is not now so common. Jacob supplanted his brother by deceiving his father, old and blind; and by a shrewd device managed to get most of the flock of his father-in-law. Yet out of such weakness these men developed by faith into moral and spiritual giants, whose names stand out on the sacred page worthy of our profound reverence and sublime admiration. But this was the development of a long life. It is a grand mistake to suppose that Abraham was capable of doing, when called out of Ur of the Chaldees, what he afterwards did at the command of God.

Also in the lives of the Apostles we see the same development out of weakness into strength. Not only did they forsake their Master; but Peter, the boldest of the lot, even cursed and swore, and denied that he ever knew Him. But when possessed of a purer faith, they were all ready to go to the stake, and thanked God that they were worthy to suffer for Him whom they once deserted and denied.

In studying the elements of weakness and strength of God's ancient people, we pass by an easy transition to the study of those elements in His people now. Hence it is my purpose today to consider the elements of strength and weakness as we understand them to exist among us as a religious people. This leads me to speak of what is generally denominated

OUR PLEA.

Whenever a people come before the world with a plea demanding its recognition, the world has a right to demand of them a reason for their claim. Hence we should be always ready to give a reason for the position we occupy in the religious world. The work in which we are engaged is generally called the Reformation, but sometimes, and more correctly, I think, the Restoration. But this depends largely on the point of view from which the work is considered. In presenting this plea today I shall speak first of its

ELEMENTS OF STRENGTH.

In considering the nature of our work as a people, I shall first mention what it is not, that we may the more clearly understand what it is. In doing this I shall be very brief, because most of you are familiar with these facts, more so, than I. But the mention of them is necessary to get other thoughts properly before us.

The work of Thomas and Alexander Campbell, if I understand it, was not to establish another church or denomination. On the contrary, they held that there were too many churches already; and that for these there is no divine warrant. They held that denominational divisions are evil, and, therefore,

240

should not exist. Hence to start another denomination, in the current sense of that term, would be to increase an existing evil. They never regarded their work in this sense during their lives. Nor are we or others justifiable in so regarding it now.

It was not the purpose of the Campbells and their co-laborers to reform the denominations as such. While there was great room for reformation in all the denominations, and is yet, still a reformation, however great, that would leave them *denominations,* would leave them in a position unsanctioned by the New Testament. A very great reformation has been gradually produced in the denominations, which we are satisfied is largely due to our plea and work as a people, but this is only an incidental result, and not the main object sought.

The primary object of the religious work in whose interests we are assembled was—

I. *To restore the Church to the world as it was when left by the Apostles.*

It must be admitted by all who respect divine example, that God cast the New Testament churches in just such a mold as He saw was best. In this respect, therefore, they were left by inspiration just as God would have them. They were left as models for our imitation. We are to copy what is approved, and avoid what is condemned. From this divine standard the Church gradually departed, till the apostasy was the result.

To restore the Church to the original model, is a work that must commend itself to every man's conscience in the sight of God, who once firmly grasps the idea. On this underlying principle rests the very pillars of the temple of faith we are trying to build. Here is the basis of our strength. The strength of God's people has ever been in their faith. Hence, if we would build strong, we must build by faith. Faith comes by the word of God. Hence, if we would build by faith, we must build by that word. What is done by faith is done by divine direction. Therefore, if we would become strong in our work, we must work by divine direction.

Men admit that our plea for restoration is a grand conception of Christian work, but say it is ideal, and can never be accomplished. Our faith is that it can be accomplished. Much has already been done, and God's word indicates that much more should and can be done. If it is never done, it will not be the fault of the plea, but of those who make it. Are the rewards of present success required to induce truth-loving men to do what God has appointed? That is the work of time-servers, and not of men who love the truth because it *is the truth*.

(1). This work of reformation demands that we accept Christ as our only creed, and the Bible as our only rule of faith and practice.

We sometimes say that the Bible is our creed. But this is to speak loosely; not accurately. Under the ministry of the Apostles the converts were not asked if they believed the Bible, nor the New Testament; for it was not then written. But they were required to believe in Christ. They were not asked to accept some theory about Christ, but were required to accept *Him,* as their personal and only saviour. Accepting Him the Bible is accepted as a consequence, because He is the central thought of the Book. Take Christ out of the Bible, and you take its life out. The Bible becomes our rule of faith and practice because it is an amplification of our creed —a divine commentary on its wonderful meaning— *Jesus is the Christ, the Son of the living God.* Whether or not we would have another creed, is not a matter of choice with us. We are compelled to have this, and this only, or abandon our plea. For this only did the churches have whose imitation our plea demands.

(2). Our work demands that we hold to the simplicity of conversion, and admission into the Church by baptism, just as we find them in the New Testament. The simple presentation of the Gospel facts to be believed, commands to be obeyed, and promises to be enjoyed, disentangled from the sectarian confusion on the subject of conversion, has ever been a tower of strength to the cause we plead. Our plea compels us to stick close to Bible *facts* on all these points, without regard to theories. Without a reproduction of these historic facts, our work of restoration would not be a restoration of New Testament Christianity.

243

(3). Our work demands that we call Bible things by Bible names. We must have the Bible *things*. We can not have a complete restoration without them. Then when we have the things which the New Testament churches had, we must give them the names that the Holy Spirit gave them. To disregard the things they had, or the names given them, is to presume to improve on divine wisdom. A departure from this principle could never result in a restoration of the Church of God as it was when these things existed. Of course I speak of things of divine appointment and approval, and not of mere incidentals.

As a natural result of the restoration of New Testament Christianity, and resting on that divine foundation, is—

II. *Our plea for Christian union.*

The union of all God's people in one harmonious body, as they were in the apostolic age, is a thing for which every one who loves the Lord should both work and pray. The necessity of this in order to the world's conversion, it is not my purpose to discuss. It is sufficient to say that its evident importance and righteousness have so struck the popular mind that it is one of our greatest elements of strength.

(1). Our plea for Christian union implies that there are Christians to unite.

It has ever been admitted that God has children

among the denominations—those who have obeyed the Gospel and are serving Him in the spirit of humility. To deny that there are Christians apart from those who stand identified with us in our work of restoration, would be to make our plea for Christian union both meaningless and senseless. While we believe that many identified with the denominations are Christians, they have taken on much that is neither Christianity nor any part of it; and this we labor to have them put away. These are the things that cause sectarian divisions, with all their evils. Such people are more than Christians; and what they have in addition is wrong. In being more than Christians they become less than what Christians should be. This may appear paradoxical, but it is true.

It will be seen, therefore, that while we claim to be Christians only, we do not claim to be the only Christians. Our principles will not allow us to be anything else; and we strive to have others satisfied with being the same. Hence the change so often made, that we arrogate to ourselves alone the name Christian, is false. We simply decline to be more than this, because God's people in New Testament times were nothing more. To those who love the simplicity of apostolic Christianity this position will commend itself with great force.

(2). Our plea for the union of God's people implies that the Church of God includes more than those engaged in this work of restoration. In other words, that the Church of God is a more comprehensive term than those descriptive of our work.

God's Church is composed of individual Christians, wherever they may be. Of His Church they become members by obedience to the Gospel. They do not forfeit their membership in God's Church till they cease to be His children. As long as they are children of God they are members of the body of Christ. Hence if there are children of God outside of what the world calls Campbellism, the Church of God extends beyond the same boundary. Consequently, while we claim to belong to the Church of God only, we do not claim to be the only people who belong to the Church of God. Others who belong to the Church of God also belong to a church *not* of God. They belong to *two* churches, while we belong to but one. Hence the whole charge of exclusiveness brought against us on this point turns on the question as to whether or not it is one's privilege to belong to but *one* church, and that the Church of God? That God's people in ancient times belonged to but one Church is simply an admitted fact; and His people now should belong to that, and that only, to which they belonged then.

In the New Testament the word *church* is applied to a local congregation and to the whole body of believers. It is never used in any denominational sense. Consequently we may not limit it to any religious people now, unless we believe that they include all God's children. While, therefore, we belong to the Church of God only, and our principles will not allow us to belong to any other, we should be careful to give to that term no mere denominational meaning. When I say I belong to the Church of God, the Church of Christ, or any other scriptural term by which the same thing is designated, I mean that I belong to God's redeemed family,

> "Part of whom have crossed the flood,
> And part are crossing now."

(3). From this it follows that our work of restoration is wholly undenominational.

When the Church of Christ shall be restored as it was at the beginning, or to the extent of that restoration, it will be wholly undenominational. This is true from the simple fact that there were no denominations then. No one then belonged to the Church of God and also to some denomination. All the Apostles belonged to the Church of God. None of them belonged to any denomination. So of all the disciples. What was true then may be true now; and to the extent that this is true, or ever shall be true, in the restoration of the Church, to that extent will denominationalism cease. Our plea means its destruction. It can mean nothing less. This is the secret of their intense hatred of it. But be it so; truth can never compromise with error.

The great objection which the world has urged

against our plea for Christian union is, that we can not all think alike. In this they have their mind more on opinion than faith. Hence we have found it necessary to urge a union on faith and not on opinion. One important item of our plea has, therefore, become

III. *Unity of faith and diversity of opinion.*

Many have thought the distinction between faith and opinion more fanciful than real. We think, however, that between the two there is a clearly-marked line in the word of God. One is a matter of divine statement, the other of human inference. Or rather, one is that which divine testimony establishes without doubt; the other that which is probable, but on which the testimony is not conclusive. The strength of one's opinion is governed by the strength of testimony. We have this strikingly illustrated in Abraham at the offering of Isaac. The test of his faith was not simply in taking the life of his son, but in taking the life of him whose posterity God had said should be as numerous as the sands on the sea-shore. The question with Abraham was, if I obey God's command, how can He fulfill His promise? His faith was that God would do what He had promised. His opinion was that He would do it by raising Isaac from the dead. (See Heb. xi :19). This was the conclusion of his reasoning; not of God's statement. In his faith he was right. In his opinion he was wrong. God did it, but did it not as Abraham expected. Abraham's opinion, though wrong, interfered not with his obedience. This has ever been the real test of the hurtfulness or innocence of one's opinion. So long as it does not stand in the way of one's obedience to God, it will not interfere with his salvation. And while it does not interfere with one's salvation, he should be permitted to enjoy it. But he should not be permitted to disturb the peace of Zion by urging it on others as an item of faith. When one's opinion, however, stands in the way of his obedience to God, it becomes fatal. Hence, after all, obedience becomes the test of acceptance and fellowship.

(1). From the distinction between faith and opinion it follows that nothing should be claimed as an item of faith that is not clearly expressed by precept, example or *necessary* inference.

What God has clearly expressed as His will, men should be required to accept and do. This faith in Christ demands. Without this there can be no unity of faith. Further than this we can not go without requiring unity of opinion; and that the Bible does not authorize.

(2). From this it follows that we may make nothing a test of fellowship that Christ has not made a condition of salvation.

If we recognize those in the fellowship of the Church of God who do not comply with the clearly expressed conditions of salvation, we break down all barriers between the Church and the world. If we refuse to fellowship obedient believers on account of something which Christ has not made a condition of salvation, we arrogate to ourselves the prerogative of binding on earth what has not been bound in heaven. Hence the whole question of fellowship turns on the conditions of salvation.

(3). While our plea demands conformity to the precepts and examples of God's word, we should carefully mark the distinction between the essentials and the incidentals of that age of the Church which we have accepted as an example for our imitation.

When we fail to insist on that which was an essential item in New Testament faith or practice, we fail to that extent in our work of restoration. When we insist on the mere incidentals of that age, which did or did not exist, according to circumstances, we contend for a religion shaped by accident, rather than by divine principles.

The observance of the foregoing principles has constituted, I think, our main elements of strength as a religious people.

ELEMENTS OF WEAKNESS.

While it is important to know our strength, it is equally important to understand our weakness. That we have elements of weakness is a painful fact. These we should study to understand, and labor to correct. Our judgment is, that prominent among the things now constituting our weakness is—

I. *The extent to which we are losing sight of our distinctive plea.*

Unless we have a distinctive plea we have no right to exist. The day we become like the denominations around us, that day ends our right to exist as a distinct religious people. If we have a distinctive plea, in that consists our strength. I believe that our distinctive principles are made less prominent in our pulpits now than formerly. I do not mean that our preachers should be always on what is called "first principles." Very far from it. But I do mean that all our members should be deeply indoctrinated in the things that distinguish us from other religious peoples. The people should understand *why* they occupy the position they do. The better this is understood the more it will be appreciated, and the more firm and consistent will be the Christian life. When people are led to believe that sectarianism is about as good as New Testament Christianity their influence for the cause we plead is positively hurtful. Whenever we begin to curry favor with the sects and fawn upon them for recognition, we are certain to say but little about a plea that lays the axe at the root of the whole denominational tree. Whenever we begin to curry favor with the world, we are certain to fall in with the world's notions, and adjust ourselves to the world's ways. Hence much of that in which churches now indulge in the way of worldly amusements, carnal methods

251

of raising money, the spirit of mere entertainment in the worship, etc., is due to the fact that they copy the sects, rather than the New Testament churches; and are filled with the spirit of the world, instead of the spirit of Christ.

The religion of Christ is a religion of spirituality. When you take the spirituality out of a church, you take the life out of it. You may have members and wealth and culture left, but the power of divine truth and love is gone. There is too much of this spirit pervading our churches. Worldly conformity in spirit, in worship, in life, is the great weakness from which our cause is suffering; and this is largely due, in my judgment, to the want of strict adherence to the fundamental plea that gave us our power in the past. If the restoration of New Testament Christianity, *in spirit and in life,* as well as in form, had full possession of our hearts, this would never be.

(1). One thing, I think, in which we have copied largely from the world, and which adds greatly to our weakness, is our practice in church government.

In large measure we borrowed from the Baptists the democrat idea of church government. We learned to decide too many things by a majority of the popular vote. We act as if the kingdom of God were a democracy, and not an absolute monarchy. This has given rise to immense trouble. It has left questions, to be settled by boys and girls who hardly know whether the Acts of the Apostles is in the Old Testament or the New, that were decided by Jesus Christ more than eighteen hundred years ago.

Much is said in this age about an inefficient eldership, and said with much truth. Truth is a natural and necessary consequence of this false idea of church government. Any man will become inefficient anywhere when he is made a mere figure-head. When the bishops are recognized as the *"overseers"* of the congregation, who are to govern the church in harmony with law so long as they are kept in that place, they will have inducement to make themselves efficient. And only those thus capacitated should be put into the position. The New Testament example is to have none, till you have men qualified for the work. And it is always safest and best to follow the Book. Democracy may be well enough in human governments, but it is unknown in the kingdom of God. When the young and giddy ignore the eldership, and take the reins in their own hands, instead of honoring them as their spiritual counselors and rulers, the restoration at this point breaks down. We are exceedingly weak here, and the symptoms are not favorable for improvement.

(2). From democratic ideas of church government have arisen extreme injurious views of congregational independence.

In breaking away from the ecclesiastical slavery of the past, my judgment is, that we have run to the opposite extreme, and become too free. Freedom is a good thing when properly used, but when it runs into licentiousness it is worse than bondage. While the churches of Christ are under no ecclesiasticism, in the current sense of that term, they sustain a close relation to one another in the "general assembly and Church of the first-born." This relation can not be disregarded without disintegration and mischief. My candid judgment is, that this has been done, and continues to be done, to the serious weakening of the bonds that should unite as one loving household of faith all who are striving for the same grand work of restoration. Each church ought to feel itself in sympathy with every other, as sisters in the great family of God, and so act as to respect the interests, the rights, and the feelings of all the others. The spirit of congregational independence that disregards this fraternal unity, is not of Christ.

Another thing which may be justly regarded as a great weakness in our cause is—

II. *A want of co-operation in church work.*

In union there is strength. In co-operation there is power. We have not worked together as we should for the accomplishment of so grand an end. As individuals and churches we have acted too much on the principle of every one for himself. We must learn to work as one body if we would ever accomplish what we should toward the world's conversion.

We think this co-operation has been hindered in several ways.

(1). Much of the indifference and opposition to co-operation has been produced doubtless by imprudence in the work.

In our mission work we have not always been just as careful as we should have been to infringe upon no New Testament legislation, and thereby create no fears or opposition. Our privileges and duties in these matters lie within certain limits, and the more careful we are to regard these limits the more unity and harmony will there be in the work. Should we differ as to the amount of liberty which the New Testament grants, it is not wise to disregard the judgment of a large and influential element of the brotherhood, and thereby provoke their opposition. Union in poorer methods is infinitely preferable to division in better ones. We plead for the union of all Christians by showing the power and divine wisdom there is in it. We censure the sects for doing that which creates unnecessary division in Christian work. In our mission work it would be well for some of us to take a dose of our own prescription. A disposition now growing to make missionary conventions, and their executive boards, high courts ecclesiastic to decide upon and officially settle controverted questions in the brotherhood, touching missionary matters, will eventually, if persisted in, drive from such societies every prudent man, in disgust.

(2). A still greater amount of this indifference is due to a false education with reference to the support of the Gospel.

The warfare that was justly made by Alexander Campbell on the "hired clergy" was largely misconstrued, and produced a general feeling of opposition to the support of preachers of the Gospel. We are very easily educated in the direction of our selfishness. From this false education the churches have never recovered. Many of them have vastly improved, but we are still suffering from the effects of that wrong idea at the start. In addition to this, the false idea of congregational independence has caused many churches to adopt as scriptural the motto that "charity begins at home." They have been slow to learn that while a church has its own local work to perform, for which it is congregationally responsible, it is only a small part of the great body whose interests are its interests, and to which it should constantly look, and for which persistently work. The church that never looks beyond its own local interests has a low and selfish conception of Christianity. When congregations become independent in their feelings and actions with reference to the welfare of others, they will soon become independent of their Master.

It is a very easy matter, therefore, for us to slight any co-operative work when we have no heart in the thing to be accomplished. We are naturally hard to please about ways and means when we are indifferent about the end. If we had the spirit of our Master we would be striving to save the world; and if we doubted the wisdom of the plan open to us for its accomplishment we would risk its want of wisdom till we could do better. The fact is, if we all had more of the spirit of Christ in our hearts we would have more regard for and confidence in one another.

Our last and greatest weakness that I shall mention is—

III. *A want of personal consecration to the work.*

No man or body of men ever succeeded grandly in any cause who did not throw into it their concentrated energies. If our affections are divided between the Church and the world, we shall accomplish but little. "This one thing I do," is the secret of success. A consecrated life is a life of power.

(1). A want of consecration is now being manifest largely on the part of preachers.

While I believe the world contains no truer and nobler men than those now engaged in pleading for the restoration of New Testament Christianity, I do not believe that the cause of Christ is absorbing our attention as it should. Many of us now seem wholly indisposed to practice that self-denial that characterized our fathers in this good work. Too many of us are hunting an easy place. We want every thing lovely. One humble, self-denying, earnest preacher of the Gospel, of mediocre ability, with the spirit of John T. Johnson, is worth a ten-acre field full of clerical babies, that whine to be dandled on the luxurious lap of the Church and fed on dainties. Our Master never had an easy place, nor should we expect to find one till we find it in the grave.

Again, there are too many of us beginning to look to secular pursuits. Circumstances may demand this in many cases, but we should be careful that it is first demanded. The man who spends the week in peddling sewing machines or patent churns, will come before his neglected and hungry congregation on the Lord's day with a dish of hash. People soon tire of theological hash. Like eating-house hash, it is difficult for them to see what it is made of. But, unlike cheap hotel hash, they generally find nothing in it. Consequently the preacher that feasts on the world all the week, and gives his congregation the scraps on Sunday, soon ceases to be in demand; and then he complains of the church. Brethren, let us be sure that a consecrated life is unappreciated by the Church before we turn to the world for our daily bread.

(2). Church officers and private members are too much disposed to look after their own private interests, and to neglect the interests of the church.

Could we all get out of this selfishness, and be consecrated to the Lord's work, our colleges, orphan schools, missionary enterprises, religious publications, and all other good works of the Church of God, would receive our sympathy and support. We could feel that they are all a part of *our* work because they are

258

a part of the *Lord's* work; hence we would never cast them aside as none of our business simply because we are not *paid* to look after them. This want of individual interest in all the work of Gods which demands a heavy outlay in time and money to enlist our attention and aid, is a paralyzing weakness to the whole body. We should seek to remedy it as soon as possible, by imbibing and cultivating the spirit of our Master, and expanding our hearts with more of His pure and undefiled religion.

THE DEATH OF CHRIST NECESSARY

By J. M. HENRY

And he said unto them, "Thus it is written, and thus it behooved Christ to suffer, and to rise from the dead the third day; and that repentance and remission of sins should be preached in His name among all nations, beginning at Jerusalem. And ye are witnesses of these things."—Luke xxiv: 46-48.

ETERNITY will never exhaust the riches of this theme. The redeemed in the heavenly world will sing forever, "Thou art worthy to take the book and to open the seals thereof; for thou wast slain, and hast redeemed us to God by thy blood out of every kindred, and tongue, and people, and nation; and hast made us unto God kings and priests; and we shall reign on the earth." The saints on earth overcome the accuser of the brethren, by the blood of the Lamb, and by the word of their testimony. Jesus was made, for a little while, lower than the angels, that he, by the grace of God, should taste death for every man. This is he by whom all things were made, and without whom was not anything made that was made. God called Him his only begotten Son—his beloved Son, in whom he is well pleased. So full was Jesus of Divinity, in the days of his pilgrimage on the earth, that all the angels, at the commandment of God, fell down and worshipped Him. His dignity is such as to entitle to the profoundest regard every thought revealed concerning Him. The richest sacrifices ever offered before, could not take away sins; but by the offering of himself, Jesus perfected forever them that are sanctified. The sufferings of Christ, and the glory that should follow, were of such importance that the prophets searched and inquired diligently concerning them, and the angels desired to look into these wonderful things. Paul, under the influence of inspiration, declared to the church at Corinth that he determined not to know anything among them, save Jesus Christ, and him crucified. The death of Christ is the ground of hope for a lost and ruined world. Ever since it occurred, it has been the joyful theme of all the holy men on earth. Let it, then, command our prayerful attention.

The death of Jesus became necessary, in order to accomplish the divine purpose in creating man.

That purpose is recorded Gen. i :26. And God said, Let us make man in our image, after our likeness; and let them have dominion over the fish of the sea, and over the fowl of the air, and over the cattle, and over all the earth, and over every creeping thing that creepeth upon the earth. David says, Ps. viii :6, Thou madest him to have dominion over the works of thy hands; thou hast put all things under his feet. Paul also says, Heb. ii :8-9, Thou hast put

261

all things in subjection under his feet. For in that he put all things in subjection under him, he left nothing not put under him. But now we see not yet all things put under him. But we see Jesus, who was made a little lower than the angels for the suffering of death, crowned with glory and honor; that he, by the grace of God, should taste death for every man.

From these passages, God's purpose in creating man was known during forty centuries of the history of our race. But Adam sinned, and lost the scepter, the crown, and all pertaining to his royal character and condition. He was sent forth from the garden, the original seat of his empire, to endure for a time, degradation and toil. To make his labor more severe, the ground was cursed for his sake; "thorns and briers shall it bring forth, and in the sweat of thy face shalt thou eat bread until thou return unto the ground." A finite intelligence having learned God's purpose in making man, and then seeing him so soon fail for that design, would probably conclude that God's plans were frustrated. That this, however, was not the case, may be indicated in his language to the serpent—"I will put enmity between thee and the woman, between thy seed and her seed, he shall bruise thy head, and thou shalt bruise his heel." Time bore the race onward through four thousand years, and with it the hope and numerous and various prophecies of him that should bring deliverance to man, and overthrow to the serpent.

"Blind unbelief is sure to err,
  And scan his work in vain;
God is his own interpreter,
  And he will make it plain."

"In the fullness of the time, God sent forth his Son, . . . that we might receive the adoption of sons." "Forasmuch, then, as the children are partakers of flesh and blood, he also himself likewise took part of the same; that through death he might destroy him that had the power of death, that is the devil; and deliver them who, through fear of death, were all their lifetime subject to bondage." The overthrow of him that had the power of death, and the adoption of men as sons of God, in order to the accomplishment of the divine purpose in man's creation, made Jesus' death necessary.

We make no inquiry of God's purposes beyond what is revealed; for all such inquiries are a virtual abandonment of faith for philosophy—of what God has written for human reason. God ordained, as it is written, that Adam should not eat of the fruit of the tree of the knowledge of good and evil. If it be said that God secretly decreed that he should eat of it, then, whether he eat or not, a decree of God will be broken; and further, faith in his word is overthrown, because what was recorded as His will, was what his secret purpose determined should not come to pass. Let us never tread the border of so dangerous a vortex as that.

Man's history does not terminate with the few

263

days of his existence on the earth, in his present condition of labor and suffering. In the sequel of God's revelations to us, man is represented as being a king and a priest to God; and having overcome, as Jesus overcame, is seated with him on his Father's throne.

The maintenance of the divine veracity made the death of Jesus necessary.

"The word of the Lord," says David, "is established in heaven forever. The word of the Lord, which by the Gospel is preached unto us, endureth forever." "These are the words that I spake unto you, while I was yet with you, that all things must be fulfilled which were written in the law of Moses, and in the prophets, and in the Psalms concerning me."

We may learn much of how God regards his word, if we remember some fifty predictions made directly concerning the Messiah, nearly all of which refer to his death, and the circumstances attending it. Not one of these fails, though Jesus must be condemned by a human tribunal to a most painful and shameful death, and their truthfulness be vindicated.

God has said, they shall look on him whom they pierced. If He is not pierced, how shall the divine veracity be maintained? His cry, "My God, my God, why hast thou forsaken me?" had been foretold, and how shall this be made true, if Jesus utter not that wail? It had been written that he should be numbered with the malefactors, hence the necessity of his death with thieves. His hands and feet were pierced, according to a prediction one thousand years old. They gave him gall for his meat, and vinegar for his drink, when he cried from the cross; for it was written. He died so soon on the cross as to cause Pilate to marvel, for it had been written in the Psalms, "Thou hast known my reproach, and my shame and my dishonor; mine adversaries are all before thee. Reproach hath broken my heart, and I am full of heaviness." It was written, "All they that see me, laugh me to scorn; they shoot out the lip, they shake the head saying, He trusted in the Lord that He would deliver him, let Him deliver Him, seeing He delighted in Him." All this was borne by him. From all this, and much more of a kindred character, the conclusion is easy that Jesus died to vindicate His Father's word. Another is equally clear, viz.: If God would allow His Son to suffer as He did, and ever forsook Him, that His word might be kept true, He will also forsake and permit every sinner to suffer who may be found in the day of judgment adverse to His word. There is no hope for us, except that which is built upon His word.

The law of Moses had a shadow of good things to come. Under it a font of beautiful and appropriate types was instituted. Among other things adumbrated there, nothing occupied a more prominent place than those typical of the death of Christ. Shall they all be abortive of the purpose for which they were given? It would have been so had not Jesus died. All the blood that had been offered by divine authority from the beginning, for remission of sins, was typical of the precious blood of Christ, who, in this manner, was as a lamb, slain from the foundation of the world. Without the shedding of blood, there was no remission. The sacrifice of bulls, calves, lambs, and goats could not take away sins, though offered according to the law of Moses. "Jesus, by his death, for the redemption of the transgressions that were under the first testament gave promise of eternal inheritance to them that are called, and offered himself through the eternal spirit without spot to God, to purge the conscience from dead works to serve the living God." The types were all fulfilled, and the prophecies concerning his sufferings verified, that our faith produced by the word of God may be strong, and our hope in his promises rest on a sure foundation.

That God may be just in saving believers in Jesus, His death was necessary.

That Jesus died as a substitute for sinners should not be overlooked. He did not, however, suffer all that the impenitent will suffer in a future state, for then he would have to endure everlasting punishment. Neither were his sufferings an equivalent for what the ungodly will suffer, for then there could be no pardon extended to those who are saved; and the Scriptures teach that the saved are all pardoned persons. He did not die because God was angry with the world, but because He loved it. Man's sins lay in the way of God's purpose in creating him, and an honorable and justifiable ground for pardoning him must be presented, or man must forever perish, and God's design in creating him, fail. God, therefore, sent forth His Son to be a propitiation through faith in His blood, to declare righteousness, for the remission of sins that are past, through the forebearance of God—to declare, at this time His righteousness; that He might be just, and the justifier of him that believeth in Jesus.—Rom. iii :25,26.

God pardons men for the sake of His Son. "I write unto you, little children, because your sins are forgiven you for His name's sake. I John ii :12. The death of Christ, considered as the divine expedient for saving men, is what is generally denominated the atonement. Such is the worth of the sacrifice of the Son of God, that sinners may be pardoned for His sake, that otherwise must perish forever. No just complaint can be brought by any intelligent being in the universe against the government of God, because He pardons the believer in Jesus.

Pardon may, and often has been extended, by human governments, to the injury of the government, for insufficient reasons. The object of government is the good of the governed. Mercy may be exercised when it can be done without weakening the government, and injuring the governed.

A familiar illustration of a government pardoning an offender, and maintaining its authority, is furnished in the history of Zaleucus, the king of the Locrians. He had enacted a law against adultery, the penalty of which was that the offender should lose both eyes. The first person convicted of this offense was the king's own son. As a father he felt anxiety to save his son, but as a king he felt disposed to maintain his authority for the good of the government. If from his paternal feelings he pardons his son, his subjects will despise him as a ruler. If he repeals the law to save his son, he may justly be charged with weakness; and if, on the other hand, the law is executed, his son must grope in blindness through the world the rest of his days. How shall he be merciful to his son, and maintain his authority over his subjects? He decided to lose one of his own eyes, and destroy one of his son's eyes. In acting thus the king exercised mercy to his son, and at the same time secured the integrity of his authority. Let us see how this transaction would affect his subjects. They would hear of the case—the king's son has violated the law. Will his father punish him? If he does, we may be sure that he will punish us, if we disobey. They learn that the king has spared one eye of his son, and had one of his own destroyed as a substitute for the son's other eye. Does one of the king's subjects say he has acted unjustly? On the contrary, every one thinks, if the king had been merciful to his son, he has shown such a regard for his law, that if I dare to violate it, I will be punished as certainly as I am convicted. The dignity of the king, as a ruler, silences all objections. He has been merciful and sustained his authority.

The case of the Prophet Daniel is an illustration of an attempt made by the king to be merciful to him, and failed. A decree had been signed by the king, that no petition should be made to any god or man, except the king himself, for thirty days, on pain of being cast into a den of lions. Daniel continued his custom of praying three times a day with the windows of his room open toward Jerusalem. His enemies watched him, and reported his disregard of the unalterable decree to the king. ''Then the king, when he heard these words, was sore displeased with himself, and set his heart on Daniel, to deliver him: and he labored till the going down of the sun to deliver him!''—Dan. vi:14. The king was doubtless striving to spare Daniel, and maintain the decree. He failed, however, and did the best thing that he could—maintained the decree, and commended Daniel to the God in whom he trusted, who delivered him. There was no honorable ground on which the king could pardon the prophet. In other words no atonement could be found. Had he substituted a less honorable man for Daniel, it would not have answered the ends of government. One equally honorable in the king's judgment, could not be found. It would not have answered the purpose to have compelled any one of the presidents or nobles of his kingdom to suffer instead of Daniel. It might have answered the purpose, if some one had voluntarily offered himself in Daniel's place.

Jesus Christ voluntarily came and suffered in our behalf, so that God does no violence to His government, in pardoning the man who complies with the terms His son submits. God accepted the offering that Jesus made of himself, and regards it sufficiently worthy and honorable to give all rule, and authority, and dominion, into the hands of His Son; and power to execute judgment also, because He as the Son of Man, partook of flesh and blood, humbled himself, and was found in fashion as a man.

To this is objected, that Jesus was innocent, and men guilty before God. The idea of the innocent suffering for the guilty, is revolting to our sense of justice. It is a fact, nevertheless, that one certain result of sin is, that the innocent suffer on account of the sins of the wicked, all around the world. For proof of this, look into any one of ten thousand households that can be found in this country. See the bare walls, the cheerless appearance of everything in that poor dilapidated hut. Contemplate the inmates. There sits, in worn and faded clothing, one young in years, but old in sorrow. Her eye, that once sparkled with joy, and was met with pleasure by numerous friends, has lost its radiance, and the cheek that once bore the impress of health and beauty, is faded and sorrowful. Her heartstrings have been relaxed and broken, one by one, until life is a burden, and hope, so often disappointed, has gone out

270

forever. Little ones gather around her knee in your presence, as if in fear, because a stranger talks to their mother. They are in clean rags, that scarcely hide their nakedness. They look pale and hungry. Their young hearts, that are capable of gladness, are being schooled to sorrow and woe. Ask the cause of all that sad condition. An honest shame mantles the cheek, with a feeble ray of former beauty, but soon fades to pallor, as she says, "My husband is an indolent drunkard."

Is she, poorer than the widow, to blame for all her sorrow? Are her little ones, less fortunate than orphans, at fault because they suffer? Answer me, you who say the innocent suffer not for the guilty. Do you say that is all wrong? So it is, but is it not a fact, that the innocent suffer for the guilty, as one of the *certain* consequences of sin? Why, then, object to the "suffering of the just for the unjust," if God in His wisdom and mercy uses this as the occasion to bring us salvation? God is just in justifying the believer in Jesus, in forgiving sins for Christ's sake.

The death of Jesus was necessary to show the love of God.

"God so loved the world, that he gave His only begotten Son, that whosoever believeth on him, should not perish, but have everlasting life."—John iii:16. The frequent repetition of this statement in the word of God, renders its quotation, in other places unnecessary, to the careful reader of the

271

Bible. How, except by what we do, say, and suffer for another, can we show him our love? In all these respects, nothing is wanting on the part of heaven, to show the most earnest love to our ruined race. Such words of grace and gentleness never fell on the human ear, as those employed by our blessed Lord, in the days of his flesh. Hear him addressing the poor miserable woman, brought before him by his enemies. After they have been conscience-smitten by His address to them, He said to her, "Has no man condemned thee?" She said, "No man, Lord." Said he, "Neither do I condemn thee; go, and sin no more." Hear Him comforting Martha, and Mary, in their bereavement. His voice is most soothing, his bosom heaves with emotion too great for words, and is feebly indicated by weeping. Listen again, as He converses with His disciples, just before His death. They are almost overcome with sorrow, because he has told them he must leave them. "Let not your heart be troubled; ye believe in God, believe also in me. In my Father's house are many mansions; if it were not so, I would have told you. I go to prepare a place for you; and if I go and prepare a place for you, I will come again and receive you unto myself; that where I am, there ye may be also." Time fails to repeat now, all that he said, expressive of His great love to us.

More forcible than his words, are his benevolent acts. He healed the sick, unstopped the ears of the deaf to the harmonies of nature, and the

272

music of his own sweet voice, opened the eyes of the blind, to see plainly, cast out demons, and restored to life and the embrace of weeping friends, the dead. His Omnipotent power was employed to do good. His miracles, excepting two, were of a merciful character. "He did all things well."

Admire, as we justly may, his love to us, as shown in what He said and did, all that is completely eclipsed in what He suffered for the world. What human tongue or pen can describe His amazing sorrows of heart! After instituting the supper, in commemoration of His body and blood, and walking toward the garden in Gethsemane with his little company of disciples, he said to them: "Now is my soul exceeding sorrowful, even unto death; and what shall I say? Father, save me from this hour? And yet for this cause came I unto this hour." When He had entered the garden, he prostrated himself on the cold earth, and being in agony, He said: "Father, if it be possible, let this cup pass from me; nevertheless, not as I will, but as Thou wilt." This He did three times. At last an angel appeared to strengthen him. But for this angelic assistance, he might have died there. He was made known to those that accompanied Judas to arrest him, by the traitor's kissing Him. He was taken to Pilate, and by him sent to Herod, because Herod was in the city, and Jesus was a Galilean. Herod had long desired to see him, and witness His performance of a miracle. Jesus will not even converse with him, which so exasperates Herod, that he and his men of war set him at naught, and arrayed him in a gorgeous robe, and returned him to Pilate. These two rulers were made friends that day. Then Pilate examined him, and reported to the Jews who sought his death, that he found no fault in him. The governor was disposed to release him, but they said if he did, he was not Cæsar's friend. He sought to reason them out of their opposition to Jesus, but to no purpose. You have a custom, said he, that I should release one prisoner at this feast to you. Here are Jesus and Barabbas in my custody; which of them will you that I release? They said, not this man, but Barabbas. He had been a leader of an insurrection in the city, and had committed murder. Think of it as we may, it is certain that Jesus was put to death instead of Barabbas, who was one of the most wicked of men. Pilate then, seeing he could not reason them out of their opposition, took Jesus and had him scourged. Presenting Him to them, bathed in His own blood, and quivering in every muscle, and His countenance so marred that there was no beauty that they should desire him, Pilate said, behold the man. His suffering does not move their hard hearts. "What shall I do with him?" asked Pilate. "Away with Him, away with Him, crucify Him, crucify Him," said the multitude. Pilate, alarmed at their wickedness, and startled by a message from his wife, who said, "See thou have nothing to do with that innocent man," said, "Shall I crucify your king?."

"We have no king but Cæsar," they answered. He then called for a basin, and in their presence washed his hands, saying, "I am clean from the blood of this innocent man, see ye to it." They said, His blood be on us, and on our children. Then Pilate gave sentence that he should be crucified. They hurry Him away with the cross upon Him. On the way He reels, faints, and falls, beneath the weight of the cross. There they met a man from Cyrene, named Simon, whom they compelled to carry the cross to the place of execution. The only act that seems to have any compassion in it, during the whole of this awful tragedy, was the offer made by one of the soldiers, that had charge of his execution, of a cup of wine, mingled with myrrh. He would do nothing that should mitigate the bitterness of the cup His Father had given Him to drink. They nailed Him to the cross, and then mocked Him, bowing before Him in worship saying, "If thou be the Christ, come down from the cross, and we will believe thee. He saved others, He can not save himself! Hail, king of the Jews! Ah, thou that destroyest the temple, and buildest it in three days! He said God was His Father!"

See His agonies! Hear His cry! "My God! My God! Why hast thou forsaken me?" He calls for water, and they offer Him vinegar and gall. After three hours of the strongest suffering ever borne on this earth, he says, "Father, into thy hands I commit my spirit," and bowed His head and died.

The heavens and earth were mantled in darkness by the time he expired. While all were in consternation, and men speak to one another in whispers, a new alarm startles the guilty consciences, for a distant rumbling is heard, the earth trembles, and the sound increases, as if the foundations of the globe were being broken. The centurion speaks, and says, "Truly, this good man is the Son of God." The darkness passes away, and many graves of the saints are found open; the vail in the temple has been rent from the top to the bottom. Pilate on being informed of the speedy death of Jesus, marveled at it.

There never was such a death, for there never was such a victim. There never was such suffering, for there never was such love to be shown by suffering. God laid on Him the iniquity of us all; the chastisement of our peace was on him; by his stripes we are healed.

By His sufferings, that He voluntarily bore, we know He loved us. He could have prayed His Father, and instantly twelve legions of angels would have hastened to His rescue from the hands of His murderers. But then how should God's purpose in creating man have been accomplished? How could sinners have been induced to love God? Without love to Him, how could they have been brought to reformation? This is love, not that we loved God, but that He loved us, and sent His Son to be the propitiation for our sins. God commended His love

276

toward us, in that, while we were yet sinners, Christ died for us.

Christ did not die a martyr for the truth, but offered himself a sacrifice for sins. If He died only as a martyr, He was less fortunate than any of His disciples that have died for their love of Him since, for He was forsaken of God, which none of them ever was. In the bitterness of His sorrows is God's love to us manifested. Jesus left heaven, and all its glories and honors, became poor as the poorest of the children of earth, that all might know He loved them. When the foxes had holes, and the birds of the air had nests, He had no place to lay His head. He became poor, that we through His poverty might be rich. When He had given all else, then He laid down His life, a ransom for all.

The death of Christ was necessary to induce men to love God and forsake sin.

"For it became him, for whom are all things, and by whom are all things, in bringing many sons to glory, to make the captain of their salvation perfect through sufferings," "and being made perfect, He became the author of eternal salvation to all them that obey him."

The perfection of Christ as a Saviour is here declared to be through suffering. His sufferings, voluntarily endured, form an honorable ground for God to pardon the believer in Jesus. To show man the sinfulness of sin, and the love of God, Jesus suffered as he did. Suffering certainly could add nothing to

277

the wisdom, goodness, power, or knowledge of the Lord. But His sufferings do perfectly adapt Him to influence the human heart to love Him, and hate sin. That Christ died for our sins according to the Scriptures, are the grand facts, declared to be the Gospel, by which men are saved, if they keep it in memory.—I Cor. xv :2-4.

The apostles were commanded to preach the Gospel. They always referred to the death of Christ for men's sins, as proof that God loved them, and that they should forsake their transgressions. ''The love of Christ constraineth us; because we thus judge, that if one died for all, then were all dead, that they who live should not henceforth live unto themselves, but unto Him, which died for them, and rose again.'' —2 Cor. v :14,15. The mind in contemplating the death of Christ for sins, easily arrives, indeed, is compelled to the conclusion, that sin is of such a nature as to make it unsafe for one longer to continue it. If I would be saved, I must turn from my iniquities to the Lord. God knows the difficulties sin has placed in the way of my salvation, and for their removal allowed His own Son to suffer as He did, that those who live should not live unto themselves, but unto Christ who died for them; then if I will not be warned, my punishment will be just.

There is a disposition in the human mind to regard sin as less obnoxious than it is, and to apologize for it. This disposition must give way in the presence of the sufferings of the Messiah, or we can not be saved. The man whose heart can remain untouched by the evangelical narratives of the sufferings of the Son of God, need look in no other direction for saving power. These narratives are the most precious and wonderful records ever known to man. They contain the power of God to save them that believe. There is a point of contact between the human heart, and the power of God. That point is Christ crucified. There is power in the death of human friends to move our souls greatly. How much more then in the death of Jesus, our heavenly friend? He whose heart is not moved to love God by the sufferings of Christ, must think too lightly of sin and the great love wherewith God has loved us, to be accepted of Him. Being made perfect by His sufferings, to lead men to love Him, and hate sin, He is the author of eternal salvation, to all them that obey Him.

"He laid down His life, that He might take it again." "He was declared to be the Son of God with power according to the Spirit of holiness by the resurrection from the dead." Through death and the resurrection, He reached the scepter and the throne of universal domination, in heaven and earth. All may trust in Him, for He is able and willing to save, to the uttermost, all that come to God by Him.

His death was necessary, that reformation and remission of sins should be preached in His name among all nations.

So Jesus declares. No terms of pardon, nor precedent for our salvation, can be found, *in his name,* before He arose from the dead. Persons were forgiven by Him during His ministry on the earth, but not by His own authority. He came in His Father's name. "My Father," said He, "He doeth the works." He was obedient to the will of His Father, whose love and authority, as manifested in the law of Moses, continued until His death on the cross. The Proclamation of reformation and pardon, he said, should begin by His authority in Jerusalem. Jesus began to preach in Galilee.—Matt. iv: 17. What He preached is called the Gospel of the kingdom. What he said was, "Reform, for the kingdom of heaven is at hand." After He arose from the dead, and ascended to heaven, no inspired man has said, the kingdom of heaven is at hand. On the contrary, the first discourse preached after His ascension, declared that God had made Jesus both Lord and Christ. This believed, caused the people to ask the apostles of Christ what they should do? They were promptly told to reform, and be immersed *in the name of the Lord Jesus Christ,* for the remission of sins and they should receive the gift of the Holy Spirit.

The fact that God has given all dominion and power, in heaven and earth, in to the hands of His Son, is repeated substantially in every discourse and epistle of the apostles after Jesus' coronation in heaven. They say that God has given Him a name

280

which is above every name; that at the name of Jesus every knee should bow; that every tongue shall confess that He is Lord, to the glory of God the Father. There is a lamentable failure among the professed friends of Jesus to confess his authority as supreme in all the matters of salvation. When he said to one man in the days of His flesh, "Thy sins are forgiven thee;" or to the thief on the cross, "This day shalt thou be with me in paradise," no precedent is thereby furnished for the way we shall be saved. These men were saved by divine authority. Jesus had not then died, nor risen from the dead; both of which were necessary in order to the proclamation of repentance and remission of sins by His authority. The apostles pleaded Jesus' authority for their preaching to the people. "He commanded us to preach unto the people," said they.—Acts x :42.

The proclamation of reformation and remission of sins was to commence in the city of Jerusalem. It was to be done by the power with which the apostles were to be endowed by an immersion in the Holy Spirit. They claimed to be ambassadors of Christ. Their credentials were shown by their power to speak in many languages, to heal the sick, to cast out demons, to raise the dead, and to do many wonderful works. They were invested with the power to submit the terms of pardon to all nations and to every creature. Through them alone, guided as they were by the Holy Spirit infallibly, can we learn the way of salvation. What they taught is sanctioned

281

by the authority of Christ, the Lord of Lords, and King of kings. How reformation and forgiveness are preached by Jesus' authority we must learn of his apostles.

They taught that men must believe in Christ, or they can not be saved. "By him all that believe are justified from all things, from which they could not be justified by the law of Moses."—Acts xiii:39. "Sirs, what must I do to be saved?" And they said, "believe on the Lord Jesus Christ, and thou shalt be saved and thy house."—Acts xvi:30, 31.

They taught repentance toward God. "The times of this ignorance, God winked at; but now commandeth all men everywhere to reform; because he hath appointed a day in the which he will judge the world in righteousness, by that man whom He hath ordained; whereof He hath given assurance unto all men, in that He hath raised Him from the dead." Acts xvii:30,31. "Repent and be converted, that your sins may be blotted out, when the times of refreshing shall come from the presence of the Lord." —Acts iii:19.

They taught that men must confess the name of Christ. "If thou believest with all thy heart, thou mayest be immersed." And he answered and said, "I believe that Jesus Christ is the Son of God." (Acts viii:39). "If thou shalt confess with thy mouth the Lord Jesus, and believe in thine heart that God hath raised Him from the dead, thou shalt be saved. For with the heart man believeth unto righteousness;

and with the mouth confession is made unto salvation." (Rom. x:9,10).

They taught that men must be baptized in order to be saved. "Reform, and be immersed every one of you, in the name of Jesus Christ, for the remission of sins, and ye shall receive the gift of the Holy Spirit." (Acts ii:38). Paul said, "Lord, what wilt thou have me to do?" And the Lord said unto him, "Arise, and go into the city, and there it shall be told thee what thou must do." (Acts ix:6). Ananias said to Paul, "And now why tarriest thou? Arise, and be baptized, and wash away thy sins, calling on the name of the Lord." (Acts xxii: 16). "The like figure whereunto even baptism doth also now save us (not the putting away the filth of the flesh, but the answer of a good conscience toward God), by the resurrection of Jesus Christ." (I. Pet. iii:21).

They taught that men should call on the name of the Lord to be saved. "And it shall come to pass, that whosoever shall call on the name of the Lord, shall be saved." (Acts ii:21). "For whosoever shall call on the name of the Lord shall be saved." (Rom. x:13). "Arise, and be baptized, and wash away thy sins, calling on the name of the Lord." (Acts xxii:16).

From the foregoing it is seen that faith, reformation, confession of Christ, immersion, and calling on the name of the Lord were all taught, and the promise of salvation connected with each. Should we refuse to obey any one of these commandments, we neglect and come short of the promise of salvation. All of them were required to be observed, by the ambassadors of Christ. He died and rose again, that they might be proclaimed by his authority. He who disregards these things, disregards to the same extent the death and resurrection of the Lord Jesus Christ. He died for all, that they who live should not henceforth live unto themselves, but unto Him who died for them, and rose again.

Those who comply with the above conditions are pardoned. Then, if they add to faith, virtue; and to virtue, knowledge; then to knowledge, temperance; and to temperance, patience; and to patience, godliness; and to godliness, brotherly kindness; and to brotherly kindness, charity, an abundant entrance will be ministered unto them, into the everlasting kingdom of our Lord and Saviour Jesus Christ.

To persons possessed of the above characteristics, the death, resurrection, and glorification of the Christ is a pleasing theme, and forever will be. They that overcome, as he overcame, shall sit with Christ on His throne. They shall inherit all things. To them crowns and scepters, and dominion over all things will be given. Then they will sing, ''Thou are worthy, O Lord, to receive glory and honor and power; for thou hast created all things, and for Thy pleasure they are and were created.'' Then it will be clearly seen, that God has not been frustrated in

His purpose in creating man. The most wonderful scene in the whole drama is, and forever will be, the death of Christ according to the Scriptures, that repentance and remission of sins should be preached in His name among all nations, beginning at Jerusalem.

> "Rock of Ages, cleft for me,
> Let me hide myself in thee;
> Let the water and the blood,
> From thy side, a healing flood,
> Be of sin the double cure—
> Save from wrath and make me pure.
> Should my tears forever flow,
> Should my zeal no languor know,
> This for sin could not atone;
> Thou must save, and thou alone:
> In my hand no price I bring;
> Simply to thy cross I cling.
> While I draw this fleeting breath,
> When my eyelids close in death,
> When I rise to worlds unknown,
> And behold thee on thy throne—
> Rock of Ages, cleft for me,
> Let me hide myself in thee!"

CHRIST'S TRANSFORMING INFLUENCE

By ALANSON WILCOX

"And be not conformed to this world; but be ye transformed by the renewing of your mind, that ye may prove what is that good and acceptable and perfect will of God."—Rom. xii:2.

I. That Christ and his Gospel have a transforming influence can not be questioned. Under it individuals, communities and States are changed.

1. *Turbid natures are subdued,* softened, sweetened and sanctified. Peter was once approached by Jesus, who was about to wash his feet, and he said, "Thou shalt never wash my feet." And when the Lord explained this matter, he so changed his mind that he said, "Not my feet only, but also my hands and head." And now, when Christ's life and character and teachings are explained and understood, they change a person's thinking, loving and acting. Hatred is changed to love, enemies to friends, the intemperate to temperate, cursing to praying, the conscience is enlightened and the will is strengthened to do the right.

2. *Communities, too, are transformed.* Nor need

286

one go to heathen lands to witness Christ's power. In the city from which I write are two communities almost as distinct as heaven and hell. One of them is under the influence of the priest and politics, and as a result poverty and drunkenness and crime of all classes abound. They would be worse than they are, did not an indirect influence from Christ reach them through "Mary, the mother of God." The protestants, less under the priest and more under Christ, are better developed, yet there is room for improvement among them; so that if Christ should be fully received, every sinner would be transformed and every house would be an asylum of peace and retreat of love.

3. *States are changed.* Right religion is not only the basis of individual character, but its power is manifest in and necessary to national greatness. The United States, partially under the influence of Christ, differs from China with its thirty centuries of Paganism. In imperial Pekin infanticide is fearfully prevalent. Scores of children, every night, are thrown into the streets and abandoned by their parents. In the morning dogs and swine are let out to devour them. Then carts are sent around and the living and dead alike are gathered and thrown into a pit. Other districts are still worse, so that nearly two-thirds of the children born are never reared. Now the Christian religion makes especial provision for such exposed children (I Tim. v:10). And, somewhat influenced by this religion, the people of

the United States provide "Orphan Homes" and "First Day Schools" for poor and abandoned children. Our Briton ancestors were no better than the Chinaman. The pen of the historian trembles to relate, and we shudder at the recital of those things they practiced. Christ's religion has changed them.

II. The manner of this influence is silent. It is like leaven in three measures of meal. In nature God's power is silent. There is no creaking to the machinery of the universe. Worlds and systems move in silent majesty. The changes of day and night and of the seasons manifest great, silent power. Nature's noises show her weakness. What is the power of electricity, manifest in the thunder, in comparison with the transformation of the winter world to the spring paradise? The Gospel, too, silently works on mind and soul and hand. No booming guns announce its progress. "My doctrine shall drop as the rain, my speech shall distil as the dew, as he shall rain upon the tender herb, and as the showers upon the grass."

Child power is wonderful. A little child's advent into the world is hailed with rejoicing. All things around are concentrated in its interest. There is a way in which children may be said to rule the world. Once strong, tall men as Saul were selected to be rulers. In time women were taken into consideration and counsel, and the world improved by the change. And now four-fifths of all legislation is in behalf of children and coming generations. Their interests control things. The child Jesus came before the man Christ. Nor does the child or man take the heart by storm. But we in our natures feel the want of such a life, such a sacrifice, such a child, such a Christ, such a God, and under their power we are silently transformed.

Little faith can be put in sudden conversions. Some speak of being changed "quick as the spark from the smitten steel." But this gospel power does not work in that way. It comes "line upon line, precept upon precept," from childhood to manhood. And at last the argument comes that turns the soul in favor of Christ. On the mountain top the dews and rains and melting snows settle through the sands and rocks, and at the mountain's base the shepherd removes a stone and the spring leaps out. The spring was not then and there formed, but was made manifest. So the influence of earlier years may be brought out to view by a sermon, and the silent influences are manifest in producing a new life. In this land none are devoid of these influences. They may be repressed, but if persons are true to themselves and Christ, the transformation must be made visible.

III. In considering some of the details of this influence, allow the *head* and *heart* and *hand* to represent the whole person. Accepting this order, there will be *light* for the head, and *love* for the heart, and *labor* for the hand.

1. *The head, or mind, has much to do in religion.*

A thing with no head or brains, though in the form of a man, can not embrace the religion of Christ. The whole person is to be transformed through the renewing of the mind (Rom. xii:2).

Some would have religion consist entirely of doing—visiting the widow and fatherless, and in deeds of mercy. These things can not be divorced from Christianity, but they receive their value from the motive prompting to them. Love and respect for God's authority lead to action, and labor performed should be guided by a sound mind. Things God never made are very religious, if doing alone is religion. God never made a mule or a mill, and they are all the time doing, packing loads and grinding grain, and no one thinks of calling them religious, or their doing religion.

Others talk of religion as consisting of love, and it is an essential part. "Though I speak with the tongues of men and of angels, and have not love, I am become as sounding brass, or a tinkling cymbal. And though I bestow all my goods to feed the poor, and though I give my body to be burned, and have not love, it profiteth me nothing." And we sing:

> "Love is the golden chain
> That binds the happy soul above,
> And he's an heir of heaven,
> That finds his bosom glow with love."

Poetic license may admit this form of expression; but is love more than a link in the chain or a strand of the cord that binds the soul to God? A man may have the ability to do, of a Samson, so that he could carry off the gates of Gaza, and may be filled with love and zeal and energy, and yet act very silly. Doing and loving need the guidance of a sound mind. Hence, "God hath not given us the spirit of fear; but of power (ability to do), and of love, and of a sound mind."

There are many crazy religionists. Ordinary lunatics we treat kindly, and put them where they can hurt no one, and use means to restore their senses. Shall we have less care for these moonstruck religionists? They live more under Moses than Christ. Christ has done something for them, and they see things dimly, men as trees walking; but their eyes are not opened sufficiently, and they have a blind religion of impulse and feelings. They are very uncertain and crazy Peter like, under certain circumstances they would smite off a man's ear with sword, and when the excitement passes away, in the presence of a damsel they'll deny the Lord. Now, God says: "Let there be light." He sent Paul to turn men from darkness to light. Truth transforms the mind, and guides the head and heart and hand and feelings for the glory of God. Rationalism is a reaction from this blind Papal and sectarian religion. Scripture teaching would lead to the golden medium where feelings and reason would sit at the feet of Jesus, and learn to glorify God through his transforming truth. Pass on the light!

2. *The heart or affections are changed by love.*

Light shows the things of heaven. We set our affections on things above. We become like what we love and worship. We think Christ, and talk Christ, and love Christ, and worship Christ, and become conformed to his image. In Central Park are globe mirrors reflecting the landscape, and a person is transfigured as he stands before them, so "we all, with open face beholding as in a glass the glory of the Lord, are changed into the same image from glory to glory even as by the Spirit of the Lord."

There is power in kindness. Dumb animals feel its influence. A balky horse is not whipped in these days by his master. He first treats him kindly, and then gives him a new idea by putting sand in his mouth or a pebble in the ear, and under these influences he forgets his stubbornness and pulls astonishingly well.

The warden of the state prison in Connecticut once received to the prison a strong, powerful man, who had been the terror of the country for seventeen years. He said to him: "I will treat you kindly and give you the largest possible liberty, if you will not get me into difficulty." The influence of this kindness was not perceptible at first. The prisoner tried to escape, and the warden was compelled to put him in irons, and was about to incarcerate him in a solitary, dark cell. Before entering it, the little, gentle warden looked him in the face, and said: "Have you treated me as I deserve?" And the great, iron-hearted criminal wept and said: "I have been a very devil for seventeen years, and you have treated me kindly and like a man.'' The warden gave him the free range of the prison, and he was a subdued man to the end of his imprisonment. Persons can not long withstand the influence of kindness.

Now, the heart is not only made for kindness, but for love. A Jesus without tears would not meet the wants of mankind. Nor would a saviour without love fill the soul, and transform the heart into that Christ-likeness which is joy and peace and eternal blessedness. This love is stronger than law or death, and is of God, and lifts us to his blessed presence, where there are pleasures forevermore.

3. The hand represents the ability to do. Under the reign of Christ, persons are to "cease to do evil and learn to do well.'' This doing, inspired by love and guided by reason, has a magical influence on our lives. We are created in Christ Jesus unto good works. Good works are those good actions that spring from good motives, are spiritual and have for their object the well-being of mankind. Failing of these, the objects of the Church are not accomplished, and the persons thus neglecting their opportunities become dwarfed and selfish and dead. Good works give life to faith and love. We show our faith by our works.

In the Church of Christ every man has something to do. Singing and praying and paying and preaching all have a reflex influence on the individual, and the hand becomes so transformed and accustomed to doing good, that it is easy and inspiring.

Dreamers are some professors. They find nothing to do, or no hands to do with, or no time to devote to good works. They dream of good singing, but never learn to sing themselves. They dream of benevolences, if they had the means, but they never give, because they can not do a big thing. They dream of happy dying, and do not seem to understand that this comes of happy living. They are enraptured with visions of heaven, but seem to have lost sight of the realities of this life, which transform us for the joys and realities of a never-ending life. They say: "Oh, if Jesus were on earth now, how we would minister to his necessities!" and seem to forget that if they do it to his brethren, it is as unto him. Let every person in the Church have an appropriate work to do, and carry it on to success. "*He* went about doing good."

IV. *A scriptural example* of this influence now remains to be presented. An illustration of a theme by a living example or a life invests it with a reality that is desirable. Our religion is a greater power in the world for having been identified with a person, a life, the life of Christ.

Now, if a person wants to become a Christian, he will find, whatever his condition may be, a living example in Acts of Apostles of his own condition. Let him find that example, and do the things he did

294

under the direction of the Apostles, and there will be certainty in his efforts that will send him on his way rejoicing.

The scriptural example selected to illustrate the present subject may not be so apparent to all, or so satisfying as others that might have been selected; but it certainly is not entirely devoid of interest and applicability. John is the man. So much of the sunny side of his life appears in the writings of the New Testament, that the impression is made that he was always gentle, good and genial. Yet he was once a Boanerges, a Son of Thunder, impetuous, vehement, unmanageable in spirit as is the thunder. With this dare-devil spirit, and ambitious for a place in Christ's kingdom, which he supposed was at hand, he once came to Jesus and asked for a position, a chief place, at his right hand or left, and he declared himself ready to face the terrors of the cup and baptism that awaited Christ, that he might serve his ambitious purposes. Jesus intimates to him that he had better wait for a fuller understanding of things. Some of this spirit of thunder must be driven out, and love must take its place.

Once he found persons casting out devils in the name of Christ, and because they did not come to his notion of things, he forbade them. This sectarian spirit which he exhibited is always contemptible, and Jesus ever condemned it. And has not the time come to rise above this dog-in-the-manger style, and admit the good wherever it is found? Truth should never be sacrificed, but goodness should be recognized wherever found.

At another time he wanted fire called down from heaven to destroy certain persons. Now, these examples indicate that he was a hard case, and truly a son of thunder. But see him when changed by Christ's presence and grace and love and gospel! He evidently had capacity and a receptive disposition, and passing through a wonderful transformation, he became the disciple whom Jesus loved. On one occasion Peter, feeling that the gulf between himself and Jesus was so great, asked John to speak to Jesus for him about a certain matter. This indicates a great change in John. And it was no small compliment to John's character, when on the cross Jesus commended to him the care of his mother.

The spirit of his Epistles is one of love. "Behold what manner of love the Father hath bestowed upon us!" And tradition says that when he was too old to meet with the disciples, he would gather his friends around him and say, "Little children, love one another." And so he was waiting to be like Him; "for we shall see him as he is."

In the Gospel which he wrote, how he is wrapped up in Jesus! He goes back to the beginning, and walks with him on the abyss of eternity. He traces his genealogy, not through patriarchs and kings, but from Jehovah's bosom, and then he is seemingly intent on catching all his heavenly words and secret spirit. Now, with this idea before the mind, we watch with interest the interview with Thomas, and Lazarus, and the blind man and the Samaritan woman, and the interview with Nicodemus, when all were sleeping save the stars and Jesus.

And we can not close this imperfect sketch without referring to him on Patmos, amid the awful glories and grandeurs of the Apocalyptic vision. He is now in the kingdom and patience of Jesus Christ a calm and unimpetuous old man, and stands amid all those strange sights and sounds unmoved by fear or impulse. It is only recorded of him once, that he fell down as dead. He had learned that the great conflict of the ages is to be carried on, not with carnal weapons, but with the word of God. His thoughts are changed. His loves are different. He is patient under very trying circumstances, while he is engaged in suffering and doing for Christ. Being now fully transformed into the likeness of Christ's character, in his everlasting presence his body shall be fashioned like unto his glorious body.

In conclusion, dear brethren in Christ, be assured that the path of the just is as a light that shines more and more unto the perfect day. Are your minds daily renewed? Remember our Bible is a daily Bible, and our light is the truth of God. Are you children of the light, shining in the midst of a perverse generation? Men are dying in darkness around us, and we must be quick. Be ye filled with this light? Do not exercise private judgment for once in your life, and never improve your conversion, but grow up into Christ in all things—grow, *grow,* GROW!

Let love also abound; it has a magical transforming power. Set your affections on things above, and

> "Dare to do right, dare to be true,
> You have a work that no other can do;
> Do it so kindly, so bravely, so well,
> That angels will hasten the story to tell."

THE FIRST PETITION

By ISAAC ERRETT

Thy Kingdom come.—Matt. vi:10.

EVERY careful reader of the New Testament will have learned that the narratives of Matthew, Mark and Luke, are largely occupied with teachings and preachings concerning the Kingdom of Heaven. There are four distinct ministers—those of John, Jesus, the Twelve, and the Seventy—whose special object is, the announcement of a Kingdom, heavenly in its origin and aims, soon to be established in the earth. Matt. iii:1-12; iv:17; x:1-7; Luke x:1-11. This approaching kingdom was the burden, not only of preaching and teaching, but of prayer, as will be seen in the language of the text. We assume here, that the limits of this discourse will not allow us to prove, that this kingdom denotes the spiritual reign of the Messiah—the gospel dispensation; that we have the history of its formal establishment in the second chapter of the Acts of Apostles; and that the embodiment is found in what is afterward known as the Church of God. But while affirming that this petition had its immediate fulfillment in the notable events narrated in the second chapter of Acts, we are far from supposing that the spirit and scope of the prayer are confined to the occurrences of that Pentecostal season. It is important to estimate aright the value of that chapter, as furnishing the *starting point* in the authoritative announcement of the kingly power of Jesus, of the terms of salvation under his reign, and of the planting of the divinely organized society, to be thenceforth known as his church. But it is only the beginning. It is the germ of an institution which is to live through all ages— the *little stone* cut out of the mountain without hands, which is to become *a great mountain* and *fill the whole earth*. Dan. ii:44,45. While, therefore, this petition has a meaning, on the lips of the original disciples, which it can not now have; we still regard it as a suitable prayer to be used by the intelligent Christian, in its wider scope, as embracing the grand objects of the reign of grace—the world-wide and age-lasting achievements of the kingdom of the heavens.

We design, in this discourse, to speak of the *nature* and *objects* of this kingdom, and of the *means by which these objects are to be accomplished.*

I. Touching the *nature* and *objects* of the kingdom of heaven, let the reader pause, and carefully peruse the second and seventh chapters of the book of Daniel. From these he will gather the following deeply interesting particulars:

1 This kingdom differs from the kingdom of this

300

world in possessing *a divine origin*. Its symbol is not an image made with human hands, but a stone cut out of the mountain *without hands*. The God of heaven was to set up this kingdom. In the seventh chapter, the symbol is not a beast rising out of a stormy sea, as with the brutal and monstrous tyrannies of earthly empires, springing from wars and revolutions; but *a son of man*, coming in the clouds of heaven, and receiving from the Ancient of Days, dominion and glory. It is therefore a spiritual kingdom, in opposition to earthly and carnal kingdoms; and is meant to redeem, elevate and glorify man, in opposition to the oppressive, corrupting and degrading tendencies of the kingdoms of this world.

2. This kingdom is essentially *aggressive* and *revolutionary* in its spirit and aims. The little stone is to *smite* the image, break it in pieces, and grind it to powder.

All who become citizens of this kingdom, are therefore enlisted in a *positive, aggressive* warfare against all that dishonors God, and degrades humanity.

3. This kingdom is to pass through *severe and protracted struggles* with opposing powers. The little horn is to make war with the saints and prevail against them. As in the personal history of her king, sufferings come before glory—the cross before the crown.

4. It aims at *universal dominion*. Its objects are world-wide in their scope.

5. It will surely triumph. However severe and protracted the struggles and the sufferings of the saints, the time will surely come when this little stone, becoming a mountain, shall fill the whole earth; when the kingdom and dominion, and greatness of the kingdom, under the whole heaven, shall be given to the people of the saints of the Most High, whose kingdom is an everlasting kingdom, and all dominions shall serve and obey him.

This petition, in the light of these prophetic announcements, is a prayer for the overthrow of all false governments and false religions; for the universal spread of the dominion of truth, holiness and love; and for the uplifting of our sin-oppressed race from the hopeless grave where human governments leave them, to the immortal glories and dominions of the everlasting kingdom of our Lord and Saviour, Jesus Christ.

In the light of these considerations, what an interest gathers about the philanthropic mission of our Saviour, as He proceeds to lay the foundations of this universal empire of truth and righteousness and peace! and what a loftiness and holiness belong to the mission of every Christian, who is enlisted as a co-worker with the Lord, in this magnificent scheme of human redemption!

II. After this rapid, but, we trust, not unsatisfactory glance at the nature and object of the kingdom of heaven, we hasten to the consideration of that which we meant to be the burden of this sermon—

the means by which these objects are to be
accomplished.

There is the most remarkable contrast, in this
respect, between earthly kingdoms and this kingdom
of the heavens. When Pilate, alarmed at the charge
preferred against Jesus, of setting up claims to
royalty, inquired anxiously, *Art thou the king of the
Jews?* the answer was, *My kingdom is not of this
world. If my kingdom were of this world, then
would my servants fight, that I should not be delivered to the Jews; but now is my kingdom not from
hence.* Pilate, not yet relieved pressed the question:
Art thou a king then? which brought out more fully
the spiritual nature of his reign: *Thou sayst that I
am a king. To this end was I born, and for this
purpose came I into the world, that I should bear
witness unto the truth. Every one that is of the
truth heareth my voice.* John xviii:33-37. This
kingdom was to be maintained by the power of truth,
and not by the power of the sword. Its conquests
were to be mighty, but bloodless.

For the greaves of the armed warrior in the conflict,
And the garment rolled in much blood,
Shall be for a burning, even for the fire.
For unto us a Child is born; unto us a Son is given;
And the government shall be upon his shoulder:
And his name shall be called Wonderful, Counsellor,
The mighty God, the Father of the everlasting age,
   the Prince of Peace
Of the increase of his government and peace there
   shall be no end;

Upon the throne of David, and upon his kingdom;
To fix it, and establish it
With judgment and with justice, henceforth and for
   ever:
The zeal of JEHOVAH God of hosts will do this.
   (Lowth's Isaiah, ix:4-7.)

At this time of bitter and bloody strife in our
land, when all our confidence seems to be centered
in military skill and prowess, and when, amidst the
professional followers of Jesus, many are abandon-
ing all hope of the conversion of the world by moral
and spiritual forces; it is important to refresh our
minds with the testimonies of the Spirit so clearly
uttered in the predictions of the Old Testament, and
the teachings of Christ and his apostles.

When Isaiah announces the establishing of the
Lord's house, the rebuking of the nations, and the
spread of peace and good will among men, he un-
covers the source of this revolutionizing and regen-
erating power in these words: *For the law shall go
forth from Zion, and the word of the Lord from
Jerusalem.* Isa. ii:2-4. In like manner, in the
eleventh chapter, when describing the king arrayed
for his conquests: *The Spirit of the Lord shall rest
upon him; the spirit of wisdom and understanding,
the spirit of counsel and might, the spirit of knowledge and of the fear of the Lord.* Isa. xi:2. And
after he has again set forth, in the most beautiful
imagery, the universal reign of peace and holy
brotherhood, he gives the reason of it in these words:

304

For the earth shall be full of the knowledge of the Lord, as the waters cover the sea. ver. 9. The word of God is living. Heb. iv:12. The word of God is powerful. The word of God is eternal. I Pet. 1:24,25. The word of God teems with the energies of spiritual life. John vi:63. From the magazines of Jehovah's power, this means has been selected as the most perfectly adapted to the wants of human nature, and to the achievement of the great ends of the kingdom of Christ. The entire harmony between Old Testament prophecies and New Testament facts and teachings on this point, may be seen by the following statements:

1. We have already heard the Saviour affirm respecting his kingdom, that he came to establish it *by bearing witness to the truth.*

2. The mission of the Holy Spirit, for the conversion of the world, is likewise associated with the utterance of truth. He is called, therefore, *the Spirit of truth*; and the express promise to the apostles was, *He shall guide you into all truth.* John xvi:13.

3. When our Lord sent his apostles forth to push the conquests of his kingdom, he bade them rely on the message of truth and grace committed to them, and on divine protection in its utterance. *Go into all the world and preach the Gospel to every creature.* Mark xvi:15. *Go teach all nations. . . . And lo I am with you always, even unto the end of the world.* Matt. xxviii:19,20.

4. The first gift bestowed by the Spirit on these

ambassadors of Christ was *the gift of tongues*, that they might speak in all languages, the words of this life; and by the spiritual energy of the truth thus divinely communicated, they pierced the hearts of sinners, and turned them by thousands to the Lord. Acts ii :1-41.

5. The kingdom of heaven is compared to a sower going forth to sow, and the *seed of the kingdom* is declared to be *the word of God*. Luke viii :11. As rationally expect wheat to grow without seed, as to look for the fruits of the Spirit where the Word of God has not been received into the heart. The *germ of the harvest is in the living seed.*

6. The failure to save men is traced to a failure in conveying the truth to their hearts. *This people's heart is waxed gross, and their ears are dull of hearing, and their eyes they have closed, lest at any time they should see with their eyes, and hear with their ears, and should understand with their heart, and should be converted, and I should heal them.* Matt. xiii :15; see also Rom. x :14-17; 2 Cor. iv :3,4.

In view of these and kindred facts, we are bold to affirm that nothing is wanting to the conversion of the world, but that all men everywhere should hear, understand, and receive the Word of God, the gospel of salvation. It is the power of God to salvation to every one that believeth, to the Jew first, and also to the Greek. We can not here enter into an analysis of this word of life, to show its adaptness to this great end. We throw ourselves on the broad

306

declarations of Holy Scripture, and in the face of all the babbling philosophies of earth, and of all the trembling doubts of the professed people of God, declare that it is so, and must be so, and will inevitably prove to be so, *for the mouth of the Lord hath spoken it.*

But let it be carefully observed, that it is the Word of God, not on the printed page, but *in the human heart,* that is to achieve this result. We have not, therefore, fully met the inquiry as to the means of success in promoting the objects of this kingdom. There must be means and agencies to convey this word to the hearts of men. These means are both divine and human. It is impossible for us to know all the providential and spiritual agencies employed by the king to give free course to his Gospel. We know that he has promised to be with the ambassadors of his reign unto the end of the world. We know that all the sufficiency, even of inspired apostles, was of God; that while, as spiritual husbandmen, they planted and watered, it was God that gave the increase. We know that they were divinely guided into some fields of labor, and divinely restrained from entering other fields. We can readily perceive how vast a space is left for providential workings, and consequently for constant and earnest prayer, after all that belongs to human agency has been accomplished. Some nations may be so far sunken in sin and delusion as to be irrecoverable; the judgments of the Almighty can exterminate them. Other nations may be in an unfavorable condition for attending to the message of life; the governor of the nation, by a train of mercies or of judgments, may prepare them to receive it. In the wide range of freedom that belongs to the human mind, there may be long and wide-spread reigns of falsehood and delusion; the earth may be deluged with error; but there is one who sitteth above the floods, and stilleth the raging of the seas, who will, after long patience, cause the waters to abate, and stretch the bow of peace over a redeemed world. Human tyrannies may forbid the spread of truth; ecclesiastical despotisms may banish the light, imprison the saints, and threaten to annihilate the kingdom of God; but *He that sitteth in the heavens shall laugh; the Lord shall have them in derision.* The Word of God is not bound. The truth never pauses. In God's own good time these tyrannies crumble to the dust, hoary systems of error sink into contempt, and the Word of God comes forth from its banishment to live and abide forever. The same principles of the divine government which we recognize in his dealings with nations and ages, are applicable likewise to communities and to individuals. So that, in all cases, we may have the cheering assurance that Christ is with his truth and with its advocates, and that *greater is he that is in us, than he that is in the world.* I John, iv:4.

Let us look now at the human instrumentalities to be employed in the salvation of the world.

In the divine arrangement, the Church is to be this light of the world. To her members—to all of them—is given the solemn charge of holding forth the word of life. In the primitive Church, there were special gifts and extraordinary offices, to meet the exigencies of the Church's infancy; but these were only *until* the weakness of infancy was outgrown, and the means of grace were perfectly developed. Eph. iv:11-16. Jesus taught his disciples that they were to be the *light of the world* and the *salt of the earth.* Matt. v:13,14. Paul taught the Philippians that they were *to shine as lights in the world, holding forth the word of life.* Peter taught Christians that they constituted a royal priesthood, a chosen race, a peculiar people, for this very purpose, that they might *show forth the praises of him that called them from darkness into his marvelous light.*

This they were to do:

1. *By the testimony of a holy life. Let your light so shine, that others seeing your good works may glorify your Father who is in heaven.* Matt. v:16. *And ye became followers of us and of the Lord, having received the word in much affliction, with joy of the Holy Spirit; so that ye were examples to all that believe in Macedonia and Achaia. For from you sounded out the word of the Lord, not only in Macedonia and Achaia, but also in every place your faith to God-ward is spread abroad, so that we need not to speak anything. For they themselves show of us what manner of entering in we had unto you, and*

how ye turned from idols to serve the living and true God. I Thess. i:6-13. *Do all things without murmurings and disputings, that ye may be blameless and harmless, the sons of God without rebuke, in the midst of a crooked and perverse nation, among whom ye shine as lights in the world, holding forth the word of life.* Phil. ii:14-16. *The kingdom of God is not meat and drink, but righteousness, peace, and joy in the Holy Spirit. For he that in these things serveth Christ, is acceptable to God, and approved of men.* Rom. xiv:17,18.

2. *More particularly, the union, harmony, and love of the saints* is to win the world to Christ.

I pray . . . that they all may be one; as thou, Father, art in me, and I in thee, that they also may be one in us, that the world may believe that thou hast sent me. John xvii:21. So peculiar to the religion of Jesus is the spirit of love and peace, that he has made this the badge of discipleship: *By this shall all men know that you are my disciples, if you have love one to another.* John xiii:35. The spirit of the world is a spirit of selfishness; and its bitter fruits are unrighteousness, oppression, anger, hatred, envy, malice, revenge. The spirit of Christ is a spirit of love, and its blessed fruits are righteousness, kindness, forgiveness, meekness, and active benevolence. To subdue the enmities and rivalries of Pharisee and Sadducee, of Jew and Samaritan, and unite them in harmonious association, was a heavenly work, and carried with it great converting power. To unite

Jew and Gentile in one body, and bring together
Pharisee, Sadducee, Samaritan, with Epicurean and
Stoic, Roman and Greek, Barbarian and Scythian,
bond and free, eliminating all the elements of discord, and binding in affectionate and happy brotherhood, men of all creeds, ranks, and conditions, was
indeed a miracle of grace, which more than all else
attracted the hearts of men to the Gospel. Nor was
this a merely theoretical oneness. While there were
occasional outbreaks of an evil spirit, it is evident
that the primitive Church was animated by such a
love, and marked by such a unity of spirit as had
never been seen before. There was *one Lord, one
faith, one baptism, one body, one spirit, one hope, one
God and Father of all.* Eph. iv:4-6. In the unity
of interest and affection, which belonged to the primitive Church, there were the most beautiful and
touching and captivating displays of the sentiment
of brotherhood, in the maintenance of the poor,
sympathy with the suffering, relief of those who
were in the bonds, and even in laying down their
lives for one another. So long as a deep spiritual
life pervaded the Church, and the spirit of sect was
subjugated by the spirit of love, the onward marches
of the soldiers of the cross were marked by a succession of gorgeous triumphs of grace. The gods of
the nations fell before the cross, like Dagon before
the Ark of Jehovah. Temples were forsaken, altars
crumbled, and the hoary superstitions of ages, more
extensive and powerful than even the political

311

despotism of the Roman empire, tottered to their foundations. The world seemed already to lie prostrate before the spiritual potencies of the kingdom of heaven. But when prosperity gave birth to pride, and pride gave birth to sects, and sects gave birth to anger, strife, and every evil work, the glory departed from Israel. Lured by the attractions of heathen philosophy, enticed by the smiles of worldly friendship, the heroes of the faith were lulled to sleep in the lap of the Delilah of earthly pride; and there, shorn of their strength, and robbed of spiritual vision, they became blind and foolish, and helpless. Let the fearful lesson be well considered. Selfishness, pride, and sectarian strife are the brood of perdition; Satan is their father, and hell their native air. Love, humility, and holy brotherhood are the fruits of the Spirit of God. They only can successfully labor for the conversion of the world, who are one with Christ, and one with each other, and who develop the spiritual life which they have received from God in brotherly affection and in a world-wide philanthropy.

3. A third means of extending the triumphs of the cross, is *the maintenance of the order and worship of the Church.* All the ordinances and appointments of the Lord's house are means of grace—ministrations of light and life. Prayer, praise, preaching, teaching, exhortation, the Lord's Day, the Lord's Supper, together with the social sympathies and affections continually cultured in a well-

ordered church, furnish heavenly influences for the salvation of the sinful. *The Spirit of God operates not only through the word spoken, but through the whole harmonious life of the body which that Spirit animates.* Thus the Church becomes *the pillar and ground of the truth.* I Tim. iii :15. Of the churches in Judea, Galilee, and Samaria it is said, that *walking in the fear of the Lord, and in the comfort of the Holy Spirit, they were multiplied.* And to the church in Corinth, Paul says, that if they faithfully perform the functions of a church, the unbeliever *is convinced of all, is judged of all; and thus are the secrets of his heart made manifest; and so falling down on his face he will worship God, and report that God is in you of a truth.* I Cor. xiv :24,25. No one can honestly pray, in the spirit of this petition, *Thy kingdom come,* who does not, to the extent of his ability, contribute to the vigor and energy of the church of which he is a member, to make it a center of living and loving influences, whence light and love may radiate to the community round about.

4. That on which the Scriptures lay most stress, for the conversion of the world, is *the public preaching of the Gospel.* This is the most popular and efficient means of promoting the blissful objects of the reign of the Messiah. *Go into all the world, and preach the Gospel to every creature.* Mark xvi :15. *It hath pleased God by the foolishness of preaching to save them that believe.* I Cor. i :21. How *shall they believe in him of whom they have not heard?*

313

and how shall they hear without a preacher. Rom. x:14. Accordingly we find the church in Jerusalem sending Barnabas to Antioch; Acts xi:22, and Antioch sending out Paul and Barnabas through an extensive region of country; Acts xiii:2,3, and the disciples, when driven from Jerusalem, *went everywhere preaching the word.* Acts viii:4.

Whether this shall be accomplished by the individual efforts of those to whom the Lord opens the way, or by the benevolence of a single church, or by a combination of the means of two, or fifty, or a thousand churches, must be decided on the ground of *expediency,* and not on the basis of a divine prescription. In a religion meant for all the world, there can be but few positive statutes. We are under *a law of liberty.* Much must be left to the judgment of the children of God, in every age and in every country, so far as matters of expediency are concerned. And if we are only studious not to trench on the few positive statutes that are given, if we duly respect the general sentiment of the Church in all expedients, and are careful to violate the Christian liberty of none of our brethren, there can be no danger in voluntary associations of Christians in a neighborhood, county, state, province, or nation, to further the aims of the kingdom of God. The matter of greatest moment is the possession by *the Church of the genuine missionary spirit.* If there is that deep and earnest consecration to the work of the Lord which distinguished the Jerusalem church, which led her members to give up all their property for the work of Christ, Acts ii :44,45 and iv :34-37, which made preachers of her deacons, Acts vii :2 and viii :5, and which finally sent out the mass of her membership to preach the word of life; Acts viii :4; we should not be long troubled about the necessary expedients. Money, personal influence, learning, talents, and labor would all be "willingly offered"; the Church would have her messengers in every scene of degradation and suffering, her colporteurs in every lane and alley, and on every highway; her tracts and sermons in every house; her preachers in every city and wilderness, in the islands of the sea, and at the ends of the earth, praying, *Thy kingdom come*, and laboring in the spirit of the prayer.

Has it ever struck your mind, that when our Lord taught his disciples to pray, *this was the first petition he taught them?* He thus instructed them that the kingdom of God was to be *first* in their thoughts and desires. Not even their daily bread was to be sought until they had first prayed, *Thy kingdom come*. Ah, my brethren, how far have we wandered from the pure spiritual loves and aims of our Saviour's teachings? How entirely have we been immersed in the cares and ambitions of earth! Who makes the kingdom of heaven *first* in his *thoughts*, *first* in his *prayers*, *first* in his *plans*, *first* in his *offerings?* We toil for wealth, and excuse ourselves from the toils of the kingdom on the score of business necessity! We use our wealth to minister to the

315

lusts of the flesh, the lust of the eyes, and the pride of life, and give whatever fragments we can spare from such purposes, to advance the interests of the Church! We bestow the strength of our days for earthly pelf, for political ambitions, or social position; and have scarcely time amidst our feverish excitements and carking cares to pause long enough to utter with thought and heart even this short prayer —*Thy kingdom come!* How few hearts are burdened with the weight of this mighty enterprise for the salvation of the lost! How few know the fellowship of the sufferings of Christ—and how few consequently know the power of his resurrection! We do not doubt that there are many thousands who have not bowed the knee to Baal, and we do not, therefore, use the language of despondency. But when we see where our blessed Lord places the interests of his kingdom—in the front rank of all interests and of all prayers, we can not but raise a voice of earnest admonition, that we may be awakened to a more entire consecration to the service of the king.

Reader! Are you a citizen of the kingdom of heaven? Have you, by *a birth of water and of the Spirit,* entered into the kingdom of God? John iii:5. Do you enjoy the peculiar treasures of this kingdom —*righteousness, peace, and joy in the Holy Spirit?* Rom. xiv:17. *Being delivered from the power of darkness,* and *translated into the kingdom of God's dear Son,* have you been made *meet for the inheritance of the saints and of the household of God?*

316

Eph. ii:19. How great the grace! how rich the mercy! how exalted your honors! how cheering your hopes! All your durable treasures are laid up in this kingdom. All earthly powers will be shaken, but the kingdom of God *can not be moved.* Heb. xii:28. In this kingdom every citizen is a king and a partner of the throne of the king eternal. He can not fail. He can not perish. He will be more than a conqueror here; and glory, honor, and immortality await him in the heavens! His ransomed nature is destined to the brightest and the noblest fame that a created intelligence can possess. Blood-bought, toiling, terrible, victorious, glorified human nature—it is, in all the universe, the grandest monument of heaven's wisdom and graces, and is worthy to stand "nearest the throne and first in song." I need not ask you if you are grateful for your inheritance, happy in your privileges, and joyful in your hopes. I will not insult you with the question if you could be induced to sell your immortal birth-right for any mess of pottage this life can afford? But let me ask you whether you may not be *more* grateful, and enlarge your own joy by an increased devotion to the work of the Lord? Jesus has done great things for you, my brother! He gave all—*all* for you and for me; became a slave, a felon, and drank the bitterest cup of death ever pressed to human lips, for our salvation. Have we given *all* for him—*all?* Have we kept back no part of the price? Are wealth, influence, mind, heart, tongue, and hands freely consecrated to his service?

Is his kingdom more than daily bread to us? Let us never feel at ease until we are sure that this is the first petition of our hearts—*Thy kingdom come* a prayer never to cease until *the kingdoms of this world become the kingdoms of our Lord and of his Christ, that he may reign for ever and ever.*

PROPHECY VINDICATED BY VOLNEY

By THOMAS HOLMAN

READER, you claim the right to judge for yourself, and you are entreated to use that right in
examining the evidences of the truth of the Scriptures. It may be that you have heard the opinions
of believers ridiculed, and their arguments treated
with scorn because they were not deemed impartial
witnesses on the subject. Should such have been
the case, we here bring before your view substantial
facts, asserted by a professed infidel, and therefore
not liable to the objections which are raised against
Christian writers. The facts to which your attention
will be called are indisputable, and most of the particulars to which they relate have been verified by
the personal examination of the most recent travelers,
and may now be scrutinized by any one who chooses
to visit Syria.

The object of the present tract is to adduce facts
which prove the divine inspiration of the Holy Scriptures, from the writings of Volney, the author of
The Ruins of Empires, and *Travels in Syria,* a most
determined infidel. Not only does he attest facts
which constitute the literal fulfillment of numerous

prophecies, but he describes the peculiar and characteristic features of the desolations foretold by them, with as much detail and precision as if he had copied the prophetic denunciations rather than related his own observations; or as if he had aimed to prove that they had been fulfilled to the very letter. Nor can any authority be adduced superior to Volney as a correct and faithful describer of the countries which he visited; and his descriptions are as minute as the testimony on the subject is unexceptionable. "It has been reserved for the genius of Volney," says Malte Brun, "so to combine the detached accounts of other travelers, antiquaries, and naturalists with the results of his own observation and study, as to offer to the world a complete description of Syria."

The present state of Judea and its inhabitants, and of adjacent countries, has been foretold by various prophecies, of the exact accomplishment of which we may have at one view the most satisfactory proof, by placing them without note or comment, beside the assertions of a decided enemy of Christianity.

EXTRACTS FROM VOLNEY.	PROPHECIES OF JUDEA AND THE ADJOINING COUNTRIES.
"Every day as I proceeded on my journey, I found fields lying waste."—*The Ruins*, c. i.	"Then shall the land enjoy her sabbaths, as long as it lieth desolate, and ye be in your enemies' land; even
"Why are these lands stript	

320

of their former blessings (numerous flocks, fertile fields, and abundant harvests)? Why have they been banished, as it were and transferred for so many ages to other nations and different climes?"—Ib., c. ii.

"During the last 2,500 years, ten invasions may be enumerated, which have successively introduced different foreign nations."—Travels in Syria, c. xxii.

"In the year 622 (636) the Arabian tribes, collected under the banners of Mohammed, seized, or rather laid it waste. Since that period, torn to pieces by the civil wars of the Fatimites and the Ommiades, wrested from the Caliphs by their rebellious governors, taken from them by the Turcoman soldiery, invaded by the European crusaders, retaken by the Mamelukes of Egypt, and ravaged by Tamerlane and his Tartars, it has at length fallen into the hands of the Ottoman Turks."— Ib., p. 352.

then shall the land rest and enjoy her sabbaths. As long as it lieth desolate, it shall rest." (Lev. xxvi:34,35.)

"Your land strangers shall devour it in your presence, and it is desolate, as overthrown by strangers." (Isaiah i:7.)

"Destruction upon destruction is cried; for the whole land is spoiled." (Jer. iv:20.) "And I will give it into the hands of the strangers for a prey, and to the wicked of the earth for a spoil; and they shall pollute it." (Ezek. vii:21.) "Wherefore I will bring the worst of the heathen, and they shall possess their houses." (Ezek. vii:24.) "Mischief shall come upon mischief." (Ezek. vii:26.) "Jerusalem shall be trodden down of the Gentiles, until the time of the Gentiles be fulfilled." (Luke xxi:24.)

"In the interior parts of the country there are neither great country roads, nor canals, nor even bridges, etc. The roads in the mountains are extremely bad. It is remarkable that throughout Syria, neither a wagon nor a cart is to be seen."—Ib., c. xxxviii.

"Your highways shall be desolate." (Lev. xxvi:22.)

"There is no establishment either of post or of public conveyance. No one dares travel alone, by reason of continual danger. It is necessary for travelers to wait till several are going to the same place; or to take the opportunity of joining the suite of some great man, who may act as protector, or, as is more frequently the case, oppressor, to the whole caravan."—Ib.

"The highways lie waste, the wayfaring man ceaseth." (Isaiah xxxiii:8.)

"These precautions are particularly necessary in those parts of the country which lie open to the Arabs, such as Palestine, and the whole frontier of the desert."—Ib.

"The spoilers are come upon all high places through the wildernesses." (Jer. xii: 12.)

"The merchants live in a state of continual alarm, etc. The same dread prevails in

"Thus saith the Lord God of the inhabitants of Jerusalem, and of the land of

the villages, every peasant fearing equally to excite the envy of his fellows, or the avarice of the Aga and his soldiery."—Ib.

"The condition of the peasantry is wretched. Their sole subsistence is a little coarse barley bread, with onions or lentils; and water their only beverage. Agriculture is in the most deplorable state, no more grain being sown than is absolutely necessary for bare subsistence."—Ib., c. xxxvii and xxxviii.

Israel: They shall eat their bread with carefulness, and drink their water with astonishment, that her land may be desolate from all that is therein, because of the violence of all them that dwell therein." (Ezek. xii:19.)

"Corruption is habitual and universal."—Ib., c. xxxiv.

"They have no music but vocal; for they neither know nor esteem that which is instrumental."—Ib., c. xxxix.

"Their singing is accompanied with sighs, etc. They may be said to excel most in the melancholy strain."—Ib.

"Good cheer would expose them to extortion, and wine to a corporal punishment."—Ib., c. xl.

"The earth is defiled under the inhabitants thereof." (Isaiah xxiv:5.)
"The mirth of the tabrets ceaseth; the joy of the harp ceaseth." (Isaiah xxiv:8.)

"All the merry-hearted do sigh." (Isaiah xxiv:7.)

"They shall not drink wine with a song." (Isaiah xxiv:9.)

"In whatever they say or do they maintain the same grave and phlegmatic air. Instead of the frank and lively manner which so universally prevails among us, their behavior is serious, austere, and melancholy. They rarely laugh; and the gayety of the French appears to them a fit of delirium."—Ib.

"The noise of them that rejoice endeth. All joy is darkened; the mirth of the land is gone." (Isaiah xxiv: 8,11.)

"The government of the Turks in Syria is a mere military despotism; that is, the bulk of the inhabitants are subject to the will of a faction of armed men who dispose of everything according to their own interest and pleasure."—Ib., c. xxxiii.

"They that dwell therein are desolate." (Isaiah xxiv: 6.)

"So feeble a population in so excellent a country may well excite our astonishment; but this will be increased if we compare the present number of inhabitants with that of ancient times."—Ib., c. xxxii.

"The appearance of the village of Loudd, formerly Lydda and Diospolis, is precisely that of a place which has been recently ravaged by

"I will bring the land into desolation; and your enemies which dwell therein shall be astonished at it." (Lev. xxvi:32.)

"Everyone that passeth thereby shall be astonished." (Jer. xviii:16.)

"Your cities are burned with fire." (Isaiah i:7.)

324

the enemy and by fire. Arimathea is almost as completely in ruins as Loudd itself."—Ib., c. xxxi.

"At every turn there are found ruins of towers, turrets, and moated castles, left as a dwelling for owls and scorpions.—Ib.

"The forts and towers shall be for dens forever." (Isaiah xxxii:14.)

"The defensed city shall be desolate, and the habitation forsaken, and left like a wilderness." (Isaiah xxvii: 10.)

"Beyond (Jaffa) the country was once full of large olive trees; but the Mamelukes having cut them all down, either for the pleasure of cutting, or to use as firewood, Jaffa has lost the benefit of them.

"When the boughs thereof are withered, they shall be broken off; the women come, and set them on fire." (Isaiah xxvii:11.)

"The country around (Arimathea) has been planted with olive trees; but they are perishing through the mischief done to them by the people, either openly or secretly."—Ib.

"A people among whom the simplest arts are in a state of barbarism; and the sciences quite unknown. The barbarism of Syria is complete."— Ib., c. xxxix.

"It is a people of no understanding." (Isaiah xxvii: 11.)

"It may be said that the means of instruction do not exist among them."—Ib.

"The Turcomans, Kurds, and Bedouins have no fixed abode, but wander about with their tents and flocks, etc. The Arabs encamp everywhere upon that part of the frontier of Syria which borders upon their deserts; and even upon the plains in the interior, as those of Palestine, Bequaa, and Galilee."—Ib., c. xxii.

"Many pastors have destroyed my vineyard; they have trodden my portion under foot." (Jer. xii:10.)

"The pastoral or wandering tribes of Syria."—*Title of* c. xxiii.

"I have visited the places that were the theatre of so much splendor, and have beheld nothing but solitude and desertion."—*The Ruins*, c. ii.

"They have made my pleasant portion a desolate wilderness." (Jer. xii:10.)

"Nothing is to be seen but solitude and sterility."—Ib.

"The whole land shall be desolate. Yet will I not make a full end." (Jer. iv: 27.) "In that day it shall come to pass, that the glory of Jacob shall be made thin. When thus it shall be in the midst of the land among the

326

people, there shall be as the shaking of an olive-tree, and as the gleaning grapes when the vintage is done." (Isaiah xvii:4; xxiv:13.)

"I looked for those ancient people and their works, and all I could find was a faint trace, like that left in the sand by the foot of the passenger." —Ib.

"Man sows in anguish, and reaps nothing but vexation and cares."—Ib.

"They have sown wheat, but shall reap thorns; they have put themselves to pain, but shall not profit." (Jer. xii:13.)

"War, famine, and pestilence assail him in turn."—Ib.

"No flesh shall have peace." (Jer. xii:12.)

"The earth produces only briars and wormwood."—Ib.

"Upon the land of my people shall come up thorns and briars." (Isaiah xxxii: 13.)

"The temples are thrown down."—Ib.

"I will destroy your high places, and cut down your images. I will bring your sanctuaries unto desolation." (Lev. xxvi:30,31.)

"The palaces are demolished."—Ib.

"The palaces shall be forsaken." (Isaiah xxxii:14.)

327

"The ports are filled up."
—Ib.

"I will destroy the remnant of the sea-coast. (Ezek. xxv:16.)

"The towns are destroyed, and the earth stript of inhabitants."—Ib.

"I will make your cities waste." (Lev. xxvi:31.)
"I beheld and all the cities thereof were broken down." (Jer. iv:26.) "Every city shall be forsaken and not a man dwell therein." (Jer. iv:29.)

"The territories of Yamnia and Yoppa, in Palestine alone, says the Philosophical Geographer Strabo, were formerly so populous that they could bring forty thousand armed men into the field. At present they could scarcely furnish three thousand.—*Travels in Syria*, c. xxxii.

"The inhabitants of the earth are burned, and few men left." (Isaiah xxiv:6.)

"Every day I met with deserted villages."—*The Ruins*, c. i.

"The cities that are inhabited shall be laid waste." (Ezek. xii:20.)

"The plain country is rich and light, calculated for the greatest fertility."—*Travels in Syria*, c. i., s. 6.

"But yet in it shall be a tenth, and it shall return, and shall be eaten; as a teil-tree, and as an oak, whose substance is in them when they cast their leaves." (Isaiah vi:13.)

"When the Ottomans wrested Syria from the Mamelukes, they only considered it as the spoil of a vanquished enemy," etc.—Ib. c. xxxiii., s. 1. "As the porte never restores anything to a nation which it has pillaged, it evidently does not disapprove of robbery which is profitable to itself."—Ib.

"I will give it into the hands of the strangers for a prey, and to the wicked of the earth for a spoil. The robbers shall enter into it, and defile it." (Ezek. vii: 21,22.)

"Like most hot countries, it is destitute of that fresh and living verdure which almost constantly adorns our own lands, and of the grassy and flowery carpet which covers the meadows of Normandy and Flanders. The earth in Syria always looks dusty. Yet, probably, the country would have been shaded by forests, had it not been laid waste by the hand of man."—Ib., c. xxxii., s. 1.

"How long shall the land mourn, and the herbs of every field wither, for the wickedness of them that dwell therein." (Jer. xii:4.)

"From whence proceed such melancholy revolutions? For what cause is the fortune of these countries so strikingly changed? Why are so many cities destroyed? Why is not that ancient population reproduced and perpetuated? Why

"And the stranger that shall come from a far land, when they see the plagues of that land, and the sicknesses which the Lord hath laid upon it, even all nations shall say: Wherefore hath the Lord done this unto this

329

are these regions deprived of the blessings they formerly enjoyed?"—*The Ruins*, c. ii.

"A mysterious God exercises his incomprehensible judgments! He has doubtless pronounced a secret malediction against this land. In what consists that anathema of Heaven? Where is the divine curse which perpetuates the desolation of these countries?"—Ib.

"The white marble ruins which are still remaining at Gaza, show that it has been at some former time the abode of wealth and luxury. At present, it is a small unfortified town."—Ib., c. xxxi.

"The waste ruins Askelon."—Ib.

"Several ruins are met with in succession, the most considerable of which is Ezdoud, at the present time noted only for scorpions."—Ib.

"All the rest of the country is a desert."—Ib.

land? What meaneth the heat of this great anger?" (Deut. xxix:22, 24.)

"The anger of the Lord was kindled against this land, to bring upon it all the curses that are written in this book." (Deut. xxix:27.)

"The earth also is defiled under the inhabitants thereof, because they have transgressed the laws, changed the ordinances, broken the everlasting covenant." (Isaiah xxiv:5.)

"I will not turn away the punishment of Gaza." (Amos i:6.) "Gaza shall be forsaken." (Zeph. ii:4.) "Baldness is come upon Gaza." (Jer. xlvii:5.)

"Ashkelon is cut off, with the remnant of their valley." (Jer. xlvii:5.)

"Ashkelon shall be a desolation." (Zeph. ii:4.)

"Ashkelon shall not be inhabited." (Zech. ix:5.)

"I will cut off the inhabitant from Ashdod." (Amos i:8.)

"The remnant of the Philistines shall perish." (Amos i:8.)

"I enumerated the kingdoms of Damascus and Idumæa, of Jerusalem and Samaria, of the warlike states of the Philistines, and the commercial republics of Phoenicia. This Syria, said I to myself, which is now almost depopulated, then contained a hundred flourishing cities, and abounded with towns, villages, and hamlets. Everywhere might have been seen cultivated fields, frequented roads, and crowded habitations. Ah! what is become of those ages of abundance and of life? What is become of so many splendid productions of the hand of man?"—*The Ruins*, c. ii.

"This country (Idumæa) has never been visited by any traveler, though it richly deserves it."—*Travels in Syria*, c. xxxi.

"From the report of the Arabs of Bakir, and the inhabitants of Gaza, who frequently go to Maan and Karak, on the road of the pilgrims, there are to the southeast of the Lake Asphaltites (Dead Sea), within three days' journey, upward of thirty ruined towns, absolutely de-

"The kingdom shall cease from Damascus, and the remnant from Syria." (Isaiah xvii:3.)

"They shall call the nobles thereof to the kingdom (in Idumæa, but none shall be there, and all her princes shall be nothing." (Isaiah xxxiv:12.) "I will cause to cease the kingdom of the house of Israel." (Hosea i:4.)

"As for Samaria, her king is cut off as the foam upon the water." (Hosea x:7.) "Samaria shall become desolate." (Hosea xiii:16.)

"I will cut off the pride of the Philistines." (Zech. ix:6.)

"None shall pass through it (Idumæa) forever and ever." (Isaiah xxxiv:10.)

"From generation to generation it shall lie waste." (Isaiah xxxiv:10.) "All the cities thereof shall be perpetual wastes." (Jer. xlix:13.) "Edom shall be a desolation; every one that goeth by it shall be astonished. No man shall abide there, saith the Lord, neither shall a son

331

serted. This was the country of the Idumæns, who, at the time of the destruction of Jerusalem, were almost as numerous as the Jews."—Ib.

"In several of them are found large colonaded buildings, which may have been ancient temples, or, at least, Greek churches. The Arabs sometimes fold their flocks in them, on account of the enormous scorpions with which they abound."—Ib.

"Where are those fleets of Tyre, those dockyards of Arad, those workshops of Sidon, and that multitude of mariners, pilots, merchants, and soldiers? Where are those laborers, those dwellings, those flocks, and that picture of animated nature of which the earth seemed proud?"—*The Ruins,* c. ii.

"The whole population of the village (Tyre) consists of fifty or sixty poor families, who live obscurely on the produce of their little ground, and a trifling fishery."—*Travels in Syria,* c. xxix.

of man dwell in it." (Jer. xlix:17,18.) "I will lay thy cities waste, and thou shalt be desolate, and thou shalt know that I am the Lord." (Ezek. xxxv:4.)

"Thorns shall come up in her palaces, nettles and brambles in the fortresses thereof; and it shall be for an habitation of dragons and a court for owls." (Isaiah xxxiv: 13.)

"Thy riches and thy fairs (O Tyrus), thy merchandise, thy mariners, and thy pilots, thy calkers, and the occupiers of thy merchandise, and all thy men of war, that are in thee, and in all thy company which is in the midst of thee, shall fall into midst of the seas in the day of thy ruin." (Ezek. xxvii: 27.)

"I will make her (Tyre) like the top of a rock. It shall be a place for the spreading of nets in the midst of the sea." (Ezek. xxvi:4,5.)

"Among the rocks appear remains of the so much boasted cedars, which, however, are anything but majestic."—*Ib.*, c. xx., s. 2.

"There are not more than four or five trees of any size." —*Ib., note.*

"Such is the state of Egypt. Deprived twenty-three centuries ago of her natural proprietors, she has been successively a prey to the Persians, the Macedonians, the Romans, the Greeks, the Arabs, the Gorgians, and, at length the race of Tartars distinguished by the name of Ottoman Turks."—*Travels,* c. vi.

"Where are those ramparts of Nineveh?"—*The Ruins,* c. ii.

"Of Nineveh, of which scarcely the name is left."— Ib., c. iv.

"Where are those walls of Babylon?"—Ib., c. ii.

"Nothing is left of Babylon but heaps of earth, trodden under foot of men."—Ib., c. iv.

"Lebanon is ashamed and hewn down." (Isaiah xxxiii: 9.) "The cedar is fallen; the defensed forest (marg.) is come down." (Zech. xi:2.)

"The rest of the trees of his forest shall be few, that a child may write them." (Isaiah x:19.)

"I will sell the land (Egypt) into the hand of the wicked: and I will make the land waste, and all that is therein, by the hand of strangers; I the Lord have spoken it." (Ezek. xxx:12.)

"She (Nineveh) is empty, and void, and waste." (Nah. ii:10.)

"Their place is not known where they are." (Nah. iii: 17.)

"The broad walls of Babylon shall be utterly broken." (Jer. li:58.)

"Cast her (Babylon) up as heaps, and destroy her utterly: let nothing of her be left." (Jer. i:26.)

"O ye solitary ruins! ye silent walls!" exclaims Volney, "how many useful lessons, how many affecting and striking reflections do ye offer to the mind which is capable of considering you aright!"—*The Ruins*, c. iii.

It is true that these ruins do afford most important lessons, and especially as to the truth of prophecy. Never was a man more completely vindicated from the charges of his enemies and calumniators, than is the truth of the Bible by the writings of the writer who has dared to call in question its divine authority. That very man, whose senses were spell-bound in the thickest darkness of error, has, however undesignedly, struck a blow powerful enough not only to shake, but to overturn, the erroneous opinions of any individual who will calmly interrogate these ruins, and listen to the voice of their reply.

It is true, as Volney affirms, that they are not the effect of chance. Chance is but an empty name invented for the purpose of hiding ignorance and sheltering sloth; not a power capable of overthrowing cities, and changing kingdoms into mighty deserts. The destruction of empires demonstrates the wickedness of the men by whom their ruin has been effected and perpetuated. Everywhere, without exception, the Scriptures point out in these ruins the punishment of sin, and thereby make manifest the moral government of God, and show the untiring vigilance with which his providence enters into the minutest details of human events. Considered in their true light, as the express and literal fulfillment of numerous prophecies, they prove, beyond all doubt, the divine inspiration of the Scriptures. We must be deaf to reason, and blind worshippers of idol chance, if, for the sake of listening to the declamations of a lying philosophy, we refuse to hear that spirit of prophecy which is the testimony of Jesus, while it proclaims: "Verily there is a God that judgeth in the earth." We here invite you, therefore, to behold the fulfillment of what the Lord has foretold, and to be convinced of the undeniable fact that the Bible is the word of God, who, having from the beginning determined the end, has caused it to be written in his book, that all men may know that he alone is God.

If you will calmly and carefully examine the prophecies of Scripture, as here confronted with the testimony of Volney, you will be compelled to submit to such satisfactory evidence. Volney, however, is but one among a multitude of witnesses, and the prophecies here cited form a small part of those contained in the Bible. The judgments of God, as written in that book, are repeated by thousands of ruins as by so many echoes. The sins of mankind are all known unto the Lord; the guilty shall find no favor in his sight, and none that riseth up against him shall prosper. The anger of nations is the rod of his displeasure. The convulsions of kingdoms and empires prove the infallible certainty of "the word of God which abideth forever;" and as the

335

most potent among them is successively laid in the dust, a voice from amidst their ruins is heard proclaiming: "One jot or one tittle shall in no wise pass from the law, till all be fulfilled." (Matt. v:18.) "Come, behold the works of the Lord, what desolations he hath made in the earth. Be still and know that I am God." (Psalm xlvi:8,10.) "Come and see the works of God. He is terrible in his doing toward the children of men. He ruleth by his power forever; his eyes behold the nations; let not the rebellious exalt themselves." (Psalm xlvi:5,7.) "Sin is the ruin of nations."

While the revolutions and overthrow of cities and empires, as described by Volney, prove that the prophets by whom they were predicted in such striking detail were divinely inspired, and that "holy men of God spake as they were moved by the Holy Spirit" (2 Pet. i:21), it must also be remembered that these very prophets all bear witness to Jesus Christ, who came into the world to make atonement for sin, and to save his people from the wrath to come. By a succession of inspired men, our attention is directed to the way of salvation which in his unbounded love to a sinful world, combined with his infinite abhorrence of sin, God has condescended to provide for the human race. His own word reveals the way of salvation. "Whosoever believeth in him shall not perish, but have everlasting life." (John iii:16.) "Search the Scriptures," said Jesus himself to the Jews, "for in them ye think ye have

eternal life; and they are they which testify of me."
(John v :39.) Whosoever, therefore, either attempts
to adulterate or wilfully to misconstrue the Scriptures for the purpose of supporting error and superstition, or to withhold it from the people, and give
them in its stead dogmas of mere human invention,
is guilty of enormous sin. What plainer proof, indeed, can be given of the weakness of a cause, than
the attempt to hinder men from examining for themselves whether it is consistent with that divine will,
which ought to be the foundation of all faith and of
every institution of religion?

If we possessed no written revelation of the will
of God, we must of necessity seek some other means
of discovering the way in which we might please him
and secure the salvation of our souls. But we are
not left to such a difficulty. God has given us the
Bible, that infallible testimony which is thus described by the Psalmist: "The law of the Lord is
perfect, converting the soul; the testimony of the
Lord is sure, making wise the simple. The statutes
of the Lord are right, rejoicing the heart; the commandment of the Lord is pure, enlightening the
eyes." (Psalm xix :8,9.) The testimony of which
Paul speaks, when he says: "All Scripture is given
by inspiration of God, and is profitable for doctrine,
for reproof, for correction, for instruction in
righteousness." The endeavor, therefore, either to
dissuade or to prevent men from reading the Scriptures, must be, in the sight of God, an offense of equal

magnitude with any of those which have brought desolation upon the finest countries on the face of the earth. Nor are they much less criminal who, for, the sake of upholding certain peculiar doctrines and ceremonies, which, in the minds of some, are identical with Christianity itself, refuse to bring them to the test of Scripture, and will not submit to its supreme authority. By such means as these, irreligion is encouraged and sanctioned, and immortal spirits are driven to perdition. It is, however, an awful truth that the blood of these lost souls will be required at the hands of those who, having taken from them the key of knowledge, have closed against them that kingdom of heaven which Jesus Christ has, by his own death, opened to all believers.

Reader, do you wish to believe what is true? Are you willing to be convinced that the word of God is of divine origin, and therefore can not fail? Take the Scriptures then; they are worthy of your perusal, and the very design of their existence is, that they may be read by every man. Get for yourself this precious book, and read it with all the attention of which you are capable. Let no man forbid what God has commanded. Let no man, be he whom he may, prevent you from acquiring the knowledge contained in the word of God. You have seen that according to the testimony of an infidel, by facts attested by himself, the very facts by which he sought to overturn the Christian faith, that the judgments of God are proved to be true, and that the same word of truth which contains the prophecies of these remarkable facts teaches also the way of salvation. Take care, then, that while you "believe the truth," you have no "pleasure in unrighteousness" (I Thess. ii:12); for as no nation can escape the just judgments of God, so neither shall any individual; and there is no other way of deliverance from the dominion and consequences of sin, but through the merits of the Lord and Saviour Jesus Christ, the only Mediator and Intercessor between God and man.

THE WORLD'S WONDERFUL BOOK

By W. J. RUSSELL

Text: "Thy testimonies are wonderful."—Psa. 119:129.

THE Bible, the Book of God, is, without any exception, the most remarkable book in existence. It is the "beau ideal of all subjects that ever engaged the powers of burning eloquence or inspired poetic fire." Carlyle well knew the sublime thoughts as well as the value of this great book, when he said: "I call the Bible apart from all theories about it, one of the grandest things ever written with pen. A noble book! All man's book!" This is true. It is unlike all other books. There is something more than human attached to this divine volume. There is a divinity in it, which makes it among books what the diamond is among stones—the most sublime and the brightest; and the most apt to scatter light and make impressions upon the human mind. While secular books have grown old and become obsolete, the teachings of the Bible are just as new and the thoughts contained in it are just as sublime as they were when they fell from the lips of Christ and the inspired writers. What care we today for the work of mythology written in ancient times? There is no room for these morning mists in the bright noonday of this intelligent age of the world. The teachings of Sappho, and the pathos of Simonides are no longer sought after. But the Bible is a book for all ages. And never was there a time when its sacred pages were perused with so much candor as they are today. While the productions of the moralists and philosophers of Greece and Rome are laid away on the shelves—kept simply as monuments of genius or chapters of intellectual history—the Bible occupies a prominent place in all of our social and religious gatherings and is recognized as the one great authoritative book of the present and all future time. We would not think of going to the works of Aristotle to solve the question: "Wherewithal shall a young man cleanse his way?" We would not think of going to the works of Plato to get a solution to the problem, "If a man die shall he live again?" or to the works of Cato to ascertain the relations and dependencies between the celestial world and this. You may look through all the Greek and Roman classics and you will find nothing but dead relics of antiquity which fail to remove the burden of sin from the human soul and lift the veil and point out the glories of that eternal home which lies beyond the shadows of this earthly existence. It is only when we turn to the Bible, the great text-book, that we find an answer to these questions. This book is the guide for all men and for all time, for the twentieth century no less than the first, for the world has not outgrown it, and never will outgrow it while the ages roll.

I wish now to call your attention to some features of the Bible which make it, pre-eminently, a wonderful book.

1. *It is wonderful in its origin. It is a revelation from God to man.*—The term "revelation," from the Latin word *revelo*, signifies that which is revealed, disclosed, or made known. In a religious sense it is used to denote a supernatural communication of such things as man had not before known, and which he could not discover by natural means. Some of these are: (1) Man's origin; (2) the true character of God; (3) the true relation which should exist between man and God; (4) how man can be saved from sin; (5) the immortality of the soul and the future life. These truths which at first were wholly hidden, or obscurely seen, like a statue before it is unveiled, have been made known, and we call them a divine revelation. It is believed that the living God has made himself known to living men. Miracles attended the utterances of His voice. The infinite is above the finite, and it is possible for God to work by laws above and beyond our comprehension; and men but show their folly when they attempt to set bounds and limits to the Infinite One. All faith in a divine revelation must imply a previous conviction that "there is a God in heaven who revealeth secrets," an Unseen Lawgiver who is capable of making known His will to mankind.

It is asked, "Can we put implicit faith in the Holy Scriptures as a divine revelation?" This is the crucial question of the theological thinking of the hour. If there is no certainty here, there is doubt everywhere. The Bible at this point is now fiercely attacked. Destructive criticism is doing its work, but God will overrule all attacks made upon His word, for its fuller confirmation. The Bible contains God's revelation to man. If this is not true, then there is no divine communication of truth from God to man. If God has not spoken here, then no man has ever heard His voice. If He has not here made known His will, then we know not what His mind concerning us may be; we know not who or what we are, whence we came, why we are here, whither we are going; existence is an enigma, life a mystery, and death a leap into darkness. No one at all conversant with the Bible will for a moment allow any other book to come into competition with it. The Greek word *Biblion,* from which the word Bible comes, signifies book, and used to denote that the sacred volume is "the book" as being superior in excellence to all other books. It is the book of God containing the instruction and counsel of the Heavenly Father to his children on earth.

In the days of Christ and his apostles the Jewish Scriptures were known as the Sacred Scriptures, and were quoted and endorsed by them as such. Jesus says: "Think not that I came to destroy the law or the prophets: I came not to destroy, but to fulfill.

For verily I say unto you, till heaven and earth pass away, one jot or one tittle shall in no wise pass away from the law, till all things be accomplished.'' (Matt. 5:17,18.) Again he says: ''All things must needs be fulfilled, which are written in the law of Moses, and the prophets, and the psalms, concerning me. Then opened He their mind, that they might understand the Scriptures'' (Luke 24:44,45.) The apostolic endorsement is given in many ways, but only two conspicuous passages will be quoted. Peter says: ''Knowing this first, that no prophecy of Scripture is of private interpretation. For no prophecy ever came by the will of man: but men spake from God, being moved by the Holy Spirit.'' (II. Pet. 1:20,21.) Paul says: ''Every Scripture inspired of God is also profitable for teaching, for reproof, for correction, for instruction which is in righteousness: that the man of God may be complete, furnished completely unto every good work.'' (II. Tim. 3:16,17.)

That the Old Testament was inspired is attested by the high moral tone throughout. Those who criticise it on the ground that its morality seems low from a Christian standpoint, should remember that its ethical principles and the actual morality of the people are two different things. The Old Testament was beyond the attainment of any actual character of those ages for which it was designed. The best Old Testament saints but partially realized the ideals that were set before them constantly in their law and in the preaching of their prophets. A certain writer has said: "If the moral pitch of the Old Testament were on the same key with the character of the age in which it originated, the book would not be exceptional; but when the tendency of the age was downward, and the thoughts of men gross, and the trend of nations was toward corruption and violence, nothing less than the guidance of a holy and just God could have directed the composition of such a volume as the Old Testament."

Inspiration is also seen in the exalted conception of God found in these writings. Only a slight familiarity with the ideas of deity prevalent among the nations surrounding the Jews, and the base submission with which the Jews themselves yielded to the religious influence exerted upon them by other people, is sufficient to demonstrate the superhuman origin of the divine character portrayed in this volume. "The just and righteous laws, the pure and harmless worship, the wise restraints placed upon the excesses of corrupt human nature, the introduction and exemplification of such vital principles in the process of ennobling humanity as repentance, obedience, mercy, and benevolence, all these prove that a divine character was being revealed to the Jews which surpassed their own power of invention. It was the peculiar office of those writings contained in the Old Testament to set forth this divine character. If the character be superhuman, the writings which first present that can not be wholly of man."

We may still further trace the divine hand in the Old Testament by the unity of its purpose. The student of the history of the Jews and influence exerted by the sacred writers and teachers upon their people, easily discerns one purpose pursued throughout all the works of their instructors. That purpose is, to bring man nearer to God and his inestimable blessings. That one writer should have followed a single purpose throughout one book, or even all his works, is not to be regarded as remarkable; but that many men, living in ages distinct from each other, under circumstances wholly different, should have pursued one principal object, and that object contrary to the tendencies of their times, is not only extraordinary, but is indicative of supernatural direction. To appreciate this strong argument for the divine origin of the Bible, try this test in a supposed case: Imagine another book, compiled by as many writers, scattered over as many centuries! Herodotus furnishes an historical statement of the origin of all things; a century later Aristotle adds a book on moral philosophy; two centuries pass and Cicero writes a valuable treatise on law and government; another hundred years elapse and Virgil's pen gives to the world a sublime poem on ethics; in the next century Plutarch supplies some biographical sketches; two hundred years after, Origen adds essays on religious creeds and conduct; a century and a half later, Augustine writes a treatise on theology, and Chrysostom a book of sermons; then seven centuries pass away and Abelard completes the compilation by a splendid series of essays on rhetoric and scholastic philosophy. And between these extremes, which, like the Bible, span fifteen centuries, let us imagine all along from Herodotus to Abelard thirty or forty other contributors whose works enter into the final result, men of different nations, periods, habits, languages, and education; under the best conditions, how much moral unity could be expected, even if each successive contributor had read all that preceded his own writings?

Have you heard Sousa's grand orchestra? You have noticed how that as the baton rises and falls in the hand of the master musician, from violin to bass viol, cornet and flute, trombone and trumpet, flageolet and clarinet, bugle and French horn, cymbals and drum, there comes one grand harmony! You are convinced at once that there is one master mind which controls all the instrumental performers. "But God makes his oratorio to play for more than a thousand years, and where one musician becomes silent another takes up the strain, and yet it is all one grand symphony—the key is never lost and never changes, except by those exquisite modulations that show the composer; and when the last strain dies away you see that all these glorious movements and melodies have been variations of one grand theme! Did each musician compose as he played, or was there one composer back of the many players? "One supreme and regulating mind" in this Oratorio of the Ages? If God was the master musician, planning the whole and arranging the parts, appointing player to succeed player, and one strain to modulate or melt into another, then we can understand how Moses' grand anthem of creation glides into Isaiah's oratorio of the Messiah, by and by sinks into Jeremiah's plaintive wail, swells into Ezekiel's awful chorus, changes into Daniel's rapturous lyric, and after the quartette of the Evangelists, closes with John's full choir of saints and angels!''

The New Testament was quite generally accepted by the Apostolic Church as of divine authority. Before the close of the second century there was an essential agreement to the fact that the New Testament Scriptures, as we have them today, were clothed with the authority of heaven, and were written, according to the promise of Christ, by inspired men. In confirmation of this we have the testimony of Christ and his apostles. Christ did not himself organize his church, but gave to his apostles all authority for this purpose. In terms the most complete and unqualified he confers upon them the power to speak and act in his name, and to be his witnesses, to organize, legislate, and even forgive sins, and that, too, because of the aid of the Holy Spirit and his own perpetual presence. As correlated with these promises and their fulfillment, the apostles constantly claim and assert this divine authority and guidance. John declares that the Apocalypse was a communication ''in the Spirit.'' Peter, in his first

348

epistle, asserts that the things testified beforehand by the Spirit of Christ in the prophets "have been announced through them that preached the gospel by the Holy Spirit sent forth from heaven." Paul declares that the gospel which he preached was not after man, nor received from men, but made known by the revelation of Jesus Christ. And again, in the First Corinthian epistle, referring directly to his writing, and vouching for all the apostles, he said: "Which things also we speak, not in words which man's wisdom teacheth, but which the Spirit teacheth; combining spiritual things with spiritual words." (I. Cor. 2:13.) It is evident from these Scriptures that inspiration is claimed on the part of the sacred writers of the New Testament and if we accept them as honest witnesses, we must admit that they spake as they were moved by the Holy Spirit.

No one can intelligently affirm that the apostles were not competent witnesses, neither will anyone dare say that they were dishonest or fanatical. Their lives were singularly transparent and beautifully consecrated. The sobriety and naturalness of their narratives are as apparent as their simplicity and honesty. In matter, effect, and motive the New Testament record is beyond all comparison superior to all other literature of its own day or any other time. In many respects, in its thought and expression it is totally opposed to the entire spirit of the age in which it was written, and to the opinions of the people to whom it was primarily given. "The development of literature in different countries," says MacArthur, "is recognized among all literary students; but the New Testament, in its pure thought, heavenly atmosphere, and divine influence, stands apart from all the law of movement, of progress, and of attainment among uninspired writers of every century and country. The volume possesses a unity, a singleness of purpose, and an elevation of tone which stamp it as a work alike of human genius and of divine inspiration. Its calmness, comprehension, reticence, and majesty differentiate it from all the literature of the world." Well may Van Oosterzee say: "He who will acknowledge in Scripture nothing higher than a purely human character comes into collision not only with our Lord's word and that of his witnesses, but also with the Christian consciousness of all ages. It is impossible to account for these exalted qualities on any other hypothesis than that the writers of this uncommon volume were under the special influence of God in thought and speech."

II. *The Bible is a Wonderful Book* on account of its antiquity. "For many centuries," says Dr. A. H. Sayce, "it was possible to describe the Pentateuch as the oldest book in the world. There was nothing with which it would be compared; it was the last relic that had survived to us out of the wreckage of the oriental past. But all this has been changed by the spade of the excavator and the patient labor of the decipherer of the buried records of antiquity. The civilizations which have been called back to life were intimately bound up with the art of writing. We have learned that long before the days of Moses, or even of Abraham, there were books and libraries, readers and writers; that schools existed in which all the arts and sciences of the day were taught, and that even a postal service had been organized from one end of Western Asia to the other. The world into which the Hebrew patriarchs were born, and of which the Book of Genesis tells us, was permeated with a literary culture, whose roots went back to an antiquity of which, but a short time ago, we could not have dreamed. There were books in Egypt and Babylonia long before the Pentateuch was written; the Mosaic age was, in fact, an age of widely-extended literary activity, and the Pentateuch was one of the latest fruits of long centuries of literary growth.''

"And yet there is a sense," says Dr. Sayce, "in which we may still say that the Pentateuch is the oldest book in the world. The books of Egypt and Babylonia have, for the most part, come down to us in a torn and fragmentary condition. And of those which are complete, there is none which can compete, either in length or unity of plan, with either the Book of Genesis or the Pentateuch as a whole. For the books of Moses have been written in accordance with a definite plan which has been worked out consistently from their beginning to their end. It is just this plan that gives them their literary form and stamps them as the first known literary example of a literary conception of history."

These early books of the Bible furnish us with the only authentic history we have of the world before the flood. They take us back to the very dawn of human life and to the beginning of all the great movements which have culminated in the civilizations of all the races of men. Moses has given us an account of the creation, brief, vivid, comprehensive, and majestic. The book of Genesis is one of the oldest trustworthy books in the world, containing about all we know of the race for more than two thousand years. Tatian, one of the Greek fathers, tells us that "Though Homer was before all poets, philosophers, and historians, and was the most ancient of all profane writers, yet Moses was more ancient than Homer himself."

Tertullian of Carthage was born about the year 160. He was bred to the Roman law, and gave himself to political and forensic labors until he reached his maturity. He then renounced paganism, embraced Christianity, abandoned his profession, and became a Presbyter. He gave his great learning, vigorous mind, and original genius to the defense and exposition of Christianity. In speaking of the antiquity of the Bible he says: "The pagans themselves have not denied that the books of Moses were extant many ages before the states and cities of

Greece; before their temples and gods; and also before the beginning of Greek letters.''

The authorship of the book of Job has been assigned to Moses by Jewish tradition as represented in the Talmud, and by such comparatively recent writers as Ebrard (1858) and Rawlinson (1891). The style has a ''grand character,'' which has been recognized by almost all critics. But if it was not written as early as some claim, and we take the date —the time of Solomon—assigned by the consensus of modern scholarship, it must be admitted that the events, the scenes, the drapery, the facts it records, and the whole tone of the book, are Patriarchal. Scientific men now turn to its allusions as the only recorded evidence we have of the state of the arts and sciences four thousand years ago. A modern writer has collated from its passages illustrative of the then existing state of knowledge respecting astronomy, geography, cosmology, precious stones, writing, medicine, music, hunting, zoology, and the military art. Surely such a book, that gives to us the state of these sciences and arts thirty or forty centuries back, ought to be hailed as a treasure worthy of a nation's purchase.

III. *The Bible is a Wonderful Book* because of its safe transmission to us from the earliest times, without being corrupted and mutilated. This fact rests on the most satisfactory evidence. The original manuscripts of the Old Testament were preserved with the utmost care by the Jews, who were famed for their faithful guardianship of the Sacred Books. This fact is confirmed by the eminent William Greenfield, who tells us that the Jews were remarkable in this respect. They not only devoted much time in copying their sacred books, but most carefully compared them with the originals, and went so far as to even number the words and letters. "That the Jews have neither mutilated nor corrupted these writings," says Greenfield, "is fully proved by the silence of the prophets as well as of Christ and his apostles, who, though they bring many heavy charges against them, never once accuse them of corrupting one of their sacred writings; and also by the agreement in every essential point, of all the versions and manuscripts amounting to nearly 1,150, which are now extant, and which furnish a clear proof of their uncorrupted preservation."

The New Testament portion of the Bible was, of course, written after Christ's coming, and within the first century. The preservation of this in its essential purity is also established by many excellent proofs, and especially by the discovery of three ancient manuscripts, one now in the British museum, bearing indubitable evidence of having been written in the fifth century; another, now in the Vatican at Rome, written in the fourth century; and the third, found at a convent on Mt. Sinai, and now at St. Petersburg, also written in the fourth century. These documents have been providentially preserved through all the dangers of fourteen or fifteen centuries, and are now delivered safe in our hands, wonderful witnesses of the general and essential accuracy of our common English Bibles.

The last book of the Bible was written nearly 1,300 years before the invention of printing. And when you think how those many centuries horde after horde of heathen barbarians swept like destroying blight over the lands where the Scriptures had a home; when you think of all the great libraries of the world, those for example at Alexandria and Constantinople, and Athens and Rome, were destroyed by fire; when you think of two systematic attempts made by the kings to exterminate the Scriptures by burning every copy in existence, the one by Antiochus Epiphanes, after the canon of the Old Testament was complete, and the other by Diocletian, emperor of Rome, after the entire Scriptures of the Old Testament and New were in the hands of the few Christians, when you think of these and many other dangers you see that it is a wonderful thing that the Bible has come to us in its integrity. How true are the words: "The grass withereth, the flower fadeth, but the word of our God shall stand forever."

Nations have been born and have passed away since the Bible was written. New customs have come into existence and formed parts of the government of the world. Manners have changed, dynasties have crumbled, while the Bible alone, in spirit, has remained the same, fresh, true, and indestructible as its Author. Linguists have assailed its language—

355

tested, tried, analyzed and weighed in the balance, and yet not an iota of its truth has grown weaker, nor one ray of its light dimmer. Age has failed to affect its power. It has flourished, while its adversaries have been entombed one after another, and it never bade so fair as at present to be the Book of Truth, and the Most High has ever been its conservator and defense.

> "The proudest works of Genius shall decay,
> And Reason's brightest lustre fade away;
> The Sophist's art, the poet's boldest flight,
> Shall sink in darkness, and conclude in night,
> But Faith triumphant over Time shall stand,
> Shall grasp the Sacred Volume in her hand,
> Back to its source the heavenly gift convey,
> Then in a flood of Glory melt away."

IV. *The Bible Is a Wonderful Book* because of its literary characteristics. It contains the highest literature of the world. It appeals to the aesthetic and intellectual as well as moral and spiritual faculties. In the words of Prof. Huxley, "it is written in the noblest and purest English, and abounds in exquisite beauties of literary form." John Ruskin considered the Bible "the grandest group of writings extant in the rational world." In the words of Theodore Parker: "This collection of books has taken such a hold as has no other. The literature of Greece, which goes up like incense from that land of temples and heroic deeds, has not half the influence of this book from a nation alike despised in ancient and modern

356

times. The sun never sets on its gleaming page. It goes equally to the cottage of the plain man and the palace of the king. It is woven into the literature of the scholar, and it colors the talk of the street.'' Hall Caine, the eminent novelist, says: ''There is no book in the world like it, and the finest novels ever written fall far short in interest of any one of the stories it tells. Whatever strong situations I have in my books are not my creation, but are taken from the Bible.'' Sir William Jones sums it all up in the following beautiful eulogy: ''The Scriptures contain, independently of a divine origin, more true sublimity, more exquisite beauty, purer morality, more important history, and finer strains both of poetry and eloquence, than could be collected, within the same compass, from all other books that were ever composed in any age or in any idiom.''

All good books are only the Bible in dilution. Its influence is seen in all other literature, and shows itself, at length, in golden veins and precious gems of thought. The most brilliant passages of Macaulay's writings are rounded with Scripture quotations. Addison's spectator is watered with the river of life. Pope saturated his writings with quotations from Isaiah and his most successful work was the Messiah. It is also easy to see that Cowper's ''Task'' drew much of its imagery from the same noble prophet; that the ''Thanatopsis'' of Bryant could never have been written but for exalted and inspired pages in Job, and that Wordsworth's ''Ode

357

on Immortality" is but the echo of glowing and glorious thoughts expressed by the Apostle Paul in his sublime and logical discussion of the doctrine of the resurrection in First Corinthians, the fifteenth chapter. Even a cursory student of Shakespeare must see that his conception of woman, of a Desdemona, and of an Ophelia, would have been impossible had not his mind been prompted by a Bible and a Christian ideal. Without the Bible, Hayden would have never chanted his "Creation," and old blind Milton's eyes would never have been illuminated to see the battle of the angels. Without the Bible, Klopstock's "Messiah" could never have been written, Raphael's master-pieces would be lost in the world, and Keats and Keble and Heber and myriads of other humble servants of Christian song would have been unknown. The Bible is the ring that unites earth with heaven as the long, mild twilight like a silver clasp unites today with yesterday. And if you would destroy this grand old volume and its influence, you must destroy the largest and most valuable portion of the literature of the world. You must tear out the leaves that have any Bible in them from every book—everything that has been quoted, suggested, derived directly or indirectly from the Bible—every allusion to it in history; every metaphor drawn from it in poetry; every quotation and thought in romance, every idea incorporated in philosophy; every passage written to defend or illustrate it in science; every principle taken from it in

358

law; every sentence that indicates any knowledge of the Bible must be cut out.

The Bible is full of the choicest gems of thought, combining a variety and richness and rareness to be found in no other book. Would you have logic? Then turn to Paul's letter to the Ephesians or his discourse on Mars Hill, recorded in Acts of Apostles. Would you be moved by the sublime? Where shall we find it if not in Job, Isaiah, the Psalms and Revelation? Would you take time to meditate upon wise sayings or maxims? Where are these to be found, so full of pith and pungency, so terse, so sharp, so vigorous as in the Proverbs of Solomon? For a story of filial affection and devotion I refer you to the book of Ruth—that book which Voltaire said was beyond anything found in Homer or in any other classic writers. Is the heart sad? Does it need tuning? Then read the sweet song of the Hebrew bard:

"Jehovah is my shepherd;
  I shall not want.
  He maketh me to lie down in green pastures;
  He leadeth me beside still waters.
  He restoreth my soul; He guideth me in the paths
      of righteousness for his name's sake. Yea,
      though I walk through the valley of the
      shadow of death,
  I will fear no evil; for thou art with me;
  Thy rod and thy staff, they comfort me.
  Thou preparest a table before me in the presence
      of mine enemies;

359

Thou hast anointed my head with oil;
My cup runneth over:
Surely goodness and loving-kindness shall follow
    me all the days of my life,
And I shall dwell in the house of Jehovah for-
    ever.''

And what beauty has been given to true and
tender fidelity in those words of Ruth, ''Entreat me
not to leave thee, and to return from following after
thee; for whither thou goest, I will go; and where
thou lodgest, I will lodge; thy people shall be my
people, and thy God my God: where thou diest will
I die, and there will I be buried; Jehovah do so to
me, and more also, if aught but death part thee and
me.'' Paul's account of ''love'' in his letter to the
Corinthians—how it glows and glistens, radiant and
beautiful, the one excelling brilliant amidst a remarkable cluster of brilliants. When the gem flashes
out in the light it outshines all the rest: ''Love suf-
fereth long, and is kind; love envieth not; love
vaunteth not itself, is not puffed up, doth not behave
itself unseemly, seeketh not its own, is not provoked,
taketh not account of evil; rejoiceth not in unrighteousness, but rejoiceth with the truth; beareth
all things, hopeth all things, endureth all things.
Love never faileth.'' Greece, whose air was redolent
of song, the land of the passions; sages, heroes, poets,
honored in every clime—these all have failed to put

into their speech the soul of love imprisoned here in apostolic word and rustling amidst the leaves of the New Testament.

In the Sermon on the Mount we have the sublimest code of morals ever proclaimed on earth. It is the Magna Charta of Christ's Kingdom. We read: "And Jesus went about in all Galilee, teaching in their synagogues, and preaching the gospel of the kingdom, and healing all manner of disease and all manner of sickness among the people. And the report of him went forth into all Syria: and they brought unto him all that were sick, holden with divers diseases and torments, possessed with demons, and epileptic, and palsied; and he healed them. And there followed him great multitudes from Galilee and Decapolis and Jerusalem and Judea and from beyond the Jordan. And seeing the multitudes, he went up into the mountain: and when he had sat down, his disciples came unto him: and he opened his mouth and taught them, saying:

"Blessed are the poor in spirit: for theirs is the kingdom of heaven. Blessed are they that mourn: for they shall be comforted. Blessed are the meek: for they shall inherit the earth. Blessed are they that hunger and thirst after righteousness: for they shall be filled. Blessed are the merciful: for they shall obtain mercy. Blessed are the pure in heart: for they shall see God. Blessed are the peacemakers: for they shall be called sons of God. Blessed are they that have been persecuted for righteousness' sake: for theirs is the kingdom of heaven. Blessed are ye when men shall reproach you and persecute you, and say all manner of evil against you falsely, for my sake. Rejoice, and be exceeding glad: for great is your reward in heaven: for so persecuted they the prophets that were before you.''

Again: ''No man can serve two masters: for either he will hate the one, and love the other; or else he will hold to one, and despise the other. Ye cannot serve God and mammon. Therefore I say unto you, Be not anxious for your life, what ye shall eat, or what ye shall drink; nor yet for your body, what ye shall put on. Is not the life more than the food, and the body than the raiment? Behold the birds of the heaven, that they sow not, neither do they reap, nor gather into barns; and your heavenly Father feedeth them. Are not ye of much more value than they? And which of you by being anxious can add one cubit unto the measure of his life? And why are ye anxious concerning raiment? Consider the lilies of the field, how they grow; they toil not, neither do they spin: yet I say unto you, that even Solomon in all his glory was not arrayed like one of these. But if God doth so clothe the grass of the field, which today is, and tomorrow is cast into the oven, shall He not much more clothe you, O ye of little faith?''

There is matchless beauty in these words. They are unlike anything that can be found in all the previous literature of the human race. What sympathy with the loveliness of the outer world! The refined intellects of cultured Athens never dreamed of this. There is but one brief description of scenery in all the "Dialogues" of Plato. It is at the beginning of the "Phædrus"; and it sounded so odd to the youth to whom Socrates addressed it as to provoke an expression of amused surprise. It was Christ who first taught us to find in the beauty even of little and unnoticed things a sacrament of goodness, and to read in the flowers a letter of the very autograph of the love toward us of our Father in Heaven. Yet in what few and simple words, in what concrete and homely images, is this instruction—which was to be so prolific hereafter for the happiness of the world—set forth! and how full of far-reaching and perpetual comfort is the loving tenderness of God's Fatherhood here demonstrated for our unending consolation.

The parable of the Prodigal Son forms part of the most beautiful chapter of "the most beautiful book in the world." It may well be called the flower and pearl of parables. It occupies less than a page; it may be read aloud in two minutes. We read: "A certain man had two sons: and the younger of them said to his father, Father, give me the portion of thy substance that falleth to me. And he divided unto them his living. And not many days after, the younger son gathered all together and took his journey into a far country; and there he wasted his substance with riotous living. And when he had spent all, there arose a mighty famine in that country; and he began to be in want. And he went and joined himself to one of the citizens of that country; and he sent him into his fields to feed swine. And he would fain have filled his belly with the husks that the swine did eat: and no man gave unto him. But when he came to himself he said, how many hired servants of my father's have bread enough and to spare, and I perish here with hunger! I will arise and go to my Father, and will say unto him, Father, I have sinned against heaven, and in thy sight: I am no more worthy to be called thy son: make me as one of thy hired servants. And he arose, and came to his father. But while he was yet afar off, his father saw him, and was moved with compassion, and ran, and fell on his neck, and kissed him. And the son said unto him, father, I have sinned against heaven, and in thy sight: I am no more worthy to be called thy son. But the father said to his servants: Bring forth quickly the best robe, and put it on him; and put a ring on his hand, and shoes on his feet: and bring the fatted calf, and kill it, and let us eat, and make merry: for this my son was dead, and is alive again; he was lost, and is found. And they began to be merry.''

Dante and John Bunyan have touched thousands of human souls; but this parable has been precious to millions of every age and every tongue, who never so much as heard of the ''Divina Commedia'' or the ''Pilgrim's Progress.'' It excells all works of fiction in its delineation of character. Mr. Hall Caine says: "I think that I know my Bible as few literary men know it. There is no book in the world like it; and the finest novels ever written fall far short in interest to any one of the stories it tells. Whatever strong situations I have in my books are not of my creation, but are taken from the Bible. "The Deemster" is the story of the "Prodigal Son.""

It is doubtful whether there is any passage in our greatest writers that is sublimer than the adoration of the angels, recorded in the last book of the Bible.

"Worthy is the lamb that hath been slain to receive the power, and riches, and wisdom, and might, and honor, and glory, and blessing.

"Unto him that sitteth on the throne, and unto the lamb, be the blessing, and the honor, and the glory, and the dominion, for ever and ever.

"Great and marvelous are thy works, O Lord God, the Almighty; righteous and true are thy ways, thou King of the ages. Who shall not fear, O Lord, and glorify thy name? For thou only art holy; for all the nations shall come and worship before thee; for thy righteous acts have been made manifest."

And what magic and haunting charm in these words recorded in the last chapter of Revelation:

"And he shewed me a pure river of Water of Life, clear as crystal, proceeding out of the throne of God and of the lamb. In the midst of the street of it, and on either side of the river, was there the

Tree of Life, which bare twelve manner of fruits, and yielded her fruit every month; and the leaves of the tree were for the healing of the nations.''

Not only does the Bible contain these choice gems of thought in poetry and words of eloquence, but it also contains the richest pearls and diamonds of all scientific discoveries. While you are gathering the richest beauties from the fields of botany, enthrone in their midst the Lily of the Valley, and breathe the perfume of the Rose of Sharon. While you are spending your vacation with geologist's hammer do not return without sounding the Rock of Ages and bringing with you ''the pearl of great price'' which is worth more than all earthly treasures. You may continue to search the vast realms of astronomy—to wander among the princes of the upper deep—but I beseech you not to miss the Morning Star or the Sun of Righteousness. Visit the art galleries of the world and stand in wonder and admiration as you gaze upon the works of the artist, but remember here in this great art gallery—the Bible—we have presented to us one picture compared with which the best work of human genius falls out of notice. Such a picture we have in Jesus, our Divine Lord and Saviour. Truly we must confess that the Bible is a wonderful book—that it is born of heaven—a child of the skies. Have you been unconscious of its worth? Has this book of infinite wealth been neglected? Get it at once and commence its study. Pore over its sacred pages until you have mastered

its contents. "No radiant hand will be thrust out of
heaven to do that for you; no aureola will play about
the book when you take it up yourselves; its characters will be but plain ink and type; no fire gleams
will leap from beneath its letters or play over the
printed page, and yet when you touch it you hold
the greatest divine work visible in the universe of
God. Be true to it! and when science has lost its
charm, when music ceases to fascinate and poetry
no longer stirs you, and the sobs of your friends no
longer recall you, this book, having given you the
greatest intellectual riches in this life, will fling its
golden baldric across the black sea of death and form
a hyaline pavement for your redeemed feet up to
your inherited home.''

V. *The Bible is a Wonderful Book* because of its
scientific wealth and accuracy. The Old Testament
Scriptures abound everywhere in scientific allusions.
They treat of biology, ethnology, astronomy, geology,
zoology, meteorology, indeed of every department of
natural science. And we marvel at the accuracy
with which the Scriptures present these various subjects. The history of science has been one of change,
and often in opposition to the Bible; but when a
true basis has been found, it has been discovered that
the Bible, far in advance, had been declaring the
same great truth. Let us notice the following conspicuous illustrations:

1. It took science many ages to reach the conclusion that the present order of things had a

beginning. There were ages of investigation, researches in the realms of physics, arguments in metaphysics, conclusions drawn from the necessities of resistless logic, before science made its declaration that there was a beginning. But the Bible from the first, on its early pages, was asserting the same great fact.

2. Science tells us that creation of matter preceded arrangement. In the beginning all was chaos —void—darkness. But the Bible, in advance of science, asserted that "the earth was waste and void; and darkness was upon the face of the deep."

3. It took science a long time to demonstrate the fact that light existed before the sun. Laplace was the author of the nebular hypothesis. According to that theory, the condensation of gaseous matter was accompanied by intense heat—emitting light. Thus is made known only what Moses declared, long before Laplace, that light existed before the sun.

4. Science has discovered the truth that the strata of the earth were formed by the action of water, and the mountains were once under the ocean. But the Bible long ago declared: "Thou coverest it with the deep as with a vesture; the waters stood above the mountains. At thy rebuke they fled; at the voice of thy thunder they hasted away. The mountains rose, the valleys sank down unto the place which thou hadst founded for them."

5. The wisdom of man for ages held that the world was flat. A long and bitter controversy took

place before the sphericity of the earth was generally accepted as true. Meanwhile, God was saying, century after century, of himself, "It is he that sitteth above the circle of the earth."

6. Science, for thousands of years, has been trying to count the stars. Hipparchus counted one thousand and twenty-two. Ptolemy counted one thousand and twenty-six. Modern appliances, including the space-penetrating telescope and tasimeters, reveal so many stars, that the best authorities tell us that the stars are innumerable to man. But long before there were any telescopes to make it known, it was declared upon the pages of inspiration that the stars were as the sands of the sea, "innumerable."

7. The discovery made by Torricelli, that the air had weight, was received with great incredulity. For ages the air had propelled ships, thrust itself against the bodies of men, and overturned their works. But no man ever dreamed that weight was necessary to give momentum. Galileo, in his day, knew, but did not dare in prison to say, that the reason why a certain pump of that day did not lift water higher than thirty-two feet was because the "weight" of the atmosphere is only fifteen pounds to the square inch. But thousands of years before Torricelli or Galileo, Job had enunciated the fact in this brief sentence: "God maketh a weight for the wind."

8. The fluctuations and variations of the weather have hitherto baffled all attempts at unraveling them.

369

This comes under the science of meteorology. But the Bible clearly stated the fundamentals of this science long ago: "The wind goeth toward the south, and turneth about unto the north; it turneth about continually in its course, and the wind returneth again to its circuits. All the rivers run into the sea, yet, the sea is not full; unto the place whither the rivers go, thither they go again."

It is Herschel who says: "All human discoveries seem to be made only for the purpose of confirming more strongly the truths that come from on high, and are contained in the sacred writings." The book of Nature and the written Revelation, teach but one set of truths. How was it possible that the writers of the earlier Scriptures described physical phenomena with such wonderful sublimity and penetrative truth? There is but one explanation. He that planned and made this vast universe inspired the Bible. It is a reliable book. In a declaration of eight hundred scientists of Great Britain, signed by such men as Thomas Bell, Adam Sedgwick and Sir David Brewster, these words are found: "We conceive that it is impossible for the Word of God, as written in the book of nature, and God's Word written in Holy Scriptures, to contradict one another." Matthew Dontaine Maury, in his physical Geography of the Sea, says: "I have always found in my scientific studies, that, when I could get the Bible to say anything on the subject it afforded me a firm platform to stand upon, and a round in the ladder by which I could safely ascend.''

VI. *The Bible is a Wonderful Book* because of its historical accuracy. This has been repeatedly confirmed by modern research. That minor errors have been inserted by copyists and interpolators is not denied; but the very fact that the mistakes of the Book are chiefly confined to that class, is the strongest argument in favor of its credibility. No other work of antiquity will stand the test to which it has been exposed. The writings of the Old Testament Scriptures touch the land and the people on every side, in the midst of which the writers lived. The story is told of a weaver in England, who had finished a beautiful piece of cloth and had taken it from the dye and stretched it upon the tenter hooks to dry. It was stolen and supposed to be lost. At last the weaver heard of a sale of valuable cloth in a remote part of the kingdom, and resolved to attend. He found there a piece of cloth he felt sure was the one he had lost. But how could he prove it? At last he thought of the holes in the selvedge and the tenter hooks on which they had hung. The cloth was taken to the hooks, and lo! each was found to fit in a corresponding hole. No one doubted the weaver's claim. So the hills and mountains, the valleys and the plains, the rivers and the seas, as well as the people who once lived among those scenes, are God's immovable and imperishable witnesses for the truthfulness of His word.

371

All other chronicles—those of Cæsar, Herodotus, and Thucydides—are but the records of an episode or period of events, but the Bible is the one universal history. It carries us back through the nations, past the earliest communities, beyond the primitive chaos, to the remotest origin of things. The earliest history of the human race, as recorded in the book of Genesis, perfectly harmonizes with modern historical research. Canon Rawlinson, the great orientalist, and the celebrated geographer, Dr. Carl Ritter, declare that of all the writings of antiquity none are receiving such confirmation from the modern researches in geography and ethnography as the tenth chapter of Genesis. The very names of the earliest peoples and countries are monumental testimony to the truth of the chapter. Here we have the genealogy of the sons of Noah. At a glance it is seen that these families expanded into nations and gave their names to the countries which they inhabited. These names and this distribution of the nations in the ancient world are confirmed by all we know from other sources. The ethnic affinities given here are in harmony with the testimony of modern science. All the various races of men are classified under three heads —the sons of Japheth, the sons of Ham, and the sons of Shem. Modern ethnological science, after a careful analysis of race peculiarities, language, and history, has agreed on a triple division of mankind, and speaks of all races as either Semitic, Aryan, or Turanian. There is truth in this chapter also concerning what were the earliest civilizations. The valleys of the Euphrates and the Nile were the homes of the most advanced nations. And all the lines of history centre back upon these lands, and there we find the most ancient ruins. Every discovery of the archaeologist among these ruins and the monuments of the past throws light upon the Bible narrative, and confirms the truth of God's Book.

The bondage of Israel in Egypt, the Exodus, and the conquest of Canaan are strongly confirmed by profane historians. The route of the Israelites from Egypt to Sinai, as given in the Bible and by modern explorers, is in perfect harmony. Nearly all of the camping places of the Israelites have been identified —thus showing that the Bible history is genuine and not mythical. The history of the Israelites from their settlement in Canaan to the close of the Old Testament history, is nowhere contradicted by profane historians, but it is strongly confirmed in many points. The Jewish people were so situated that they came in contact with all the great historic nations of antiquity, so that the great facts of their history are being continually illustrated by the ethnologist and archæologist. This line of history is very long—forty centuries—with many turns and windings in and out. How ample the opportunity to detect errors. But no errors have been discovered; not a single landmark has been changed. There stand the mountains outlining the progress of the nations, and there lie the historic continents, teeming with the art, science, laws and customs of ancient times. The Bible is, indeed, a wonderful book; venerable as the high antiquity whence it comes; and marvelous in its vitality which keeps it fresh and vigorous in the midst of perished literature and mouldering superstitions.

VII. *The Bible is a Wonderful Book* because it is incomparable as a book of ethics. No height of intellectual culture can purify the heart and make it what it ought to be—an altar of sweet incense to the Eternal One. It remains for the Bible alone to purify and ennoble man's nature. Christ presents the first and highest example of the purest teaching and holiest life in perfect harmony. His advent was a new moral creation. The extant and depth of His influence upon all future ages is beyond calculation. "The simple record of His three short years of active life," says Mr. Lecky in his History of European Morals, "has done more to regenerate and soften mankind than all the disquisitions of philosophers and all the exhortations of moralists."

Let us now examine some of the ethical teachings of the Bible. We can only glance at a few. So lavishly are the great truths of God scattered over these sublime pages, that the study of the most learned has hardly touched the theme. Every age throws a brighter light over this volume; and time's ages, and earth's greatest scholars, will be exhausted before it will be known in all its length and breadth and fulness. Those who love its truths, never get

wearied in its study. Books written by the most
gifted of earth's geniuses, after two or three read-
ings fatigue us; and we push them away, and sigh
for something new. God's Book, like Himself, is
inexhaustible; the deeper we go the brighter and
richer the ore; the higher we soar into the heavens
the more brilliant becomes the burning blazonry of
God. Let us commence our study:

1. The duties man owes himself are clearly defined and forcibly elaborated. The decalogue forms
the ethic basis of the religion of the Old Testament,
and requires the suppression of inordinate ambition
and lust for honor or power; also, the extinction of
covetousness or the desire to amass wealth from
selfish motives. In the 15th Psalm David asks,
"Jehovah, who shall sojourn in thy tabernacle?
Who shall dwell in thy holy hill?" His answer is
"He that walketh uprightly, and worketh righteousness, and speaketh truth in his heart." From the
New Testament we have many passages of Scripture,
such as these: "Know ye not that your body is a
temple of the Holy Spirit?" "Keep thyself pure."
"I beseech you therefore, brethren, by the mercies
of God, to present your bodies a living sacrifice, holy,
acceptable to God, which is your spiritual service."
A man upon whose heart these Scriptures are en-
graven will be likely to make the most of his body
without allowing it ever to be uppermost. They
demand the denial of every vice and the practice of
every virtue. They require humility, temperance,

and purity of heart and life, and declare that without holiness no man shall see the Lord.

2. The duties man owes to others are, also, clearly set forth. In the decalogue we read, "Thou shalt not kill. Neither shalt thou commit adultery. Neither shalt thou steal. Neither shalt thou bear false witness against thy neighbor." Another precept in the Bible is, "Thou shalt love thy neighbor as thyself." The question, "Who is my neighbor?" is answered by our Saviour in the parable of the good Samaritan. He there teaches us that our neighbor is *man* as *man*. And in the Golden Rule he says, "All things therefore whatsoever ye would that men should do unto you, even so do ye also unto them." The precept teaches us to estimate the rights of others by the consciousness of individual right in our bosoms. The Apostle Paul gives us these beautiful words: "Let love be without hypocrisy. Abhor that which is evil; cleave to that which is good. In love of the brethren be tenderly affectioned one to another; in honor preferring one another; communicating to the necessities of the saints; given to hospitality." And what can be more beautiful than the words of the apostle when he speaks of the mutual affection between husband and wife: "Wives, be in subjection unto your own husbands, as unto the Lord. For the husband is the head of the wife, as Christ also is the head of the Church, being himself the Saviour of the body. Husbands, love your wives, even as Christ also loved the Church, and gave him-

self up for it." Parents are exhorted to "train up a child in the way he should go." Paul says, "Fathers, provoke not your children, that they be not discouraged." The relation of children to parents is just as explicit. We read, "Honor thy father and thy mother." Again, "Children, obey your parents in the Lord: for this is right." These are only a few of the passages that might be quoted setting forth the duties that man owes to others.

3. The duties man owes to God are specifically enjoined. We read, "Thou shalt love Jehovah thy God with all thy heart, and with all thy soul, and with all thy might." The Psalmist says: "Make a joyful noise unto Jehovah, all ye lands. Serve Jehovah with gladness: come before his presence with singing, Know ye that Jehovah is God: it is He that hath made us, and we are His; we are His people, and the sheep of His pasture. Enter into His gates with thanksgiving, and into His courts with praise: give thanks unto Him, and bless His name."

The degree of enlightenment in the world is in exact ratio with the prevalence of these ethical principles. Are England, Scotland, the United States, and Germany in the lead? it is there you will find an open Bible and an efficient Christian ministry who are holding up before the people, the Christ in all of His glory and excellence of character. Are Italy, Spain, Austria, and the states of South America scarcely half enlightened? there the Bible is kept from the people, and the currents of religious

377

thought are obstructed and corrupt. Are large portions of the earth in the darkness and crime of paganism? There as yet, the Bible has not been opened and Christ has not been made known to the people. The religion of Jesus Christ is the only religion that can lead our race to the highest forms of civilization. "The Bible," says William Magill, "stands forth in its integrity, the palladium of moral freedom, the only true spring of individual and rational excellence, the conservatory of all the roots and fruits of divine virtue, which alone has power to cleanse the earth of Paganism, and restore man to himself and to God by the science of right and truth."

VIII. *The Bible is a Wonderful Book* because it reveals God's plan of human redemption. Sin and guilt are recognized as universal. In the Roman letter it is asserted that all have sinned, Jew and Gentile. In response to this every man is compelled to say, "It is true; I have sinned." Not only so, but there is in human nature the conviction that sin causes suffering, and will continue to do so till it is removed. Hence the whole world is interested in knowing how sin can be blotted out. And man also wants the way of obtaining this pardon to be made so plain that he will know certainly that he is at peace with God. He longs for definiteness and not uncertainty in this most important matter.

The Bible is the book, and the only book, that presents the way of escape, or the antidote for sin.

378

"For God so loved the world, that He gave His only begotten Son, that whosoever believeth on Him should not perish, but have eternal life." In the gospel of divine love we have the remedy for sin. This most blessed book brings to us the manna for a hungry world. Milton grandly describes the Archangel Uriel as descending to earth in a sunbeam. The revelation of the Bible is a beam on which the Father of light descends unto men to dwell with them. Sweeter than the dews of six thousand summers is the living bread which the Bible brings to a perishing world. What though it rained gold and pearls, and king's crowns on our guilty race, it were better to give them the Bible. Salvation! Behold the Lamb of God! Look unto Christ, who, in the Bread of Life. Gaze upon Him, as he hangs upon the cross, bleeding, suffering, dying for you. Love Him, trust Him, accept Him, enter into sympathy with His great heart of love, and know that it is God's heart. He is ready, willing, waiting to be gracious to you and to save you from your sins. A wonderful Saviour! Words cannot estimate the salvation he offers. "Weigh it against all created things. Measure it by eternity. Lay the plummet of infinity to its blessings. Appeal to Him who weighs the mountains in scales and the hills in a balance to teach you its worth. Climb to the throne of the Eternal, where the Universe collects her glories to decorate the palace of our King, and thence survey

all things that are made. Salvation excels all you
know and see; for it makes God himself your everlasting portion.''

The following illustration has been repeated
many times but it will never wear threadbare. A
stranger was seen one day planting a flower over a
grave in the cemetery at Nashville, Tenn. A gentleman passing by asked him, ''Is your son buried
there?'' ''No.'' ''A brother?'' ''No.'' ''A rela-
tive?'' ''No.'' After a moment's pause, the
stranger said, ''I will tell thee. When the war broke
out, I lived in Illinois. I had a large family de-
pendent upon my daily labor for support. I was
drafted. Having no means to pay for a substitute,
I prepared to go to the war. In the neighborhood
was a young man who had heard of my circumstances. On the day I was to start, he came to me
and said, ''You have a large family to care for; I
will go in your place.'' He did go, was killed, and
here in this grave rest his remains.'' The stranger,
with tears of gratitude, told of his long journey to
see this grave, and delighted to recall the fact that
''he died for me.''

This Wonderful Book, the Bible, tells how the
beloved Son of God bore our sins on Calvary's cross
to give us life. He suffered in your stead, and in
mine. He relieved us from the consequences of an
eternal lost and ruined state, and set before us a
plain road to everlasting life. Such a Saviour should
not be rejected. By his death he has elevated the

world, snapped the shackles of doom from human feet, bore the race upon his bosom and carried it to highest plains of purest civilization. This Jesus who reveals Himself from heaven to every weeping eye and aching heart, who reaches down the hand of love and lifts a faltering frame—this is the Christ, the Saviour of men, who says: "Come unto me, all ye that labor and are heavy laden, and I will give you rest. Take my yoke upon you, and learn of me; for I am meek and lowly in heart: and ye shall find rest unto your souls. For my yoke is easy, and my burden is light."

IX. *And finally, the Bible is a Wonderful Book* because it is the only telescope that reveals the world beyond the grave. "If you destroy my confidence in the Bible," says Dr. Wiley, "where am I? I know I go hence ere long, but what then? I take my place by the side of Socrates. Surely if there was ever a man who never knew the revealed word of God, whose ideas were worthy of my respect it is Socrates. I ask him about the future, and in reply I hear him say: "I am to die, you are to live; but for which of us is the better none can tell. I think the lives of good men continue beyond; but of this wise men are not confident." And that is the very best that the wisdom of this world can do for me. Destroy my confidence in the Bible, and the future which I must face is all darkness. I know well the burden of self-condemnation which I carry. I know where I am according to justice. I need nobody to

381

tell me that. But when I am induced to give up the Bible I know no more. I need deliverance but there is no deliverer. I need help but there is no helper. I have been persuaded to give up the Bible, and I find nothing to take its place. The brightness and blessedness of human life are gone, and the sun of human hope has entered into total, disastrous and perpetual eclipse."

The poet says:

> "O listen man!
> A voice within us speaks the startling word
> Man thou shalt never die!
> Celestial voices hymn it into our souls,
> According harps
> By angel fingers touched when the mild stars
> Of morning sang together, sound forth still,
> The song of man's Immortality."

Revelation corroborates the sentiments of the poet in declaring that this life is but the morning of existence. It comes to us with no guesses, doubts, or uncertainties, but with facts and living proofs. Jesus, by his teaching and resurrection has made it a certainty. He brought life and immortality to light. "We know that if the earthly house of our tabernacle be dissolved, we have a building from God, a house not made with hands, eternal, in the heavens."

"Eternity to finite thought is an unfathomable void; here are heights without a summit, depths without a bottom, lengths and breadths without

382

limits of extension. Would mere human philosophy ascend these heights? She soars at best but on conjecture's trembling wing; doubt, uncertainty and despair are the result of her inquiries. Christianity, on the other hand, crosses death's narrow isthmus with firm and undaunted steps; over a pathway of glory she ascends to the summit of everlasting hills, and gazes with open vision upon, to her, a real scene of sublimity and beauty, without a cloud to dim, or limit to obstruct, the sight.''

In John's Apocalyptic vision we have a picture of man redeemed. ''And one of the elders answered, saying unto me, These that are arrayed in the white robes, who are they, and whence came they? And I say unto him, My Lord, thou knowest. And He said to me, These are they that came out of the great tribulation, and they washed their robes, and made them white in the blood of the lamb.''

"Hast thou ever heard
   Of such a Book? the Author—God himself,
   The subject—God and man, salvation, life,
   And death—eternal life, eternal death—
   Dread words! whose meaning has no end, no bounds!
   Most wondrous book! bright candle of the Lord!
   Star of eternity! the only star
   By which the bark of man could navigate
   The sea of life, and gain the coast of bliss
   Securely."

HEARTFELT RELIGION

By JAMES C. CREEL

"Lay up for yourselves treasures in heaven, where neither moth nor rust doth corrupt, and where thieves do not break through nor steal; for where your treasure is, there will your heart be also." (Matt. 6:20,21.) "Either make the tree good and his fruit good; or else make the tree corrupt and his fruit corrupt; for the tree is known by his fruit. O, generation of vipers, how can ye, being evil, speak good things? For out of the abundance of the heart the mouth speaketh. A good man out of the good treasure of the heart bringeth forth good things; and an evil man out of the evil treasure bringeth forth evil things." (Matt. 12:33-35.) "Blessed are the pure in heart; for they shall see God." (Matt. 5:8.)

THESE verses of Scripture are not quoted simply as a text, but they are quoted because they contain some beautiful thoughts which I desire to bring out in this discourse.

The English word "Religion," is derived from a word in the Latin language which means: "To bind anew or back, to bind fast." The Christian Religion, subjectively, is piety or holiness; objectively it is that system of divine truth revealed in the New Testament which binds man "anew or back" to God. Man by his own wicked works is separated from God. The office of religion is to bring man back to God.

The expression, *Heartfelt Religion,* in so many words, is not found in the Bible; but the idea contained in the expression is found in the Bible, or rather the idea contained in the expression, *Religion of the Heart,* is contained in the Word of God. The religion of Christ has much to do with the heart of man. In fact the religion of Christ may be termed a great heart work. A religion that does not touch and control the heart is worthless. A man will derive no benefit from a religion that does not affect his heart and whole life.

What is Heartfelt Religion? There seems to be much confusion in the minds of many as to what heartfelt religion really is. The religious parties who have said so much about heartfelt religion, and who have accused others of not knowing anything about heartfelt religion, have given us no well defined and intelligent answer to this question. With some, heartfelt religion is a change of heart; with some it is regeneration; with some it is the work of the Holy Spirit in the heart; with some, it is conversion; and with others it is the pardon of sins. The best answer I am able to give this question in a brief definition is this: Heartfelt religion is the Christian religion cordially received into the heart, accepted by the heart, felt in the heart, enjoyed in the heart, producing the change of heart, purity of heart and holiness of life. The whole subject of heartfelt religion is made very plain by learning from the Holy Scriptures *what* is the heart, the

385

character of the heart, the *exercises* of the heart, the *change* of the heart, the *purity* of heart. Hence, my sermon on heartfelt religion will consist in bringing out, in the light of divine truth, the following points:

I. *The Heart.*

II. *The Character of the Heart.*

III. *The Exercises of the Heart.*

IV. *The Change of Heart.*

V. *The Purity of Heart.*

These points would indicate that the heart is really the subject of this discourse. While this is true from one point of view, yet we deem it proper to call the sermon Heartfelt Religion, from the fact that we are endeavoring to show from the teachings of the Scriptures what heartfelt religion is, by showing what the Scriptures teach in reference to the human heart.

I. *The Heart.*

What is the heart? This is a very important question, just here, in the beginning of our investigation. I have heard some persons speak of the heart as though the heart of flesh was the subject of religion. I have heard them talk in reference to the change of heart as though this literal heart of flesh was taken out of the human body and a new one put in its place. When the Bible speaks of the heart, morally, it means far more than this little throbbing

386

muscle, located in the left bosom, which beats away the seconds of time.

1. The heart, morally and religiously speaking, means *the affections of the mind*. In proof of this we invite attention to the following Scriptures. Jesus says: "Lay up for yourselves treasures in heaven, where neither moth nor rust doth corrupt, and where thieves do not break through nor steal; for where your treasure is, there will your heart be also." (Matt. 6:20,21.) Here we learn that persons may be living here in this world and at the same time have their hearts in heaven, where their treasures are; that is, their affections are in heaven with their treasures. This is true. Wherever we have our "treasures" deposited, there our affections are entwined.

Solomon says: "The heart of the wise is in the house of mourning; but the heart of fools is in the house of mirth." (Ecc. 7:4.) In order to see the force of the term "heart" in this quotation, we will suppose something like this was in the mind of the inspired writer when he uttered this language: Here is a good man—a "wise" man, who learns that in an adjacent community, where a friend resides, that death has visited that friend's family and severed some of the dearest ties on earth, that sadness and gloom have thrown their dark mantle around that once happy family, but now a "house of mourning." This good man is so situated that he cannot go there in person to minister words of comfort to the bereaved, but his heart is there! That is, his affections and sympathies are there. Here is a young man whose whole life is given to gaiety, pleasure and "mirth;" who, in a Bible sense, may be truly called a "fool." He has a special invitation to attend a grand "ball," a place of gaiety, the "house of mirth." He makes great preparations for his affections are much set upon this place of worldly pleasure. Ere the hour arrives for the giddy dance to begin he happens to a serious accident, perhaps a limb is broken and he is closely confined to his bed. The hour for the dance to begin has now come, but he in person is not there. He imagines himself there. He can scarcely keep his feet still. He imagines he can hear the delightful music of that occasion, yet he is far away; but *his heart is there,* engaged in the merry dance. *His affections* are there.

Again, in the fifteenth chapter and sixth verse of Second Samuel, we have these words: "So Absalom stole the hearts of the men of Israel." When King David's subjects came to him for judgment, Absalom, his son, stood by the way of "the gate," and when "any man came nigh to him to do him obeisance, he put forth his hand and took him and kissed him." By this act of kindness he stole their *"hearts."* What did he steal? He stole their *affections.* That is, Absalom, by his great tenderness and kindness, won the affections of "the men of Israel" and in this way stole their hearts.

2. The word "heart" in the Scriptures is also used in a more comprehensive sense than simply the affections. It is used in a broad sense to mean *the mind, the understanding, the whole moral inner man.* In support of this we ask attention to the following declarations of God's word: "And he said unto them why are ye troubled? and why do *thoughts arise•in your hearts?*" (Luke 24:38.) "Repent therefore of this, thy wickedness, and pray God, if perhaps the *thought of thine heart* may be forgiven thee." (Acts 8:22.) Here we see the heart is represented as having "thoughts." A thought is a mental act. A mental act is an operation of the mind. It is the mind that thinks and the mind only. Therefore, the word "heart" in these citations means *the mind.* Paul says: "With the heart man believeth unto righteousness." (Rom. 10:10.) Now belief is an exercise of the mind. But the apostle says: "With the heart man believeth." Therefore the word "heart" in this passage must mean the mind.

Again: "Ephraim also is like a silly dove without a heart." (Hosea 7:11.) The word "heart" in this passage seems to mean just the opposite of the word "silly." A "silly" person is one without understanding. Hence, Ephraim also is like a silly dove without *understanding.* But the text says: "Without heart." Hence, I conclude the word "heart" in this passage means *the understanding.* As the word "heart" in its broadest sense means the mind itself, the understanding, it must also mean the whole *moral inner man.*

From all the passages of Scripture now adduced we arrive at this conclusion, namely: First, the word "heart," in the Scriptures, in its primary sense means *the affections of the mind.* Second, the word "heart" is used in the Scriptures in a broad sense to mean *the mind itself, the understanding, the moral inner man.* Having now a clear and complete and scriptural definition of the whole heart, we are now prepared to proceed to our second point in the discourse.

II. *The Character of the Heart.*

When we come to speak of the character of the heart we mean the unregenerated heart; the heart that has been defiled by sin; the heart that has never been changed from the love of sin to the love of holiness; the heart that has never been melted and subdued by that divine love exhibited in the gospel of the grace of God.

1. The Bible, when it speaks of the character of the unconverted heart, draws a very dark picture. The prophet Jeremiah says: "The heart is deceitful above all things and desperately wicked; who can know it?" (Jeremiah 17:9.) Jesus who knew the human heart "and needed not that any should testify of man; for he knew what was in man," said: "For out of the heart proceed evil thoughts, murders, adulteries, fornications, thefts, false witness,

390

blasphemies.'' (Matt. 15:19.) The heart that has been defiled by sin possesses a very black character. The unconverted heart is fearfully depraved. I would to God I could draw a vail over this dark picture of the unrenewed heart; but this dark picture is the awful consequences of sin in the soul. While the heart is depraved and morally deformed by committing sin, yet it is capable of being aroused to moral action by the power of motive. The Holy Spirit presents to the heart through the gospel the great motive, the love of God as exhibited in the awful death of His dear son, which moves it to love and serve God. Then if this is true, the heart, ''by nature,'' is not *''totally''* depraved; for if it was it could not be moved to moral action by the power of motive.

The heart is the great workshop where all our wicked actions are coined. Murder, lying, adultery, and all heinous sins ever committed first began in the heart. If we keep murder, lying and stealing out of the heart these terrible sins will be committed no more. If the source is kept pure, the stream will be pure. ''Either make the tree good and his fruit good, or else make the tree corrupt and his fruit corrupt.'' This is an unerring law in nature that if the tree is good the fruit will be good. Just so in religion. If the heart is good the conduct will be good; and if the heart is corrupt the conduct will be corrupt. The old saying that ''if the heart is right, all is right,'' is most certainly true. A truer

391

saying was never uttered by man. If we can only get men right in heart we can very soon get them right in their conduct. The great object of the religion of Jesus Christ is to make men right in heart and thereby make them right in life.

2. The character of the heart is exhibited in the conduct. If it is a good heart it will show itself in the practice of good things. "A good man out of the good treasure of the heart bringeth forth good things." If it is an evil heart it will show itself in the practice of evil things. "An evil man out of the evil treasure bringeth forth evil things." The best way to learn the character of the heart of an individual is to examine closely the conduct of that individual. For it is said: "The tree is always known by its fruit." Sometimes in criticising the conduct of one we will say: "O, well, he does these wrong things, yet he is a good man at heart." Now, I deny that such a person is good at heart, for we know a good tree will not bring forth corrupt fruit. What is the fruit of this tree? Is it not bad, Therefore the tree must be bad. Men are wrong at heart when they do wrong, and that is the reason why they do wrong. Let us get our hearts right in the sight of God and our conduct will be all right. When Simon the Sorcerer, offered the Apostle Peter money to purchase the power of conferring the Holy Spirit by laying on of hands, Peter answered: "Thou hast neither part nor lot in this matter, for thy *heart* is

not right in the sight of God.'' His heart was not right, hence his great sin.

3. The words of the mouth tell what is in the heart. The text says: *"For out of the abundance of the heart the mouth speaketh."* It is perfectly natural for us to talk about those things that are in our hearts. If you find a person always talking about the things of God and Christ and the church, you will find a person whose heart is filled with these things; and his conversation is an evidence of that fact. Again, if an individual's conversation is continually given to the things of the world, such as worldly pleasures, the fashions of the day, making money, that individual's heart is filled to the brim with these things: "Out of the abundance of the heart the mouth speaketh." As a further illustration of this thought, the following incident is in point: On one beautiful Lord's day morning in May, I rode out some four or five miles into the country to an appointment, accompanied by a friend and a brother in Christ, who was a tobacconist. We had not gone far before he began to tell me about his business; how many hogsheads of tobacco he had bought; what it had cost him and what he expected to realize for it. I was glad to learn that my friend and brother was getting along so well, but I did not care about having my mind filled so much with these things on the Lord's day when we were going to His house of worship. So I changed the subject to some religious topic; but soon the subject of tobacco was

brought up again *and again*. Now the trouble was, this dear brother's heart was filled with hogsheads of tobocco! I am afraid Christ can not dwell in a heart that is so filled up with the things of the world.

III. *The Exercise of the Heart.*

The heart in accepting the religion of Jesus Christ undergoes quite a series of moral exercises. In fact, nearly every exercise of the mind is attributed to the heart in the Scriptures. We are said to *think* in the heart. Jesus said to the scribes: "Wherefore think ye evil in your hearts?" (Matt. 9:4.) We *reason* in the heart. Jesus said on another occasion to the scribes: "Why reason ye these things in your hearts?" (Mark 2:8.) We *meditate* in the heart. David says: "Let the words of my mouth, and the meditation of my heart, be acceptable in thy sight, O Lord, my strength and my redeemer." (Psalms 19:14.) We *imagine* in the heart. God said to Noah: "The imagination of man's heart is evil from his youth." (Gen. 8:21.) We *purpose* in the heart. Paul says: Every man according as he purposeth in his heart, so let him give." (2 Cor. 9:7.) As a further illustration of the exercises of the heart, we ask attention to the following points:

1. In accepting the religion of Christ, which is pre-eminently a religion of the heart, we first *understand with the heart*. The Saviour says: "Understand with their heart and be converted and I should heal them." (Matt. 13:15.) We must understand

394

with the heart if we would intelligently receive the religion of Christ. From the much confusion of mind that is exhibited sometimes on the part of some persons, it seems they do not "understand with their heart." The religion of Christ is plain and simple; and is adapted to the humblest mind and heart. There is no reason for confusion nor doubt in this matter if we first understand with the heart.

2. *We Believe with the Heart.* "With the heart man believeth unto righteousness." (Rom. 10:10.) When the Eunuch demanded baptism at the hands of Philip, Philip said to him, "If thou believest with all thy heart thou mayest." (Acts 8:37.) The Christian religion requires a faith which is with the whole heart. A mere assent of the mind to the truth is not the faith required in the gospel, but the faith of the *whole heart.* The reason why so many have such weak faith is, because they do not believe with *all the heart.* This is a vital point and should be emphasized and impressed upon those who are called upon to exercise faith in the Lord Jesus Christ. We want no half-hearted work here, but with the whole heart we are commanded to believe; and any other faith is not gospel faith.

3. *Obey from the Heart.* Paul says: "But God be thanked that (though) ye were the servants of sin, but ye have obeyed from the heart that form of doctrine which was delivered you. Being then made free from sin ye became the servants of righteousness." (Rom. 6:17,18.) Only that obedi-

ence which is "from the heart" is acceptable to God. A mere formal obedience to the commandments will avail nothing; but obedience from the very heart will always meet God's approval, and enable us to receive his blessings.

4. *We Love with All the Heart.* The Saviour said the first of all the commandments is this: "Love the Lord thy God with all thy heart, and with all thy soul, and with all thy strength; this is the first commandment." (Mark 12:30.) When we love God with all the heart, we love him to the full extent of our ability. When we thus love God we will serve him, we will obey him. The Apostle John says: "For this is the love of God (that is, the love we have for God). that we keep his commandments." (I John 5:3.)

5. *We Feel with the Heart.* When I say we feel with the heart I mean the moral feelings in the affections and soul. Paul, in speaking of the Gentiles hardening their hearts, says: "Who being past feeling have given themselves over unto lasciviousness." (See R. V. Eph. 4:19.) Here we learn that when we harden our hearts we are susceptible of moral feeling in the heart. When the religion of Jesus with all its softening power and influence is cordially received into the heart, then the heart feels the happy effects of this power and influence; and every emotion and noble feeling of the heart is aroused to exercise. A religion that we can not feel in our hearts is certainly a very cold and formal

396

religion and, therefore, worthless. The religion of
Jesus received into the heart and obeyed from the
heart will certainly produce in the heart a most delightful feeling of peace and happiness. If you
want to feel religion in your hearts, just open the
doors of your hard hearts, receive it, believe it and
obey it, then you will certainly feel it. Do right
and you will have good feeling in the heart. Do
wrong and you will have bad feeling in the heart.

6. *We Enjoy with the Heart.* In Ecclesiastes,
second chapter and first verse, we have these words:
"I said in mine heart, go to now, I will prove thee
with mirth; therefore enjoy pleasure." In this
passage is taught that we enjoy with the heart. The
intelligent Christian in the practice of religion enjoys much with the heart. He enjoys its pleasures,
its comforts and its rewards. He can truly say:

> "'Tis religion that can give,
> Sweetest pleasures while we live;
> 'Tis religion must supply
> Solid comfort when we die."

Then as the sum total of the exercises of the heart
in submitting to the religion of Jesus our Lord, we
have this: *Understanding* with the heart, *believe* with
the heart, *obey* from the heart, *love* with the heart,
feel with the heart and *enjoy* with the heart. Can
we get any more of the heart into religion? Certainly not. A religion that embraces all of this is
surely a religion of the heart, or if you please,
heart-felt religion.

IV. *Change of Heart.*

This is one of the most vital points in the religion of Jesus. We cannot put too much stress on the great necessity of the change of heart. If the sinful heart is unchanged man's religion is all worthless. There must be a *thorough, radical change of the whole heart* in entering into the Christian life. It gives me great pleasure to make strong emphasis on this point, as my brethren have been accused of denying the change of heart. This is one of the most unjust and wicked charges that has ever been made against that religious body known as Disciples of Christ. Permit me to say, and reiterate, in behalf of my brethren, that we do believe and teach from all our pulpits and in our literature, "that the heart of the sinner must be wholly changed in his conversion to Christ." There must be a moral revolution in the whole inner man in becoming a Christian. The heart must be changed from the love of sin and the world to the love of the Lord Jesus Christ. The heart must be changed from the love of sin to the love of holiness. The heart must be changed from the state of rebellion against Christ to a state of willing, loving and cheerful obedience to Christ. The whole heart must be completely swallowed up in the holy will of Jesus. All of this must absolutely take place in the heart of a person before that person is a proper or scriptural subject for Christian baptism. *Baptism in no sense changes the heart.* All the oceans of water can never change the heart of the poor sinner. The sinner that looks to baptism for the change of heart is fearfully deluded. Further, it is not only sinful, but it is morally impossible, to *scripturally* baptize a person whose heart is unchanged. Why, I would not baptize a person to save my right arm if I did not have *sufficient* evidence to believe his heart was changed. If his heart was not changed before baptism his baptism with an unchanged heart would be solemn mockery in the sight of God. Let me say here that it is a *capital item* with the Disciples of Christ that *the heart must be changed* in the sinner's turning to God. To substantiate this I will quote a few extracts from the writings of some of my brethren:

Bro. Moses E. Lard in his ''Review of Campbellism Examined,'' page 162, says: ''If, it may be truly said, there is any one subject on which Mr. Campbell has shed the whole splendor of peculiar eloquence, *it is the necessity—the absolute necessity —of a change, a moral change, a spiritual change, a deep, vital, pervading change of the whole inner man, preparatory to baptism.*'' Grand words! Can there be any more emphasis put upon the necessity of the change of heart than we find here in these emphatic words?

I now give a quotation from the great and good A. Campbell, found in the ''Campbell-Rice Debate,'' page 544: ''But our opponents have done us a great deal of injustice, in representing us as pleading for *'water regeneration.'* They have endeavored to preach us down, and sing us down, and write us down, by holding us up to public reprobation, as advocates of a mere baptismal regeneration; but they have not succeeded, nor will they succeed, with any who will hear us or read us on these subjects. No man believes more cordially, or teaches more fully, the necessity of a spiritual change of our affections—a change of heart—than I do. I have said a thousand times, that if a person were immersed twice seven times in the Jordan for the remission of his sins, or for the reception of the Holy Spirit, it would avail nothing more than wetting the face of a babe, unless, his heart is changed by the word and spirit of God. I have no confidence in any instrumentality, ordinance, means, or observance, unless the *heart is turned to God.*"

Now, then, away with that old false charge that, the Disciples of Christ, do not believe in the change of the heart before baptism. It is a great pity, that right here, on this all important and capital point, the disciples are greatly misunderstood and often shamefully misrepresented. It is exceedingly painful to hear the false charge often made that we, the disciples, believe and teach the *abominable* doctrine of "baptismal regeneration," or "water salvation." A doctrine which we abhor with all our hearts. Only a short time since, I noticed in Philip Schaff's "History of the Christian Church," if I mistake not, these words: *"Alexander Campbell, who believed baptism was regeneration."* How could this learned and eminent gentleman make such a statement, when Mr. Campbell has made such plain declarations just to the opposite in the above extract from "Campbell-Rice Debate," page 544. Surely this eminent scholar did not intend to misrepresent Mr. Campbell.

Having now sufficiently emphasized the absolute necessity of the change of heart before one can be baptized, we ask the question:

1. *What Is the Change of Heart?* In order to answer this question we must keep before our minds that other question: What is the heart? We have already learned from the Scriptures that the heart, primarily, is *the affections of the mind;* and, secondly, the heart is *the mind itself, the moral inner man.* Then it follows that the change of heart is the change of affections, the change of mind. This change of affections has reference to sin. That is, the heart is changed from the love of sin to the love of holiness; from the love of sin and the world to the love of Christ; from the sin of disobedience to the loving and cheerful obedience to Christ. All this is the change of heart. The change of heart may imply more than this; but one thing is certain, it can never mean less than this radical and thorough change of the affections in reference to sin.

2. *How Is the Change of Heart Produced?* This is very important. I answer this important question in this way: The heart is changed *by faith in the Lord Jesus Christ.* Faith controls and directs the affections of the mind. We can have no love or

401

affection for any object till we first believe that object possesses something worthy of our affections. It is utterly impossible for us to love an object that we do not believe possesses any quality worthy of our affection or love. The affections or the heart is changed from one object to another object just as we have faith in that object. Illustration: A young man believes that a certain young lady possesses those traits of mind and heart that are lovely and worthy of his affections; he believing this, centers his love and affection upon this lovely object. After while he sees another young lady, a superior lady to the first one in every respect, more lovely and beautiful in all the graces of mind and heart, a far more worthy object of his heart's love. He believes all this in reference to this other lady; and believing this, his heart is changed from the love of the first lady to the love of the second lady. Just so: The sinner loves sin and the world. His heart is given to these. The gospel presents Jesus to the lost sinner in all his beauty, love, purity. One "altogether lovely," one worthy of all the affections of his mind, one who is "able to save to the uttermost." The sinner believes all this; and thus by his faith in the Lord Jesus Christ his heart is changed from the love of sin to the love of Christ. He is now subdued in heart. He hates what he once loved, and loves what he once hated. He humbly cries: "My Lord, my Saviour, what wilt thou have me do?"

In the conversion of the Apostle Paul, there is to

my mind, a beautiful illustration of the change of heart. Paul had no love for Christ nor his disciples. He hated them with intense hatred. In speaking of his hatred toward the innocent disciples of Christ, he says: "Being exceedingly mad against them I persecuted them even unto strange cities." (Acts 26:11.) He was a blood-thirsty persecutor, a hater of Christ; for he says: "I verily thought with myself that I ought to do many things contrary to the name of Jesus of Nazareth." (Acts 26:9.) With this feeling of hatred in his heart he starts to the city of Damascus on his bloody errand of persecution against Christ and his disciples. As he journeyed near the city, "suddenly there shone around him a light from Heaven; and he fell to the earth, and heard a voice saying to him, Saul, Saul, why persecutest thou me? And he said, who art thou, Lord? and the Lord said, I am Jesus whom thou persecutest; it is hard for thee to kick against the pricks; and he trembling and astonished said: Lord what wilt thou have me do? The Lord said unto him, arise and go into the city, and it shall be told thee what thou must do." (Acts 9:3-6.) What a wonderful change has taken place in the heart of Saul! A few hours since he was a hater and a persecutor of Christ. Now he is an humble penitent at the feet of Jesus crying with great anguish of soul: *"Lord, what wilt thou have me do?"* What Saul now saw and *heard* forced the great conviction into his heart that he was a great sinner, a persecutor, lost and ruined; and that the despised Jesus of Nazareth was indeed his long looked for Messiah, his only Saviour. He believed all this with all his heart. His faith in Jesus changed his heart from hatred and persecution to that state of love and submission to Jesus which caused him to tremble and cry to Jesus for salvation in the touching words: *"Lord, what wilt thou have me do?"*

"But," says one, "is not this great change of heart which you have emphasized so much produced by the Holy Spirit operating on the heart?" Certainly, this change of heart is produced by the Holy Spirit. There could be no change of heart in the religion of Christ without the influence of the Holy Spirit upon the heart. But the real question is: How does the Holy Spirit produce this change in the heart? I answer: By producing faith in the heart which produces the change of heart. And *how* does the Holy Spirit produce faith in the heart? Answer: By and through the word of God. "So then faith cometh by hearing, and hearing by the word of God." (Rom. 10:17.) So then it is just from the point of view we look at this matter. If we look at the agent, the Holy Spirit, in the conversion of the sinner we say the Holy Spirit produces this change in the heart; and if we look at the office of faith in conversion we say the heart is changed by faith. Both ideas are true when looked at properly.

Perhaps some one is ready to ask: "How can faith change the heart?" Strictly speaking, *it is the thing believed* that produces the change in the affections and mind. It is not the kind of faith we have, but the thing believed. The Scriptures know nothing of kinds of faith. There may be little faith, much faith, weak faith or strong faith; but not kinds of faith. These words express degree, not kinds. "All faith is one, not in kind, but in object the difference lay." Now the effects of faith grow out of the thing believed. Sadness, joy, love and hatred are produced in the heart by the thing believed. If we were to believe that in one hour we should be put to death, our hearts would be filled with overwhelming sorrow. Then if we could believe that this terrible sentence of death had been recalled, our hearts would be changed from great sorrow to great joy. If we have an object of hatred and could be induced to believe that this object is really an object of love and devotion, believing this fact, our hearts would be changed from hatred to love. Just so in the gospel we have the Lord Jesus Christ presented to us in his agony and death on the cross. We believe he died for us. We believe he went down to the cold grave and abolished death and brought life and immortality to light by his glorious resurrection. We believe he is our only Saviour, believing all this, our hearts are changed from the love of sin to the love of Jesus our Saviour.

405

V. *The Purity of Heart.*

Jesus in his sermon on the "Mount" in describing the moral character of the subjects of his kingdom, which was then "at hand," says: "Blessed are the pure in heart; for they shall see God." (Matt. 5:8.) No man can see, or enjoy God with an impure heart. It is only the pure in heart that can have sweet communion and fellowship with God in this world and in the world to come. Christians are commanded to love one another with a pure heart. "See that ye love another with a pure heart fervently." (I Peter 1:22.) Paul said to Timothy: "Follow righteousness, faith, charity, peace, with them that call on the Lord out of a pure heart." (II Tim. 2:22.) The great end or purpose of the gospel is a pure heart. "Now the end of the commandment is charity out of a pure heart, and a good conscience, and of faith unfeigned." (I Tim. 1:5.) From these Scriptures we learn that *Purity of Heart* is a most vital point in the Christian religion.

1. *What Is the Purity of Heart?* It is not simply the change of heart. The change of heart is absolutely necessary to the purity of heart, and always precedes the purity of heart, but the purity of heart is far more. The purity of heart is not conversion. Conversion is essential to, and goes before the purity of heart; but the purity of heart is still a great deal more. The purity of heart *is the heart cleansed, purified and made free from sin and the guilt of sin,*

406

involving purification of the soul. So then the purity of heart implies the forgiveness or remission of sins; for as long as there is sin or guilt in the heart there will be an impure heart.

2. *How Is the Heart Made Pure or Cleansed?* By the blood of Jesus Christ. In the gospel there is revealed but one cleansing element. That element is *"The Precious blood of Christ."* The Apostle John says: The blood of Jesus Christ his Son cleanseth us from all sin." (I John 1:7.) In the book of Revelation we have these words: "Unto him that loved us, and washed us from our sins in his own blood." (Rev. 1:5.) The Apostle Paul says: "In whom we have redemption through his blood, even the forgiveness of sins." (Col. 1:14.) These passages of Scripture clearly prove that the one cleansing and purifying element, in the purification of the heart and soul, is the blood of Jesus Christ. I do not mean here that the *literal* blood of Christ *literally* cleanses the heart and soul from sin. I mean that by *virtue* of the shedding of the precious blood of Christ that God *can* and *does* take away all sin and guilt from the heart and soul of the *obedient* character. Thus it is that the blood of Christ cleanses or purifies the heart and soul from all sin and guilt. It is a great mistake to represent the Holy Spirit as a cleansing element or agent. Nowhere in the Bible is it said that the Holy Spirit cleanses or purifies the heart. The office of the Holy Spirit in the salvation of the sinner is

to convert and sanctify through the word of truth. So we may say, the work of conversion and sanctification is *begun, carried on,* and *consummated, by the Holy Spirit, through the instrumentality of the divine truth.*

The Apostle James in writing to those persons whom he addresses as my "brethren" (see James 1:2), says: "Purify your hearts, ye double-minded." (James 4:8.) I do not understand the apostle here to mean that the Christian can really purify his heart in the sense of purifying it from sin and guilt; for we have seen that the blood of Christ alone can do this; but the two-minded, or double-minded Christian is to put away from his heart all the evil thoughts, desires and passions, and thus purify his heart.

3. *When Is the Heart Made Pure or Cleansed?* There is a time when this purification, cleansing and freedom from sin takes place. Let us lay aside all opinions and notions of men; and be guided solely by divine truth. What say the Scriptures? The Scriptures teach *when we obey from the heart, the divine truth, then our hearts are purified, cleansed, and made free from sin.* In other words, when we turn to God, in obeying the truth, *then* our sins are forgiven and *then* our hearts are made pure. Now, for the Scripture proof:

The Apostle Paul says: "Ye were the servants of sin, but ye have obeyed from the heart that form of doctrine which was delivered you. *Being then*

408

made free from sin, ye became the servants of righteousness.'' (Rom. 6:17,18.) When were they made free from sin and thus had their hearts made pure? *When* they obeyed from the heart that form of doctrine or divine truth. Is not this exceedingly plain?

The Apostle Peter says: ''Seeing ye have purified your souls in obeying the truth through the spirit unto unfeigned love of the brethren, see that ye love one another with a pure heart fervently.'' (I Peter 1:22.) Here we have purification of soul and heart. When do we have this purification of soul and heart? ''In obeying the truth,'' *then* we have this purification of soul and heart.

The apostle in speaking of what God has done for both Gentile and Jew, says: ''And put no difference between us and them, purifying their hearts by faith.'' (Acts 15:9.) The word ''faith'' in this passage is used in its objective sense meaning *''The Faith,''* the truth, the gospel. In the original we have *tee* (the) *pistei* (faith). In Acts 6:7 we have: ''And a great company of the priests were obedient to *the faith.''* Now we know in this second passage that the express *''the faith''* means the truth or the gospel. But in the original, in both passages, it is precisely the same expression, *tee pistei,* the faith, the truth. (See Westcott & Hort's Revised Greek—English New Testament). Therefore, the word ''faith'' in Acts 15:9, means the truth. Then the correct idea is, ''purifying their hearts by the

409

truth.'' Now, in what sense can it be said that our hearts are purified by the truth? In this sense: When we *obey* the truth *then* our hearts are made pure by the blood of Christ.

The Apostle John says: "If we walk in the light, as he is in the light, we have fellowship with one another, and the blood of Jesus Christ his Son cleanseth us from all sin." (I John 1:7.) The words, "the light," in this passage means the truth. To walk in the light is to walk in the truth; to walk in the truth is to *obey* the truth. Now, the apostle says: "If we walk in the light," that is, obey the truth, the blood of Christ will cleanse us from all sin. Therefore, *when* we do walk in the light, or obey the truth, *then* our hearts are made pure by being cleansed from all sin with the blood of Christ. Now, the whole conclusion, from the foregoing, is this: By turning to God, in obeying the divine truth, our hearts are then made pure by being cleansed from all sin and guilt with "the precious blood of Christ." In other words: When we believe in Jesus with *all our hearts,* confess the name of Jesus with our mouths, repent *sincerely* of all our sins, and are baptized into the name of the Father, Son and Holy Spirit, *then* we have the forgiveness of sins; and thus our hearts are made pure by being cleansed from all sin.

Then, we say to the poor sinner: *Understand* with the heart, *believe* with the heart, *obey* from the heart, *love* with all the heart; and you will have *the*

410

change of heart; *the purity* of heart; and then you will feel and enjoy *heartfelt religion.* What more heartfelt religion could any one desire? This is the religion that "will do to die with." This is the religion that will enable the saint of God to sing the song of triumph in the hour of death. This is the religion that will cheer our poor, weary hearts as we toil for Jesus amid the conflicting fortunes of this life of sorrow and tears. This is the religion that will at least give us a happy home in the "sweet by and by" where we shall bask in the sunlight of our Saviour's love throughout the great eternity of God! Amen.

INFANT BAPTISM

By JOHN S. SWEENEY

ONE of the questions about baptism concerning which there is difference and discussion is as to the proper *subject* of the ordinance—that is, who may be scripturally baptized? It is about universally admitted that a penitent believer in Jesus Christ, who has not been baptized, is a scriptural subject of the ordinance. It might be worth while to mention that some Baptists who take pride in being somewhat exclusive try to make it appear that even more than penitence and belief in Jesus, on the part of the candidate, is necessary—that is, what they call an "experimental knowledge of sins forgiven." But there is nothing in the scriptures about any such "experimental knowledge" as a prerequisite to baptism, and those who profess to have it have never succeeded in making anything intelligible of it. What is an "experimental knowledge of sins forgiven?" We are told that it is a certain state of feeling, or condition of soul, and we have no right or inclination to call in question any one's state of feelings; for the feelings of a man are known only to "the spirit of the man which is in him." But who is authorized to interpret *any* state of feeling as an "evidence of sins forgiven?" Forgiveness of sins is one of "the things of God, that none knoweth save the Spirit of God." How are we to know the things in the mind of God? The Apostle Paul tells us: "But we (the apostles) received, not the spirit of the world, but the Spirit which is of God; that we might know the things that are freely given to us by God; which things also *we speak,* not in words which man's wisdom teacheth, but which the Spirit teacheth." (I Cor. ii:12,13.) God conveys to us, then, a knowledge of the things in his mind, which he freely gives us, *by his Spirit, in words;* so that no man is left to interpret a mere state of feeling as the evidence of sins forgiven. If each man's interpretation of his own state of feeling is the only evidence he has of his pardon, then it would be difficult to show what advantage, in this respect, the Christian has of the Jew, or of the Mohammedan, or of the Pagan; would it not? But we intend no discussion now of the evidence of pardon; and refer to this matter only to pay a passing notice to a seeming exception to the general admission that a penitent believer in Jesus Christ is a scriptural subject of baptism. That's all now.

While, as has been said, there is very general agreement that penitent believers are scriptural subjects of baptism, some say that only such persons are. Then there are others who contend that infant children also are proper subjects of the ordinance.

413

These are the two sides to the most important point of difference on the question. It might be worth while to note the fact that those who believe in and practice infant baptism, so-called, are divided among themselves as to the extent of it, scripturally. Some confine the right of it to infants of believing parents; others to infants of parents one of whom is a believer; and others extend it to all infants. We shall not stop, however, to discuss these questions of difference among pedo-baptists, but will leave that to them; while we shall discuss the primary and more fundamental question as to whether *any* infants are scriptural subjects of this ordinance. It being admitted generally by pedo-baptists that penitent believers who have not been baptized are proper subjects of the ordinance, the only question between them and disciples about the *subject* of baptism is as to the baptism of infants; and in the discussion of this question, the disciples are in the negative. So that my discourse on the *subject* of baptism, if to any purpose at all, will really be one against infant baptism.

METHODS OF PROOF.

To establish such a practice as the baptism of infants, it has been held and it seems to me properly and correctly, that there are but three possible methods of proof—that is, of course, from the Protestant standpoint. With such persons as believe in high churchism, the authority of the church is all-sufficient. But with these I shall not reason in this discourse. If I were going to argue with them about infant baptism, or about sprinkling and pouring for baptism, or about any one of several other questions, I would begin with the fundamental question of church authority.

The three methods of proof among Protestants, then, are (1) Precept of scripture, (2) Example of scripture, and (3) Inference of scripture. By precept of scripture is meant an express commandment, recorded in scripture, either by our Lord himself of by someone unquestionably authorized by him, that infants should be baptized. Such a commandment would settle the question in favor of the practice in the judgment of all who recognize the supreme authority of the scripture in all matters of our religion. By example of scripture is meant a recorded instance of the baptism of an infant with the approval either of our Lord himself or any one of the inspired men of the New Testament. This also would settle the question in favor of the practice with all who make the Bible the supreme authority upon the subject. By inference from scripture is meant a logical deduction from scripture either that infants were baptized by our Lord or some one or more of his authorized teachers in New Testament times, or that he or they said that they should be.

But now of the first and second methods: What can be claimed as to express scripture precept or example for the baptism of infants? Let us attend

415

to this question for a few moments. I am not going myself to answer this question, but to take the answer from pedo-baptists themselves, and from such as are confessedly eminent and scholarly among them.

Bishop Burnett.—''There is no express precept, or rule, given in the New Testament for baptism of infants.'' Exposit of Thirty-nine Articles, Art. xxvii.

Dr. Wall.—''Among all the persons that are recorded as baptized by the apostles there is no express mention of any infant.'' Hist. Inf. Bap. Introduct. p. 1. '

Luther.—''It cannot be proved by the sacred scripture that infant baptism was 'instituted by Christ, or begun by the first Christians after the Apostles'.'' In A.R's Vanity of Inf. Bap. part ii. p. 8.

Samuel Palmer.—''There is nothing in the words of the institution, nor in any after accounts of the administration of this rite, respecting the baptism of infants; there is not a single precept for, nor example of, this practice through the whole New Testament.'' Ans. to Dr. Priestley's Address on the Lord's Supper, p. 7.

Bishop Sanderson.—''The baptism of infants, and the sprinkling of water in baptism instead of immersing the whole body, must be exterminated from the Church, according to their principle; i.e., that nothing can be lawfully performed, much less required, in the affairs of religion which is not either commanded by God in the scripture, or at least recommended by a laudable example." De Obligat. Conscient. Prelect iv. pp. 17, 18.

Dr. Freeman.—"The traditions of the whole Catholic church confirm us in many of our doctrines; which, though they may be gathered out of scripture, yet are not laid down there in so many words: such as infant baptism, and of episcopal authority above presbyters." Preservative against popery, Title iii: p. 19.

Walker.—"Where authority from the scripture fails there the authority of the Church is to be held as a law. . . . . It doth not follow that our Saviour gave no precept for the baptizing of infants, because no such precept is particularly expressed in the scripture; for our Saviour spoke many things to his disciples concerning the kingdom of God, both before his passion and also after his resurrection, which are not written in the scriptures; and who can say but that among those *unwritten* sayings of his, there might be an express precept for infant baptism." Modest Plea for Inf. Bap. pp. 221, 368.

Mr. Fuller.—"We do freely confess that there is neither express precept, nor precedent, in the New Testament for the baptizing of infants. . . . . There were many things which Jesus did which are not written; among which, for aught appears to the contrary, the baptism of these infants (Luke xviii: 15,16,17), might be one of them." Infants Advocate, pp. 71, 150.

I have made these quotations second-hand, from a work by Abraham Booth, entitled *Pedo-baptism Examined,* Vol. i, pp. 303-307. Booth was an English Baptist. I have never heard the correctness of his quotations questioned, though his work has been read and used for more than a half-century. I might read some more extracts, from pedo-baptist authors, of the same import, from the same volume, but what I have read are quite sufficient for my purpose. I would not be misunderstood as to the use of these authors. Most of them, while they accept the scriptures as authoritative in religion, believed also in tradition and the authority of the church in such matters as the baptism of infants, etc. etc., as their own language shows. They were all pedo-baptists; that is, they all believed in and practiced infant baptism; but they did not claim any express scriptural precept or example in its support. And it is for this purpose—to show this fact—that I have adduced their writings. With them tradition and church authority were all-sufficient authority in such matters. And while they were, in a sense, Protestants, they did not fully endorse what we now call the great principle of Protestantism—"that the Bible and the Bible alone is the religion of Protestants"— or if they did, they did not extend that principle to such matters as the baptizing of infants, and of sprinkling instead of immersing. The supposed unwritten sayings and acts of our Lord handed down to us by the Church, and backed by its authority in such matters, was all the authority these men wanted for infant baptism and sprinkling for baptism. But such authority will not do for those who fully endorse and live up to the Protestant principle. If we are all to have the liberty of turning our imaginations loose among the supposed unwritten sayings and doings of our Lord and his apostles, we can exhume thence a good deal more than infant baptism. And if we are to trust the traditions and authority of the Catholic church in bringing down to us those unwritten things, we shall not be able to stop short of popery and all its claims.

In the next place, we shall see what some very eminent and scholarly pedo-baptists, who repudiate tradition and church authority altogether, have to say on the question as to scripture precept and example for infant baptism—some more recent writers than those quoted from Mr. Booth.

I read from the *Southern Review* (Methodist) Vol. xiv: No. 30, pp. 334-336. In an article on the *"History of Infant Baptism"* the editor, A. T. Bledsoe, LL.D., says: "It is an article of our faith, that the baptism of young children (infants) is in anywise to be retained in the church, *as most agreeable to the institution of Christ.*" But yet, with all our searching we have been unable to find, in the New Testament, a single express declaration, or word, in favor of infant baptism. We justify the rite, therefore, solely on the ground of logical inference, and not on any express word of Christ or his apostles.

This may, perhaps, be deemed, by some of our readers, a strange position for a pedo-baptist. It is by no means, however, a singular opinion. Hundreds of learned pedo-baptists have come to the same conclusion; especially since the New Testament has been subjected to a closer, more conscientious, and more candid exegesis than was formerly practiced by controversialists.'' Then, to justify his statement that his was not "a singular opinion," the writer cites other distinguished pedo-baptist writers as follows:

Knapp's Theology.—"There is no decisive example of this practice in the New Testament. . . . There is, therefore, no express command for infant baptism found in the New Testament, as *Morus* justly concedes." (Vol. ii:p. 524.)

Dr. Jacob.—"However reasonably we may be convinced that we find in the Christian scriptures 'the fundamental idea from which infant baptism was afterward developed,' and by which it may now be justified, *it ought to be distinctly acknowledged that it is not an apostolic ordinance.*"

Neander.—"Originally baptism was administered to adults; nor is the general spread of infant baptism at a later period any proof to the contrary; for even after infant baptism had been set forth as an apostolic institution its introduction into the general practice of the church was but slow. Had it rested upon apostolic authority, there would have been a difficulty in explaining its late approval, and that even in the third century, it was opposed by at least one eminent father of the church.''

Dr. Bledsoe, after making quotations just read, adds: ''We might, if necessary, adduce the admission of *many other* profoundly learned pedo-baptists, that their doctrine is not found in the New Testament, either in express terms or by implication from any portion of its language.'' And again he says: ''But what we wish, in this connection, to emphasize most particularly, is the wonderful contrast between the silence of Christ and the everlasting clamors of his church. Though he uttered not one express word on the subject of infant baptism, yet, on this very subject, have his professed followers filled the world with sound and fury. The apostles imitated his silence. But yet, in spite of all this, have the self-styled 'successors of the apostles,' and the advocates of their claims, made the universal Church, and all the ages, ring controversies, loud and long and deep, respecting the rite of infant baptism.''

I will read one other testimony on this point— that is, showing that the eminent and scholarly among the pedo-baptists, who do not accept the authority of the church or of tradition, frankly concede that the practice in question has no scripture precept or example in its support. I read from a little volume entitled *''Doctrinal Tracts,''* published for the General Conference of the Methodist Episcopal church, containing an article on baptism especially for the volume, and to take the place of one by Mr. Wesley which had been published in the little volume for almost a generation before. The new tract was prepared by a committee appointed by conference for that very purpose. Here is what that new tract says on the point in hand:

"They (anti-pedo-baptists) object that there is no explicit warrant for baptizing infants in the New Testament, and they conclude that infants should not be baptized. By an explicit warrant they mean some express declaration either that infants should be or that they were baptized. . . . . That there is no such explicit warrant for the baptism of infants is freely acknowledged." (*Doct. Tracts* p. 250.)

It is needless to multiply concessions on this point. Enough has been adduced to show that many of the most eminent and scholarly pedo-baptists admit what we claim, namely, that there is no express scripture precept or example for infant baptism. There are, we concede, many among the advocates of this practice, who, for want of the necessary information, it may be, or, possibly, for want of sufficient candor, refuse to make this admission. But such persons can do little else than wrangle about it. At any rate they have failed to show even to their own brethren the precept or example.

LOGICAL INFERENCE,

then, is the only remaining method of proof by which any respectable effort can be made to sustain this practice. Hence said Dr. Bledsoe correctly and candidly: "We justify the rite, therefore, *solely* on the ground of logical inference, and *not* on any express word of Christ or his apostles." And now, what shall we say of this method of sustaining such a practice as the one in question? Is "logical inference," be it ever so strong *as such,* a sufficient ground for it? Has God made it the duty of Christian parents to have their infant children baptized and left them to find out that such is their duty solely by logical inference? In other words, has he made it their duty, without saying one word about it in his entire revelation to men? Now, if infant baptism were a thing of indifference, a mere matter of expediency, and hence one that needed no proof, then, I grant that we might accept and practice it solely on the ground of logical inference. But it is no matter of this kind. Any one can see that it is calculated to, and that to the extent of its prevalence it does, completely set aside the baptism of believers. If it ever comes to prevail universally over christendom, then, thereafter there will be no such thing in christendom as the baptism of believers. And there will stand the *express words* of our Lord in the commission, "He that *believes* and is baptized," completely nullified—nullified, too, by a practice justified solely on the ground of logical inference! Infant baptism will then stand as the only institution under heaven having written upon it "the name of the Father and of the Son, and of the Holy Spirit." And it will stand solely on the ground of logical inference! Can a logical inference do all this? If so, it seems to me that it ought to be no doubtful one. It ought to be such an inference as all logicians can see. And even then there would be a very grave if not insuperable difficulty about it, arising out of the fact that all parents are not good logicians. Logic, I know, is supposed to be perfect; but there are very few people who perfectly understand it. There are very few perfect logicians. People differ often and widely as to logical inferences. They often draw different conclusions from the same premises —make different inferences from the same facts. This, true enough, may not be the fault of logic, but the misfortune of the people, that they are not all good logicians.

There are inferences, I grant, so very plain that all responsible persons must see them. But is infant baptism supported by any such inferences? Has there ever been a logical inference drawn in support of this practice that even all pedo-baptists could see? I believe it can be shown that every inference that has ever been brought to support this practice has been disputed even by those who practice it. True, it may be, that they all justify their practice in their own estimation by inference, but they do not all agree on any one inference. There is no one inference that is not disputed by some of them. Then how can they expect unbelievers in the practice to adopt it upon an inference that is so doubtful that it is disputed even by some who believe in the prac-

424

tice? Some believe upon one inference, disputed by others; and others believe upon another inference, disputed by some. And yet they would all have us believe upon such proof, that God has made it the duty of all Christian parents to have their children baptized.

In the next place we shall notice a few of the arguments, or inferences, brought forward to support this practice. Here is one contributed by Dr. Bledsoe, in the same article from which we have already quoted his concession as to precept and example:

"Since the first disciples of Christ, as native Jews, never doubted that children were to be introduced into the Israelitish church by circumcision, it was natural that they should include children also in baptism, if Christ did not expressly forbid it. . . . It was not only natural that they *should*, it was absolutely certain that they *would*, include children in baptism, as the event has shown. Yet Christ foreseeing the event, did not forbid it. Hence it must have been agreeable to his will." There! that's an inference which in the judgment of Dr. Bledsoe and some other great men is quite sufficient to justify infant baptism. It has failed, however, to convince the doubters; and is not satisfactory to all believers in infant baptism—believers on other grounds. Let us see: It assumes that owing to the bias the custom of circumcising infant children under the former dispensation had given to their minds, "the first disciples of Christ, as native Jews" began the practice of baptizing infants. But is this true? Do all pedo-baptists, even, accept it? No indeed! Let us hear Martin Luther on it: "It cannot be proved by the sacred scripture that infant baptism was instituted by Christ, *or begun by the first Christians after the apostles.*" As a matter of historical fact infant baptism was not begun by Jewish Christians at all; but in Africa, and long after the "first disciples of Christ" were dead. Many of the "first disciples of Christ, as native Jews," with too strong a leaning to the circumcision of infant children, and to Mosaism, generally, did a good many things they ought not to have done, and brought a good deal of trouble into the church of God; but the introduction of infant baptism is not one of the sins they will have to answer for. Give every one his due.

But the Doctor says, "Christ foreseeing the event, did not forbid it. Hence it must have been agreeable to his will." There is a sweeping inference for you! If that justifies infant baptism, it must also justify *every* event foreseen and not forbidden by Christ. Logic is always fair. Those who undertake to inform us about the foreknowledge of God— experts in this field—tell us that he foresaw *all* things that come to pass. Then all things that come to pass, which he has not expressly forbidden, are "agreeable to his will." But that proves too much for Dr. Bledsoe, or for anybody else, excepting perhaps some very old Calvinists: and, proving too

426

much, it proves nothing at all. Just think of it! Setting aside the command of God, that believers should be baptized, and justifying the substitution of infant baptism for it "solely on the ground of logical inference," and no better inference than that "Christ foreseeing the event, did not forbid it: hence it must have been agreeable to his will!"

HOUSEHOLD BAPTISM.

Or, as our pedo-baptist friends prefer to call it, "the inference from the baptism of whole families recorded in the New Testament." Among the unlearned of the rank and file there is perhaps no inference more confidently relied on as justifying the practice in question than this one. With them a household means exactly a family, in the modern sense; and a family always includes at least one infant; family baptism therefore involves infant baptism, as one of the inexorable necessities of logic. Well, let us see about it.

It has never yet been shown, that anybody knows of, that the word "house" or "household" (from the same Greek word), in the New Testament, ever means family, in the sense of parents, or parent and children. This has only been assumed; and assumed, too, contrary to very significant facts. It is a fact, that when a writer of New Testament times meant to include little children in any statement, he did not rely upon the word house or household to do it; but even where the word house was used, he would use other words in the same sentence to indicate little children. Of course, I speak not now of writers in the New Testament, but of writers as nearly contemporaneous as we can get. Let us read a few examples from the "Pastor of Hermas," a production of Hermas, the same, most likely, mentioned by Paul (Rom. xvi:14), as his contemporary. In his work, divided into Commandments and Chapters, Hermas says:

"Now I say to you, if you do not keep them, but neglect them, you will not be saved, nor your *children,* nor your *house.*" (Com. xii:Chap. 3.) Again he says: "These things, therefore, shall you thus observe with your *children,* and all your *house.*" (Similitude v:Chap. 3.) Once more, the same writer says: "Only continue humble, and serve the Lord in all purity of heart, you and your *children,* and your *house.*" (Sim. vii.)

A little later lived Ignatius, the father of Episcopacy. He wrote a letter of Polycarp, and in that epistle (Chap. viii) he says, "I salute all by name, and in particular the wife of Epitropus, with all her *house* and *children.*" Now, we can get no nearer the New Testament writers on this side than these writers take us, and we see that by "House" they did not mean "children." When they meant to include children they said children, even though it was the next word after house and in the same sentence. And what has been said of these writers immediately succeeding the New Testament was true

428

of Moses. He says: (Gen. xlvii:24.) "Ye shall give the fifth part unto Pharaoh, and four parts shall be your own, for seed of the field, and for your food, and for them of your *households* and for food for your *little ones.*" Here we find Moses the giver of God's law, using the word "household" as not including "little ones." When he means both "households" and "little ones," he says both in the same sentence.

These quotations are sufficient to show that the word "house" or "household" did not necessarily include "children" or "little ones," as, when they were meant to be included in any statement, they were named in *addition* to household in the same statement, and in the same sentence. Just what the writers of those times did mean to include in the word household we may not be able to determine to our entire satisfaction: nor is it necessary that we should do so to refute the pedo-baptists in their effort to infer infant baptism from the baptism of households, which is all I am aiming to do.

While on this question about households let us go a little further, and examine its use in the New Testament.

1. In Acts x:2, Luke, speaking of Cornelius, the centurion, says he was "a devout man, and one that feared God with all his house." This language precludes the idea of infant children in the house of Cornelius, by predicating of "all his house" what

429

infants are clearly incapable of. He *feared* God with *all* his house.

2. In Acts xviii:8, we are told that, "Crispus, the chief ruler of the synagogue, believed on the Lord with all his house." Here again, clearly infants are precluded, as *faith* is predicated of "all his house." Infants could not have "believed on the Lord."

3. In Acts xvi:32-34, "And they (Paul and Silas) spake unto him (the jailer at Philippi) the word of the Lord, and to all that were in his house. And he took them the same hour of the night, and washed their stripes; and was baptized, he and all his, straightway. And when he had brought them into his house, he set meat before them, and rejoiced, believing in God with all his house." In this case, the word of the Lord was spoken to all in the house; and all *"rejoiced, believing* in God." No infants in this house.

4. In Acts xvi:15, we are told of Lydia that "she was baptized and all her house." There is nothing said here either to include or preclude infants. We have a right to demand, however, in view of what we have seen as to use of house and household, that they should be named, before granting that they are included in the statement here made. We have also the further right, to turn back and read the commission under which the apostles were working: "Preach the gospel to every creature: he that *believes* and is baptized shall be saved." The pre-

sumption is that they didn't transcend the authority given by that commission. We have a right to note the fact that Lydia, was "of the city of Thyatira;" that consequently she was a long way from home, trading in purple at Philippi, and that even if she was a married woman, and even if she was a mother, and even if any one or more of her children were infants, she would not likely have them with her. And this is the only case of household baptism on which pedo-baptist debaters now make any stand at all!

5. Paul says (I Cor. 1:16), "I baptized also the household of Stephanas." No word or words added to include infants, as was the custom when they were meant to be included, as we have seen.

Now, we have a right to the commission here also. And we have a right also to read the account of Paul's visit to Corinth where he baptized Crispus, Gaius, and the "household of Stephanas," as given in Acts xviii:7,8. Here it is: "And he (Paul) departed thence and entered into a certain man's house, named Justus, one that worshipped God, whose house joined hard to the synagogue. And Crispus the chief ruler of the synagogue believed on the Lord with all his house; and *many* of the Corinthians *hearing, believed* and were baptized."

There is another fact in connection with this "household of Stephanas" that ought to be noted, which brings us to another instance of the use of household in the New Testament.

431

6. In his first epistle to the Corinthians, the same in which he says he baptized the household of Stephanas, the apostle speaks again of this same "house," on this wise: (xvi:15,16) "I beseech you, brethren, as ye know the house of Stephanas, that it is the first fruits of Achaia and that they have addicted themselves to the ministry of the saints, that ye submit yourselves unto such."

Now, this epistle was written not more than five years after Paul's first visit to Corinth, when he baptized the "household of Stephanas;" and here he speaks of the "house of Stephanas" as having "addicted themselves to the ministry of the saints," and tells the brethren there to "submit yourselves unto such." In the persons here included in the house of Stephanas were infants, any of them, when baptized five years before, they had come up to the "ministry of the saints" pretty rapidly. So much on this passage as it relates to the baptism of the house of Stephanas. Then, secondly, we certainly have here another use of "house" from which infants are precluded.

We have noticed six New Testament households, now, and have seen that from five of them, the very language in which they are described, excludes infants. And in the other case, that of Lydia, the circumstances are strongly against our pedo-baptist friends in the use they attempt to make of it. Can infant baptism be justified by such an inference as this is? Why, many learned pedo-baptists themselves admit the insufficiency of it. For instance, in Knapp's Theology, it is said: "There is no decisive example of this practice in the New Testament; for it may be objected against those passages where the baptism of whole families is mentioned, (viz: Acts x:42-48; xvi:15-33; 1. Cor. i:16), that it is *doubtful whether there were any children in those families,* and if there were, *whether they were then baptized.*" (Vol. ii, p. 524.) So that even in this great pedobaptist's estimation this inference is doubly doubtful: doubtful whether any infants were in the households; and if there were, doubtful whether they were then baptized. Can an inference thus confessedly doubly doubtful be relied on to convince the unbeliever in the practice?

INFERENCE FROM CIRCUMCISION.

Just what the argument is, in this case, it is not easy to state right definitely and satisfactorily. It has nothing like the antiquity of other inferences for the practice in question, and it has been relied on mostly by controversialists in the discussion of the question, in later years. These controversialists are by no means agreed among themselves as to *what the argument is.* In their discussions they have a good deal to say about the church, as to when and where it began, differing among themselves as widely as from Abel to Abraham. They claim that the church of the old dispensation is identical with that of the new, in *some* sense; but as to what sense and to what extent the alleged identity obtains they again differ among themselves widely, holding nothing in common that needs to be replied to by the opponent of infant baptism. They very generally contend that in some sense—and here there is no agreement among them as to what sense—baptism now stands to its subject and the church as circumcision did under the former dispensation. They generally agree that as infants were circumcised under the former dispensation they ought to be baptized under the Christian dispensation. The strong point, the one in which they all agree, is that *infants* were circumcised by the command of God under the former dispensation. They all emphasize this unquestioned fact; and seem to think there ought to be something in it, somewhere or somehow in favor of *infant* baptism; but just what, or just how, or just where, they are by no means of one kind. Some of them have it, that circumcision was *initiative* to the church under the former dispensation, and that baptism is initiative now; and that infants were formerly initiated by circumcision, and should now be initiated by baptism. Others tell us that circumcision was only a recognition—or declaration—of church membership under the former dispensation; and that baptism is a recognition, or declaration, of membership now; and that as circumcision was extended to infants, so baptism ought to be. They go on to argue, that infants were put in the church when it was organized in the family of Abraham—that is, such as say the church was then organized—and that no law has

434

since been given for putting them out; and that they were then initiated (some say—others, that their membership was recognized) by circumcision; and that as baptism has superceded circumcision, infants should now be initiated (or recognized) by baptism. That is about the process of the argument. Now, the great strength and merit of the argument is, that it is of such a character as to open up an immense field for pedo-baptist debaters to skirmish in. They can find a good deal to say about "covenants," about "churches," about "ordinances," and occasionally something about "infants;" and the field is large enough for them to find a good deal to talk about without having anything to say about "infant *baptism*"—the real point in their line of battle.

I have seen and heard a good many of the champions of infant baptism tug through the tedious processes of this alleged argument from the covenants, and church identity, and circumcision, with all the variations; and I have never yet heard it without finding my mind impressed most of all with the question: Is it possible that the God of infinite wisdom has made it the duty of Christian parents to have their infant children baptized and left them to find out that it is their duty by such a process as this? It seems to me that this question alone ought to condemn the alleged argument forever in the estimation of sensible and fair-minded people. Other insuperable objections to the argument are:

1. ''The covenant of circumcision'' (Acts vii:8) was a covenant ''in the flesh'' of Abraham and his descendants, (Gen. xvii:12,13); while the ''new covenant'' is in the spirit, and knows no flesh. (Heb. viii:8-12.) The covenant of circumcision embraced Abraham, and such as were born in his house and bought with his money; while the new covenant embraces believers in Jesus Christ, without respect to Abraham's flesh or money, or anybody else's flesh or money. (2. Cor. v:16,17—Gal. iii:26-29.)

2. When God wanted parents to have their children circumcised in the old covenant, he *said* so in so many words: ''And he that is eight days old shall be circumcised among you.'' (Gen. xvii:12.) Had he wanted infant children baptized in the new covenant, he would have said so, undoubtedly. Let us try a pedo-baptist argument just here, for their benefit: The Lord certainly foresaw that many Christian parents would refuse to have their infants baptized without either a scripture precept or example, yet, ''foreseeing the event,'' he did not give the command. ''Hence it must have been agreeable to his will'' that they should so refuse. How will that do for an inference against infant baptism?

3. Under the former covenant only male infants, born of Abraham's flesh or bought with his money, were circumcised; while under the new covenant pedo-baptists contend for the baptism of infants without respect to *sex, flesh,* or *money!* How is

that for *identity!* and for baptism *instead* of circumcision?

4. If the Church is one and the same under both dispensations, and baptism now sustains the same relation to it that circumcision did under the former dispensation, then why were all circumcised persons commanded to be baptized as well as uncircumcised ones? Why were the Jews twice initiated into the church—or twice recognized? Could they not *hold over* from the old to the new dispensation (the church being the same) in virtue of their initiation or recognition by circumcision? They didn't. And as they didn't hold over was there not a loss of identity? Either there was a loss of identity, or the church held over from one dispensation to the other without members.

Let us hear what one of the most eminent and scholarly of all American pedo-baptists had to say on this *inference from circumcision*. I mean Moses Stuart, Professor of Sacred Literature in the Theological Seminary, Andover. He says: "How unwary, too, are many excellent men in contending for infant baptism on the ground of the Jewish analogy of circumcision. . . . . *Numberless difficulties* present themselves in our way, as soon as we begin to argue in such a manner as this."—Com. O. T. ch. 22. And again he says: "The covenant of circumcision furnishes no ground for infant baptism."— Lecture on Gal.

INFERENCE FROM ORIGINAL SIN.

After all, this is the real ground of the practice. It was on this ground that it was first brought into the Church, about the beginning of the third century, and on this ground it was defended down to the beginning of the nineteenth century. "If infants are guilty of original sin then they are proper subjects of baptism," said John Wesley, and that was the ground on which its advocates put it from its origin. It was brought in as a deduction, and has been justified by the same deduction or inference throughout its history until within the last forty or fifty years. Of course, I do not mean that it was a deduction from original sin alone, but that that doctrine was one of the premises from which it was deduced. The other was baptism for remission of sins. From these premises infant baptism was a conclusion.

At the time infant baptism first appears in history, about the beginning of the third century, baptism as a necessity to salvation was universally taught. The church fathers not only accepted fully the words of our Lord and his apostles upon this subject, but many of them went further and ascribed to the water of baptism an intrinsic virtue to wash away sins and purify the soul. In fact, that was a time in the history of the church when almost everything was carried to an extreme. If there were any very safe and conservative men among the church

438

fathers they didn't write any; or, if they did, their writings have not been preserved.

Now, "He that believeth and is baptized shall be saved" (Mark xvi:16), is scripture. "Repent and be baptized every one of you in the name of Jesus Christ for the remission of sins" (Acts ii:38), is scripture also. "Except a man be born of water and of the Spirit he cannot enter into the kingdom of God" (John iii:5), is scripture too. "Arise and be baptized and wash away thy sins calling on the name of the Lord" (Acts xxii:16), is another passage of holy scripture. And, "Baptism doth also now save us" (1. Pet. iii:21), is still another passage, bearing upon the same subject. They are all plain. They are all true, of course. But it will be observed that none of these scriptures ascribe any intrinsic virtue to the water of baptism. It is in itself nothing. Baptism is what it is, is all that these scriptures ascribe to it, as an expression of faith in Jesus Christ, as an act of obedience and loyalty to him—as a trustful submission to the divine will. But the church fathers, among other extravagancies and vagaries began, in the second century to ascribe to this ordinance a virtue even dissociated from faith, or anything else in the creature—an intrinsic virtue for purification from sin.

About this time the doctrine of original sin came in. This, too, was an exaggeration and perversion of scripture teaching. According to many of the leading church fathers, everybody was born a sinner;

that is, *guilty of Adam's sin*. Infants were all sinners at birth—guilty of Adam's first sin, and for that reason must be damned forever, if not washed, or regenerated. Baptism was the washing of regeneration. Infants must be washed. Therefore infants must be baptized. These are the premises and the conclusion! That's the logic of infant baptism, as every one acquainted with its history knows. When thus reduced to a syllogism both premises are false. And that's a good deal to be the matter with a syllogism. Baptism dissociated from faith in Jesus Christ saves nobody, is not for remission of sins to anybody; nor is it the washing of the regeneration. So that the doctrine of baptism for remission of sins, as interpreted by the church fathers of that time, was false. So also was their doctrine of original sin. And both premises being false, of course the conclusion was also.

On this question as to the origin of the practice in question it is worth while to spend a little time. The first mention, in any form, of infant baptism was in the first quarter of the third century, and by Tertullian, one of the most distinguished of the Latin fathers. On this point, says Dr. Bledsoe, in an article already cited in this discourse: "Tertullian is the first writer in the church who makes any express mention of the custom of infant baptism. Before his time, A. D. 200, there is not an allusion to the custom from which its existence may be fairly inferred." (Southern Review, Vol. xiv, p. 339.) Now, Tertullian opposed the practice; and here are his words, as translated by the distinguished pedo-baptist, Dr. Wall, in his History of Inft. Bapt. Vol. i:p. 94: "Our Lord says indeed, do not forbid them to come. Therefore let them come when they are grown up; let them come when they understand; when they are instructed whither it is that they come; let them be made Christians when they can know Christ. '*What need their guiltless age* make such haste to the forgiveness of sins!'" I have made this quotation mainly for this last sentence, in which this eminent father argues the needlessness of baptizing infants from "their *guiltless* age." He didn't believe infants were guilty of sin. He opposed baptizing them. He grounded his opposition, certainly in part, upon his notion of "their guiltless age."

Now Origen wrote in the same quarter of the third century. They were contemporaries. The one lived and wrote at Carthage; the other at Alexandria. They were the most eminent fathers of the age. Origen advocated infant baptism, and was the first man to do so, that anybody knows of. Let us see on what he grounds it. (Wall's Hist. Inft. Bapt. Vol. i; pp. 104,105.) Here are his words: "If there were nothing in infants that wanted forgiveness and mercy, the grace of baptism would be needless to them." And again he says: "Having occasion given in this place, I will mention a thing that causes frequent inquiries among the brethren. Infants are baptized for the forgiveness of sins. Of what sins.

441

Or when have they sinned? Or how can any reason of the laver in their case hold good, but according to that sense that we mentioned even now; none is free from pollution though his life be but of the length of one day upon the earth? And it is for that reason because by the sacrament of baptism the pollution of our birth is taken away, that infants are baptized.'' There is no mistaking the ground on which Origen puts the new custom, in the words we have read. He puts it on the ground that infants need ''forgiveness.'' He admits that otherwise ''baptism would be needless to them.'' There stand the two great fathers! One believes infants are sinners, and hence the grace of baptism; the other believes infants are guiltless, and that the grace of baptism is needless to them. Can anything be plainer than that the ground of the practice—the ''reason,'' as Origen puts it—was original sin; that is, that infants one day old were sinners, and needed the ''grace of baptism'' for forgiveness. This, too, it should be remembered, is the beginning of the custom. We have gotten back to the origin of the custom, and to the original ground of it. If anyone doubts that the custom was *new* when Origen wrote, read his words again: ''I will mention a thing,'' says he, ''that causes *frequent inquiries* among the brethren.'' Then, his *answer* shows the nature of these ''inquiries.'' Here is the answer: ''Infants are baptized for the forgiveness of sins.'' The inquiries must have been, ''*Why* are you baptizing *infants?"* Origen was a very great man in the church, and lived in the very great city of Alexandria; and the doctrine that infants are all guilty of sin from their birth, had brought in the custom of baptizing infants; and it being new, "caused frequent inquiries among the brethren" of the smaller towns and rural districts.

It is worth while for us, while standing here with Tertullian and Origen; the one opposing this custom because infants were in his estimation "guiltless;" the other advocating it, because they were in his estimation sinful and in need of forgiveness—the custom a *new* one, and, therefore, causing its advocate to be plied with "frequent inquiries among the brethren" —it is worth while, from this standpoint, to look back toward the apostles, and see if the history we have affords us anything bearing upon our subject. Do the earlier fathers—earlier than Tertullian and Origen—teach that infants are sinners. They do not. Hear Hermas, one of the apostolic fathers, who, it is supposed, saw and heard the apostle Paul: (Pastor of Hermas, chap. xxix.) "And they that believed from the twelfth mountain which was white, are the following: They are as *infant children in whose hearts no evil originates.*"

Barnabas (not later than the middle of the second century) says: "He hath made us after another pattern, that we should possess the soul of *children.*" (Epistle, chap. vi.) These references to infant children—and others might be cited—by writers between the apostles and the beginning of the third century show that the doctrine of original sin had not yet come in; and no such thing as infant baptism is mentioned in that period. The first two centuries of the Christian era are as silent as the grave on the custom of infant baptism; and on the *necessity* for it, the guilt of infants.

The fathers of the second century were as silent about infant baptism and infant guilt as the apostles were; and "the apostles," as Dr. Bledsoe would say, "imitated the silence of Christ" upon the subject.

But now taking our stand with Origen and Tertullian and looking this way, we see the doctrine of original sin and the custom of infant baptism spreading, and, like a mighty river, flowing on down the ages, sweeping everything before it, east and west, until it reaches the nineteenth century—the doctrine and the custom always going together, as the foundation and the structure built thereupon.

So intimately and indissolubly were the doctrine of the sinfulness and guilt of infants, and the custom of baptizing them, linked together in the teaching of the whole Catholic church in the centuries following Origen that in the latter part of the fourth century when Pelagius denied that infants were by nature sinful in such a sense as to be liable to eternal damnation if they died unbaptized, he was accused of denying the right of infants to baptism; that is, he was accused of denying infant baptism because he denied the doctrine which was the sole ground of

444

it in the Catholic church at that time. Hence this distinguished heretic said in his letter to Pope Innocent: (Wall's Hist. of Inft. Bap. Vol. 1, p. 450.) "Men slander me as if I denied the sacrament of baptism to infants, or did promise the kingdom of heaven to some persons without the redemption of Christ." But the renowned Augustin understood him more accurately than many who agreed with him: "So that the thing he complains he is slandered in, he has set down so as that he might easily answer to the crime objected, and yet keep his opinion. But the thing that is objected to then is this, that they will not own that unbaptized infants are liable to the condemnation of the first man and that there has passed upon them original sin, which is to be cleansed by regeneration; but do contend that they are to be baptized only for their receiving the kingdom of heaven, etc." (Ibid 447.) These quotations show that it was at that time a heresy—or as Augustin puts it, a "crime"—not to "own that unbaptized infants are liable to the condemnation of the first man;" and that one not so owning was set down as denying the right of baptism to infants, because he denied the doctrine upon which it was universally grounded. There was at that time no other known reason why anyone should believe in infant baptism than the doctrine of original sin. If one denied that doctrine, he was at once set down as opposed to infant baptism. Now, would this have been the case had infant baptism been instituted by

445

Jesus or his apostles and practiced from the beginning? It is not reasonable to suppose that it
would. Had it been grounded upon the authority
of Jesus or his apostles, and practiced from the beginning, as the baptism of believers, it would not
have been necessary for the church councils of the
third century to be settling questions about it and
adjusting it to the common practice, as we know
they had to do. Neither would Origen have been
under the necessity of answering" frequent inquiries
among the brethren" as to why "infants are
baptized."

Thus infant baptism came into the church with
the doctrine of original sin, and thus it came down
through the ages into the nineteenth century.

Now let us see how it was grounded in the early
part of this century. John Wesley may be said to
have represented the views of the English church
as well of the Methodist church of which he was the
acknowledged founder. I read from a little volume
entitled *"Doctrinal Tracts,* published by order of
the General Conference" of the Methodist Episcopal
church. The preface to the edition from which I
read says: "Several new tracts are included in this
volume, and Mr. Wesley's short treatise on baptism
is substituted in the place of the extract from Mʳ
Edwards on that subject." From this "short
treatise of baptism" by Mr. Wesley, I read, showing
the ground of infant baptism as Mr. Wesley understood it when he wrote it, and as the General Con-

ference understood it, when in 1832, it ordered its publication in the *Doctrinal Tracts*.

Mr. Wesley says: "But the grand question is, who are the proper subjects of baptism? grown persons only, or infants also? In order to answer this fully, I shall, first, lay down the *grounds* of infant baptism, taken from scripture, reason, and primitive, *universal* practice." Then he says: "As to the *grounds* of it: If infants are guilty of original sin, then they are proper subjects of baptism; seeing in the ordinary way they cannot be saved unless this be washed away by baptism. It has been already proved that this original stain cleaves to every child of man; and that thereby they are children of wrath, and liable to eternal damnation." (Doctrinal Tracts, p. 251.) There it is! Just as it started out in the first quarter of the third century, when Origen was so pressed by "frequent questions among the brethren." And notice, Mr. Wesley says, that the ground of it is taken from *"universal practice"*— that is, "primitive universal practice."

And in accordance with Mr. Wesley's teaching, the Ritual for baptism in the Discipline of the Methodist church puts it upon the same ground, or, rather, *did* put it upon the same ground, almost in Mr. Wesley's words, until within the last twenty-five or thirty years. The Ritual has been considerably modified of late years. And, no doubt, the good work of modification will go on, as there is still room for improvement.

447

It is due to Protestant pedo-baptists as well as to the subject in hand to say that they have very generally abandoned the doctrine of original sin as the ground of infant baptism; and as fast as they can, they are getting it and all correlated notions out of their creeds and rituals. And in so doing they are leaving infant baptism without any ground or reason or meaning. In the ages from Origen down to Wesley it *meant* something to baptize an infant. It meant "salvation from the condemnation of the first man." It meant that they might be "delivered from the wrath of God." It meant regeneration. Now, however, it doesn't mean much. The ground of it is gone, and it is a castle in the air. It is an empty ceremony. One advocate, nowadays, grounds it upon one thing and another upon another. One says infants are saved and are members of the church, and as such have a right to baptism. Another says they are saved by the grace of God in Christ Jesus, and should be baptized to bring them into the church. Another says they are all in the "invisible church," and ought to be baptized into the "visible church." Every Protestant pedo-baptist scribe or debater puts the practice upon a ground to suit him.

No wonder the people are losing faith in the custom. No wonder we see in the papers frequently and hear from the pulpits complaints that the baptism of infants is being neglected—is in many parts of the country falling into desuetude. It is about as hard to hold up a custom without meaning, without any reason for it, as to hold up a house against the winds without any foundation. It will have to go where Protestantism prevails. The abandonment of the doctrine of original sin is the death knell of infant baptism. It is only a question of time.

WHY I AM A CHRISTIAN

By A. J. WHITE

"ARE you a minister?" said a stranger, as he took a seat by my side in a railway car.

"Yes," I answered.

"To what branch of the Church do you belong?" said he.

"I do not belong to a branch, I belong to the Church itself. Christ said to his disciples, '*Ye* are the branches,' and 'if a *man* abide not in me, *he* is cast forth as a *branch.*'"

"Well!" said he, "to what denomination of Christians do you belong?"

"I do not belong to any denomination or sect of Christians, I belong to Christ, by whose precious blood all Christians were redeemed."

"Well," said he, "what name do you go by?"

"The name that the Book of God gives to a child of God, Christian."

"What creed do you have?" said he.

"Christ is our creed. Christ is the original Apostles' Creed. Jesus said, 'Will ye also go away?' Peter said, 'Lord, to *whom* shall we go? Thou hast the words of eternal life, and we believe and are sure thou art the *Christ*, the *Son* of the *Living God.'* (John 6:67-69.) 'For other foundation can no man lay than that is laid, which is Jesus Christ.' (1 Cor. 3:11.) 'Christ is the end of the law for righteousness to every one that believeth.' If thou shalt confess with thy mouth the Lord Jesus and shalt believe in thine heart that God raised him from the dead, thou shalt be saved.' (Rom. 10:4, 9.) 'So must the Son of Man be lifted up, that whosoever *believeth in him* should not perish, but have eternal life.' (John 3:14,15.) 'For ye are all the children of God *by faith in Christ Jesus.'* (Gal. 3:26.) The creed of Christianity is not doctrinal, but personal; it centers in, rests upon, and lays hold of the person of the Son of God.''

''But,'' said he, ''have you no book of instruction in religious history and doctrine?''

''Yes, the Bible.''

''Have you any discipline?''

''Yes, the New Testament.''

''Have you no articles of faith?''

''Just one—the creed of Christianity—the creed of the Church that Christ built—the great central, fundamental, life-giving, soul-saving truth of revelation, so simple and grand, and yet so comprehensive and exalted, that by it man apprehends and lays hold of the Son of God, as meeting all his needs as a sinner, and as the source of his life and strength, as a child and servant of God. Again I answer,

Christ is our creed. The acceptance of Jesus as the Christ, the Son of God, is the faith, and the only faith, the Scriptures demand, and is the one thing the apostles everywhere urged upon the faith of the people in order to salvation and church membership. Listen to a few, out of the scores of Scripture passages that might be presented: 'Thou art the Christ, the Son of the living God. (Peter.) . . . . Upon this rock I will build my Church.' (Jesus. Matt. 16:16-18.) . . . . 'These things are written that ye might believe that Jesus is the Christ, the Son of God, and that believing ye might have life through His name.' (John 20:31.) 'As many as *received Him* to them gave he power to become sons of God, even to them that believe on His name.' (John 1:12.) 'Whosoever believeth that Jesus is the Christ is born of God.' (1 John 5:1.) 'This (Jesus) is my beloved Son, in whom I am well pleased.' 'Hear ye him.' (Matt. 3:17; 17:5.) 'And straightway he preached Christ in the synagogues, that he is the Son of God.' (Acts 9:20.) 'This Jesus whom I preach unto you, is Christ.' (Acts 17:3.) 'They ceased not to teach and preach Jesus Christ.' (Acts 5:42.) 'And He mightily convinced the Jews, publicly, shewing by the Scriptures that Jesus was Christ.' (Acts 18:28.) 'And testified to the Jews, that Jesus is the Christ.' (Acts 18:5.) 'But we preach Christ crucified, . . . Christ the power of God, and the wisdom of God. He that glorieth, let him glory in the Lord.' (1 Cor. 1:23,24,

452

31.) 'Who is he that overcometh the world, but he that believeth that Jesus is the Son of God?' (1 John 3:23.) This creed that the Bible presents is divine. One that is longer is too long. One that is shorter is too short. One that differs is wrong. It is useless to revise man-made creeds. The thing to do is to throw them away and take Christ—the creed of the Bible. (Gal. 6:14,15.)''

"I see," said he, "you are a Campbellite."

"No, indeed, I am not a Campbellite. I should think it a great sin either to be, or to call myself a Campbellite. In the church at Corinth they had begun to follow human leaders. Some were Cephasites, some were Apollosites, and some were Paulites, and some were simply Christians. Paul rebuked them sharply for following human leaders. He asked, 'Was Paul crucified for you?' 'Were you baptized in the name of Paul?' If so, then there would have been some reason why they should be Paulites. But if Christ was crucified for you and you were baptized in his name, then you are, or ought to be, Christians. So as Campbell was not crucified for me, and I was not baptized in the name of Campbell, and Campbell is not the author of anything I believe, teach, or practice, and had no more to do with originating the Church of Christ, to which I belong, than I had with creating the world, I am not a Campbellite. It would be a great sin to exalt the name of Campbell above the name of Christ, or the teachings of Campbell above the teaching of Christ. The same is true of the name and teaching of Luther, Calvin, Wesley, and of all other men, and systems. And so if neither Methodism, nor Baptistism, nor Presbyterianism, nor Lutheranism, nor Congregationalism, nor Episcopalianism, nor Catholicism, nor any other ism was crucified for us, and we were not baptized in the name of any of these isms, we ought not to be called after any of them. By so doing we hinder the answer of Christ's prayer that his people may be one, and thus the conversion of the world (John 17:20,21), and put ourselves in opposition to the word of God. (Eph. 3:15.) Paul's exhortation, 'Let every one that nameth the name of Christ depart from iniquity' (2 Tim. 2:19), assumes that all the people of God wear the name of the Christ. James 2:7 assumes the same.''

''You folks,'' said my passenger friend, ''use the name Christian in an exclusive sense.''

''No, we are doing our best to get everybody to adopt it. 'For there is none other name under heaven given among men whereby we must be saved.' Jesus said, 'There is one fold and one shepherd.' He is our shepherd, and we are His sheep, and He wishes us to wear His name and hear His voice, in preference to every other name and in opposition to every other voice. In Ephesians 4:3, which is addressed 'To the faithful in Christ Jesus' as well as to 'the saints at Ephesus,' the apostle beseeches us 'to keep the unity of the Spirit,' and immediately gives the items of that unity. Eph. 4:4-6:

One body, Church.

One Spirit.

One hope.

One Lord.

One faith.

One baptism.

One God.

In 1 Cor. 1:10, which is addressed to all Christians, Paul most earnestly beseeches 'all to speak the same things and that there be no divisions among them.' We can all agree where the Bible requires agreement—on all fully taught questions—just as all agree that the sky is blue, the grass green, the flowers beautiful, the summer showers refreshing, the ice cooling, the sleep and rest and food invigorating.''

"Will you," said my friend, "give me your reasons for taking the name Christian?"

"In the name Christian is wrapped up everything that is of highest interest and importance, and of lasting value to humanity, therefore I am a Christian and not a Campbellite. We do not claim to be the *only* Christians, but we seek to be *Christians* only.

"I am a Christian, because this name above every other name represents my interest in, relation to, and dependence upon Christ, the first-born of all the sons of God, who is head over all to his Church (Eph. 1:22), and after whom God has named his whole family in heaven and earth. (Eph. 3:15; Acts 11:26; Isa. 62:2.)

"I am a Christian, because 'the name of the Lord is a strong tower.' (Prov. 18:10.)

"I am a Christian, because this is the best, dearest and most precious name in heaven or earth, and a 'good name is rather to be chosen than great riches.' (Prov. 22:1.)

"I am a Christian, because among the children of God, 'There is neither Jew nor Greek, there is neither male nor female.' (Gal. 3:28.) 'Circumcision nor uncircumcision, barbarian nor Scythian . . . . but Christ is all and in all.' (Col. 3:11.)

"I am a Christian, because as 'in Christ Jesus neither circumcision availeth anything, nor uncircumcision, but a *new creature*' (Gal. 6:15), so in Christ Jesus neither being a Lutheran, nor an Episcopalian, nor a Baptist availeth anything but a *new creature*, that is, a *Christian*.

"I am a Christian, because this name is broad enough to take in all the people of God, and yet narrow enough to shut out Pagans, Infidels, and Mohammedans. Methodist Christians, Presbyterian Christians, and Baptist Christians have but to give up their Methodism, Presbyterianism, and Baptistism, and hold on to the Christ of God, by faith in him alone, wearing his name, and glorying only in his cross, and all others wearing human names and having human creeds to do the same, and the prayer of the World's Redeemer for the union of those that believe in him, is answered.

"I am a Christian, because Christ is the author and finisher of my faith (Heb. 12:2), and Paul said, 'Be ye imitators of me, even as I also am of Christ.' (1 Cor. 11:1.)

"I am a Christian, because I have put on Christ (Gal. 3:27), that is, I am to stand for Him, to be filled with His spirit and to reproduce His character and life, and thus prove that I have been with Him and learned of Him.

"I am a Christian, because I was baptized into the name of Christ. (Acts 19:5; 8:16.)

"I am a Christian, because I was justified through Christ's name. (Acts 10:43.)

"I am a Christian, because Christ's is the only name by which men can be saved. (Acts 4:12.)

"I am a Christian, because I must not 'deny the name' of him who gave himself for me. (Rev. 3:8.)

"I am a Christian, because I must 'hold fast' the name of him who liveth in me. (Rev. 2:13.)

"I am a Christian, because the disciples were called Christians in Antioch *first*, afterward so called everywhere. (Acts 11:26.)

"I am a Christian, because Peter says (1. Pet. 4:14), 'If ye be reproached for the name of Christ, happy are ye,' and again in the sixteenth verse he expresses the same thought and shows what he means by the name of Christ, and its meaning everywhere in the Scriptures when applied to his disciples, namely, Christian. 'For if any man suffer as a Christian let him not be ashamed.'

"I am a Christian, because this is 'the worth while name by which' (James 2:7) the children of God among the twelve tribes scattered abroad (James 1:1) were called.

"I am a Christian, because Christ's name is more excellent than that given to any angel (Heb. 1:4), and is above every name, and every knee is to bow to it, and every tongue confess the Christ. (Phil. 2:9-11.)

"I am a Christian, because Christ is the 'Alpha and Omega, the beginning and the end, the first and the last' (Rev. 22:13), the sun, center, light, life and power—the all in all—of the religion that I profess.

"I am a Christian, because Christ was crucified for me (1 Cor. 1:13), and it is the Father's purpose that he should have the pre-eminence in all things. (Col. 1:18.)

"I am a Christian, because Paul said, 'Whatsoever ye do, in word or in deed, do all in the *name* of the Lord Jesus.' (Col. 3:17.)

"I am a Christian, because the supreme questions of God's Holy Book are, 'What think ye of Christ?' (Matt. 22:42) and 'What shall I do then with Jesus which is called Christ?' (Matt. 27:22.) I think him to be, and take him to be, my Saviour, the Son of God, *the* Christ. I take his name to be my name,

458

his service to be my work, his joy and love to be my portion, his home to be my home.

"I am a Christian, because it is better to be a Christian than to gain the whole world. (Matt. 16:26.)

"I am not a Campbellite, or a Baptist, or a Lutheran, because Jesus prayed that his people might be one (John 17:21), and Paul says, 'There is one body,' or church, and all God's people never can, nor will be *one*, as Campbellites, or Baptists, or Lutherans. They may and shall be one under the name that is above every name.

"I call myself a Christian, because every motive and incentive that the Word of God furnishes for being a Christian is equally a reason for calling one's self a Christian. The Christian Church, or the Church of Christ—and these expressions represent pricisely the same thought—is the Church that Christ built, and of which He is the head, the *one* Church known on the pages of the New Testament.

"I call myself a Christian, because it is *the one purpose of my life* to be such, and a life of eternal blessedness depends on being one. One must be a Christian to be saved, for 'if any man have not the spirit of Christ, he is none of his' (Rom. 8:9), but one need not be a Presbyterian, or a Methodist, or a Campbellite, in order to be a Christian. Hear the words of the inspired apostle Paul in his first epistle to the Corinthians, also addressed to 'all that in every place call upon the name of Jesus Christ'

(I Cor. 1:2), 'Now I beseech you, brethren, by the
name of our Lord Jesus Christ, that ye all speak the
same thing (have the same name, etc.), and that
there be no divisions (different denominations)
among you, but that you be perfectly joined together
in the same mind and in the same judgment.' (1. Cor.
1:10.) 'For other foundation can no man lay than
that is laid which is Jesus Christ.' (1 Co. 3:11.)
'Therefore let no man glory in men' (or in the doctrines, systems, or names, or creeds of men). 'For
all things are yours; and ye are Christ's.' (1 Cor.
3:21,23.) 'If any man speak, let him speak as the
oracles of God' (1 Pet. 4:11), remembering that
Jesus said 'Every plant that my heavenly Father
hath not planted, shall be rooted up'."

We had reached my friend's station. He said,
"Well, you must excuse me. I'll see you again,"
and left the train.

BIBLICAL ANTHROPOLOGY, THE KEY TO SOME RELIGIOUS PROBLEMS

By J. H. GARRISON

"And God said, Let us make man in our image, after our likeness . . . So God created man in his own image, in the image of God created he him; male and female created he them."—Gen. i:26, 27.

PERHAPS the symbol or character that would most fitly represent this age is the interrogation point. It is an age of profound questioning of everything in the heavens above and in the earth beneath. There is nothing so sacred or so venerable as to escape the interrogation point. The three great questions of this age, and of the ages, are:

1. What is man, what kind of a being is he?
2. Who is Christ, and the God whom He reveals?
3. What salvation or destiny has He prepared for man?

The man that is not interested in these questions gives evidence of partial, or total, obscuration of that which is most distinctive of our human nature —its rational and moral faculties.

It is proof of the superiority of the Bible to all other books in the world, that it is the only book that furnishes satisfactory answers to these great questions; and in that fact, in my judgment, lies the Bible's supreme claim to the confidence and acceptance of men, and also its character for an assured immortality in the literature of the world. The fact that this book alone, among all the volumes and tomes of the libraries of the world, answers these three great questions of the human soul, makes it *the Book of books.* Think you that the destructive critics are likely to overthrow such a book as this? And the sooner we come to recognize the fact that it is because the Bible speaks to the human heart as no other book does on these great themes, that it is a Divine book, the sooner we will cease to be alarmed at the inquiries and investigations concerning its genuineness. The fact that the Bible opens to us more windows in heaven than all the libraries of the earth, and has a dynamic force which they do not possess, is the reason why it has such a hold upon our humanity, and the reason why we need entertain no fears whatever as to its destiny. Its safety is secure. We may look on undaunted at all the crucial investigations it is now undergoing at the hands of critics. A book that brings satisfactory answers to these great questions, the world will not easily let go. Until somebody invents a better book—one that will furnish more satisfactory answers to these vital questions—the world will hold on to the Bible.

Now let us test this old Book on one of these questions I have suggested, namely, "What is man?" If we put the question to materialistic science for an answer—that part of science which takes no note of man's spiritual nature or of the phenomena associated therewith—the answer is, "Man is a splendid animal. He stands at the very summit of the animal creation. He is a piece of finely organized clay. He is a marvelous organism; but at death he is dissolved back into his original elements, and that is all there is of him. There is no part of him that survives the grave, for we have analyzed him scientifically, and we find nothing in him but the material." Are you satisfied with that answer? Does it meet the demands of your heart? Nay, it does not meet the demands of your reason. If that is all there is of man, why these longings and aspirations after something better, something higher? Why would God mock us by putting in our hearts this deathless aspiration, to end only in the grave?

Turn from materialism, and make your inquiry of Agnosticism, "What is man?" and it replies with a show of modesty: "We do not know that there is, or that there is not, anything in man that will survive the grave. We do not know that there is any God. If there be a God, He is unknowable. The whole question of God's existence and man's destiny lies beyond the range of any evidence we can accept. We do not know." Does that satisfy? Are you willing to take that to the death-bed of your dying mother and read it? Are you willing to lie down on your own death-bed with only that for a pillow? No; you turn away heart-sick from science and philosophy, and, turning to the old Bible your mother

loved so well, you open its lids, and on its faded
pages, bearing, it may be, the tear-stains of your
mother or of your father, you read the answer to
the question, "What is man?" in these marvelous
words I have quoted: "Let us make man in our
image, after our likeness. . . . So God created man
in his own image, in the image of God created he
him; male and female created he them."

These are, indeed, wonderful words. We fail to
be startled at them and their wonderful significance
only because of their familiar sound. Prof. Caird,
in his "Evolution of Religion," sees in Greek art,
sculpture and poetry, evidence that the Grecian
mind recognized in man a higher expression of Divinity than was to be found in the works of nature,
and argues that the Greek religion was therefore
an upward step from the grosser idolatry of the
East in the direction of monotheism. I ask you to
consider the fact that the author of Genesis, whoever
he may have been, writing centuries before Grecian
philosophy had reached its acme, not only recognized
the one true God, but saw in man an incarnation of
Divinity, and rose to the sublime thought, above all
pantheism and idolatry, that "man is created in the
image of God." Now let us approach that passage
reverently, while we ask in what sense it can be true
that man, whom science pronounces to be simply
clay, is akin to God, and has been made in His likeness. It can not be that he is in the corporeal image
of God, for "God is a spirit," and, for that matter,

man is a spirit too. He may exist in the body or out of the body; it is no essential part of man. It is, therefore, in his immaterial nature that he must look for this likeness.

Affirmatively, then, we may say that man is created in the image of God *intellectually,* or mentally, because, as the astronomer Kepler expressed it, "We can think God's thoughts after Him." We are capable of seeing God's plan in the numerous adaptations of this material world to man's wants. Because we can trace out the laws that govern the material universe and see how God made it, and why He made it, and thus follow God's plan in the material world, we are sure that man is created in the mental image of God. Otherwise, the universe would appear to him as it does to other animals. It presents no plan or purpose to the mere animal. Man is the only creature who is capable of seeing God's thoughts materialized in order and beauty. And again, the very fact that God has spoken to man is evidence that he is created in God's image intellectually; otherwise, God's revelation would be unintelligible. We do not speak to those who do not understand us. We do not enter into moral discussions with our horse, our dog, or even the anthropoid ape. Why not? Because, not being in our image mentally, we can not convey to them these great thoughts. I hold that God's revelation made to man is evidence of his creation in the intellectual image of God.

Man is created in the *moral* image of God. How do we know that? Because man's moral sense approves the moral law of God. When God says in His moral law "Thou shalt not steal; Thou shalt not murder; Thou shalt not lie," man's moral nature responds at once: "That is right; a man ought not to do these things." He may steal, he may lie, he may murder, but he knows that in doing these things he is doing wrong, and violating not only God's moral law as written in the decalogue, but the same moral law as written upon man's own nature. God so made man that he can not disobey His will without at the same time doing violence to his own nature. You can see at once that if man did not have a moral nature like that of God, it would do away with all accountability to God. If, for instance, when God says "Thou shalt not murder," man's moral nature should say, "It is right to murder, and I must murder, my conscience condemns me if I fail to murder," then, if God should condemn man for committing murder, He would condemn him for being true to his own nature, which we can not conceive. I take it then as beyond contradiction that man's moral nature is like God's; that God created him in His own image morally, and placed in every man's bosom a witness (some one has called it God's vicegerent on earth) which condemns him when he goes contrary to its behest, and which approves him when he does that which he believes to be right.

But still further: Man is created in the image of God *volitionally;* that is, as to his will. The latest word in science is, that behind all phenomena in the material universe, behind all motion, behind all force, is the will of the Supreme Being of the universe. We know that behind all man's acts lies the decision of his will. God is a free, self-determining Being, who chooses, decides and acts. In creating man, He gave him the same freedom of will, the power to choose his own destiny, free from any compulsion, and to act according to his own choosing. I know there is a school of theologians, and of philosophers, too, for that matter, that call in question this freedom of the will. But against all the theological reasoning and all the philosophical speculation, I place the testimony of every man's consciousness—that he has the power to do or not to do certain acts. You simply *know* that. You can not be beguiled into believing anything to the contrary. Otherwise, it would be impossible for you to feel any sense of remorse. No man's conscience condemns him for doing what he can not avoid doing. It is only what we have the power to do, and ought to do, but do not; or what we have the power to refrain from doing, and ought to refrain from doing, and yet *do,* that gives us a sense of demerit. So the very fact that our conscience condemns us for any act is evidence of our freedom of will. This truth has a very wide application.

467

The whole realm of theology and soteriology hangs upon it.

Someone may say: "That was a very dangerous sort of being for God to turn loose in the universe— a man made in God's image morally, intellectually, volitionally, and yet put into clay and allied to the earth." Yes, there is no question about that. Somebody has said that nothing creates such a commotion as a thinker turned loose in the world. But here is not only a thinker turned loose, but a moral judge and a chooser as well. But God had this alternative: He must either create a being who would have the power to do evil if he desired to do it, or He must make a machine, whose action would possess no moral quality. God did not care to make a machine. Men could make machines. He wanted to create a man. He wanted to create a being who would reflect His glory and His character. They could not be fully reflected in the material universe nor in all the lower orders of life. I think, too, that the In- finite Being, who is most fitly described by the name Love, wanted a being in the universe that could love Him. In all the material universe—mountains, seas, lakes, and among all the lower animals—there was not a being susceptible of a single emotion of grati- tude to the Divine hand that gave it being. Think you not that God hungered for some response, some being that would love Him? And so, with the alternative before Him, knowing that if He made a being that could do no wrong, He would make at the same time a being that could not do right, He accepted the responsibility, and created man in His own image. And here, my brethren, is the true basis for an optimistic view of the world.

I am an optimist; and I like to have a rational basis for any view I may hold. The infinite God, as gracious and benevolent as He is omniscient and omnipotent, with all the pages of human history unfolded before Him—pages of crime, of sorrow, of struggle and defeat, of progress and victory—chose to create, and, as a matter of fact, did create man in His own image. That would have been impossible had not God foreseen that the final outcome of human history would be a justification for creating man in His image. So, whatever clouds may obscure the sun, and whatever reflex currents there may be in the tide of human progress, I still believe that the God who made and rules the universe, and who created man in His own image, will bring order and harmony and victory at last out of all this struggle and apparent defeat.

THE KEY APPLIED

Now, I want to take this great, luminous truth that stands in the forefront of the Bible and apply it to some of the difficult problems in religion. Others will occur to you capable of solution by the same key. When we get a great truth like this, it is not wise to lay it away as if it had no vital relation to other truths. One truth will help us to understand another. Tennyson expressed this thought in the profound lines:

> "Flower in the crannied wall,
>   I pluck you out of the crannies;
> Hold you here, root and all, in my hand,
>   Little flower—but if I could understand
> What you are, root and all, and all in all,
> I should know what God and man is."

To know one truth, in all its relations, is to know all truth. And so let us take this truth and apply it to the solution of some of those great problems that have puzzled so many thoughtful, serious people. One of the great problems to which I would apply this truth is

I. POSSIBILITY OF THE INCARNATION

Today the most prominent word in religious discussion is the incarnation, and a great many good people stumble at that doctrine. They see the moral beauty of Christ's character, and are willing to crown Him master or king of men; but they cannot accept the supreme truth of the incarnation—the stooping down of the Son of God from heavenly heights to earthly conditions. It seems to me this great truth of man's nature throws light on this question. If man is created morally, intellectually and volitionally in God's image, I can understand the possibility of the incarnation. Reverently let me say it, I cannot see how the doctrine of the incarnation could be held independently of this great truth of man's creation in the image of God. I cannot see how God could manifest His character in a being not created in His own image. Try to think of the possibility of God's taking the form of any lower animal—say a dog, or a horse, or an ape—and in either of these forms manifesting His glory, righteousness, truth, and His infinite love for the world! It is inconceivable. Why? Because these lower orders of beings were not created in the image of God, and are incapable of receiving into themselves the divinity to express the Divine character. Ah! that is a marvelous fact, that the eternal Logos, existing before all worlds, should clothe Himself in flesh, and fill out to its utmost possibility this human nature with the inflowing life of God! He thus manifests to principalities and to powers His glory, His character and His truth.

Of course, if God is to manifest Himself in the flesh, it must be subject to human conditions and limitations. Some, as it seems to me, superficial critics have been unable to accept the doctrine of the true and essential divinity of Jesus Christ, because, when in the world, He hungered, He was weary, He wept, He died. There are indications of certain self-limitations which are necessarily involved in His taking our human nature. He said, "The time of the coming of the Son of man is known only to the Father, not to the angels, not even to the Son." Is that a reason to call in question His divinity? He said again, "My Father is greater than I." Read

471

that grand word of Paul: "Who, being in the form of God, counted it not a prize—a thing to be seized —to be on an equality with God, but emptied Himself, taking the form of a servant, being made in the likeness of men." What a fact! The infinite Son of God took upon Him this self-limitation as a necessary result of His incarnation, that He might work the great problem of human redemption on a common plane with man. Was He less divine for so doing? Was King Alfred less a king when he went down among his subjects in the garb of a peasant and visited their humble homes, and shared their poverty, that he might understand and better their condition? Was he not all the more a king because he was willing to do that for the love he bore his subjects? Shall we pay less honor to Jesus Christ because He was willing to stoop down and take upon Himself these necessary limitations in order to bear our sins, and thus accomplish the redemption of the race? A thousand times, No!

Not only does this primal truth show the possibility of the incarnation, but it furnishes or suggests, also,

II. Motive of the Incarnation

Now, a great many good people have been seriously puzzled as to why the Son of God should come to this earth, which, astronomy tells us, is a very small speck in the universe. Why, it is asked, should God make this planet the scene of the marvelous tragedy of the crucifixion? I remember there came to my camp once in the mountains a man who announced to me, almost under his breath, that he had lost faith in God. He could not believe that God would send His only begotten Son to an insignificant world like this, to become incarnate, to suffer, bleed and die for such a race. That was more than he could accept. And I think the Psalmist had some such thought when he said: "When I consider thy heavens, the work of thy fingers, the moon and the stars, which thou hast ordained, what is man that thou art mindful of him? and the son of man, that thou visitest him?" I find the answer to these questions in the fact that man is the child of God, created in His image. Is not that a sufficient motive for the incarnation, and for all the suffering of the Son of God?

Has anybody been puzzled to understand why the father of Charlie Ross traveled all over the world, following every rumor, that he might find his boy? Did you need any explanation of that fact? Not if you had a boy. How far would you follow your boy? Would you stop at the Mississippi River, state lines, or national boundaries? No, you would cross the ocean, go round the world, spend all your money, mortgage the farm and homestead, that you might find the dear boy and bring him back to the old home. Certainly you would. I know you would if you have a paternal heart. But man is the child of God. I know we have obscured that truth, or let it fall into the background for fear we would in some way lower the necessity of regeneration, and of adoption into the family of God, and becoming children of God by grace. But this cannot be; for this fact of our being children of God by grace has no meaning only as it is based on the primal sonship—our having been created in the image of God mentally, morally and volitionally. I know of no truth that has more power to win man than to go and tell him: "No matter how sinful you are, no matter how low you have fallen, you are a child of God; you bear the stamp of Divinity upon you. Come home, wandering child, come home!" The prodigal son was still a son out in the swinefields. He was a lost son, it is true, but he was a son. Let us lift up that old truth that stands in the forefront of the Bible, give it its original prominence, and we shall find the true motive of the incarnation, and understand that the long journey of the Son of God to this earth was to search for His Father's lost children, to bring them back to the Father's house. I see also in this truth

III. NECESSITY OF THE INCARNATION

With certain theories of man's nature and condition, there is no necessity for the incarnation, and the cross is without meaning. It has no place in such a theory. If a man is to be converted and regenerated independently of the laws of his mental and moral nature, by naked omnipotence, there is

474

no meaning in the incarnation and the cross. But a being created in the image of God, mentally, morally and volitionally, cannot be driven into the kingdom of God; he must be won by high and mighty motives. God knew man was such a being, and so furnished the mightiest motives known to God: He sent His Son into this world—His only begotten Son —as the highest possible exhibition of His love. And the divine Son hurried to the world that God so loved, to rescue man from his lost condition. That was the measure of God's love, and it is God's argument and motive to win man. Whatever else it accomplishes, it breaks down the stubborn will of man, convincing him of the love and compassion of God, and drawing him by moral force back into the arms of the Father. I can see the necessity for the incarnation and the cross to save such a being as man, with a mind to see, a heart to feel, and a will to decide. No being of less dignity and power than the Son of God could be the Saviour of men. So much as to the bearing of this truth on Christology. It has an important bearing, also, on

IV. Soteriology, or the Nature and Scope of the Salvation Promised to Man in the Gospel

The author of the Hebrew letter speaks of "so great salvation" offered to man. A being possessed of these great possibilities—great even in his ruins, defaced by sin, and out of harmony with his own

475

nature and with the moral universe—is to be saved. He is so great a being that the world cannot satisfy the hunger of his soul. We have an explanation here, too, of that great restlessness that marks the human race. Away from God it cannot be satisfied. The spirit came from Him, and can find complete satisfaction only in Him. It is said if you take a shell from the ocean's shore thousands of miles inland, and put it to your ear, it will sing of its ocean home. Its convolutions murmur the music of the deep sea. So of the soul wandering far from God. A superficial observer will say, "It is all bad, and wholly evil;" but bend down your ear close enough to its inmost heart, and you find it moaning out its lamentation for God—the great and mighty God. Not always conscious of its needs, the heart of man yet hungers for God, and in its blindness runs into all manner of excess and dissipation to find rest. Such a being requires a "great salvation" to be commensurate with the greatness of the being that is to be saved, and the greatness of his needs.

Again, this key-truth marks out the boundaries of this great salvation. If man was created in the image of God mentally, morally and volitionally, salvation means nothing less than the restoration of God's image to man in all these departments of his nature. Mentally, man has been dwarfed by sin. He sees but a few things, and these imperfectly. Instead of walking the earth the glorious being he might have been had not sin obscured his vision, he is a mere pigmy. This "great salvation" will make him whole in intellect. He knows here only in part; after a while he will know even as he is known. This is to me one of the most entrancing visions of the future life. We are to go on and on forever advancing in knowledge. Freed from the blinding power of sin, unfettered by the limitations of the body, and under the direct tuition of the great Teacher, we shall scale the higher to inaccessible heights of wisdom, and shall have such visions of God and of His moral universe as are impossible to us while we are in the flesh. We shall be saved intellectually.

And so, too, morally, man is maimed, wounded, dwarfed; but he is, under happier influences, to be developed and rounded out in beautiful symmetry like his Master, in the society of "the spirits of just men made perfect." You say, "Not now." Then hereafter, for this work must go on and on until it is accomplished. It is God's predestined purpose that we be conformed to the image of His Son. Our Presbyterian friends silenced Professor Briggs for believing, among other things, in progressive sanctification after death. I do not know that I ever believed or preached anything else. I declare my faith, my untroubled faith, in the progressive sanctification, both now and on the other side of the death line, of every Christian until he be brought into the complete image of Jesus Christ; and if that be heresy, my brethren, you must make the most of it.

Man's will, too, is to be so harmonized with the will of God, that in doing the very things he desires he will be acting along the line of God's will and purposes. All conflict between man's will and God's will must end in his will's being merged into that of God. Not that man will lose his individuality, but his volitions will spring from a will harmonized with God's will. And the body of our humiliation —even that is to be fashioned like unto the glorious body of our Lord Jesus Christ, according to the working whereby He is able to subdue all things unto Himself. This is, indeed, a glorious salvation. It is not the mechanical idea of salvation—that a man is to be saved because he gets into a place called heaven, or is lost if he is put into a place called hell. Salvation consists, rather, according to the view I have presented, in being restored to the image of God. It is character built after the Divine pattern. Nothing short of this is salvation in its highest Biblical meaning, and no other salvation would be adequate for a being created in the image of God.

THE CONSUMMATION

Sometimes I have a vision—it must be a dim one compared with the reality—of redeemed manhood. I see a being of wondrous beauty standing beside His Master, and looking like Him. He has a kingly bearing, and from his eye there flashes the fire of an immortal genius. There is a crown upon his brow,

478

a scepter is in his hand, and he is sharing lordship
in the universe with the Lord Jesus Christ. I ask,
who is that wonderful being? and an angel answers,
"It is man, redeemed and glorified, and made like
unto his Master—God's work completed in him."
That is only one man. Take human society, for this
great salvation does not stop at the individual man.
It saves society, breaking down all caste, all division-
walls, severing all chains, lifting all men up to a
common level under the great Fatherhood of God.
This is an essential part of the truth that "Man is
created in the image of God." When that truth is
rightly understood, society will be reconstructed,
and men will crown Jesus Christ King of kings, and
He shall rule in business, in commerce, in politics,
in social life. And God's will shall be done on earth,
even as it is done in heaven. The New Jerusalem
will have descended from God out of heaven, and
the glad earth, redeemed from sin, will reflect back
the smile of God. Then shall we hear the grand
hallelujah chorus, "Worthy is the Lamb that was
slain to receive power, and riches, and wisdom, and
strength, and honor, and glory, and blessing, forever and ever." Amen and amen!